LIVING
GEL
BEYOND THE BASICS

LIVING LANGUAGE®

GERMAN

BEYOND THE BASICS

Written by
PETER KELLERSMANN

Edited by
CHRISTOPHER A. WARNASCH

LIVING LANGUAGE®

Copyright © 2005 by Living Language, A Random House Company

Living Language is a member of the Random House Information Group

Living Language and colophon are registered trademarks of Random House, Inc.

Published in the United States by Living Language, A Random House Company

www.livinglanguage.com

Editor: Christopher A. Warnasch
Production Editor: John Whitman
Production Manager: Heather Lanigan
Interior Design: Sophie Ye Chin

ISBN 1-4000-2169-3

PRINTED IN THE UNITED STATES OF AMERICA

10 9 8 7 6 5 4 3 2 1

ACKNOWLEDGMENTS

Thanks to the Living Language staff: Tom Russell, Sanam Zubli, Christopher Warnasch, Zviezdana Verzich, Suzanne McQuade, Suzanne Podhurst, Sophie Chin, Denise De Gennaro, Linda Schmidt, Alison Skrabek, John Whitman, Helen Kilcullen, and Heather Lanigan. Special thanks to Leslie Weissgerber.

CONTENTS

LESSON 9

LESSON 10

LESSON 11

LESSON 12

LESSON 13

LESSON 14

INTRODUCTION

Living Language® *German: Beyond the Basics* is a perfect follow-up to any beginner-level German course. It focuses on the specific needs of the intermediate student—vocabulary expansion, review of basic grammar, introduction of more challenging grammatical constructions, and natural conversational and idiomatic speech. If you've recently completed a beginner-level course in German, or if you're looking for a way to reactivate the German that you may have studied years ago, *German: Beyond the Basics* is a great course for you.

The complete program includes this course book, four hours of recordings, and a reference dictionary. The recordings include the dialogues and other material from the course book; they're an essential tool for perfecting pronunciation and intonation as well as building listening comprehension. The book may also be used on its own if you're confident in your pronunciation.

COURSE MATERIALS

There are twenty lessons in *German: Beyond the Basics*. Each lesson begins with a dialogue that focuses on a particular setting designed to highlight certain vocabulary or grammatical constructions. These settings will also give you a good idea of various cultural issues and put the language you're learning into a realistic context. In addition to the dialogues, each of the twenty lessons contains language notes, grammar and usage explanations and examples, and several exercises. There is also a reference section at the end of the book containing a grammar summary, a section on letter writing, and one on e-mail and Internet resources.

DIALOGUE: The dialogue in each lesson features standard, idiomatic German and presents a realistic situation that demonstrates natural language use in a real context. The idiomatic English translation is provided below each line of dialogue.

NOTES: The notes refer to specific words, expressions, or cultural items used in the dialogue that are worthy of further comment. A note may clarify a translation, expand on a grammatical construction, or provide a cultural context. The notes are numbered to refer back to particular lines of dialogue for easy reference.

GRAMMAR AND USAGE: This section focuses on a few key grammatical or structural points. There is a clear and simple explanation first, followed by examples to further illustrate the point. Many of the grammar points are included as a review of key basic structures, but the overall scope of this course also includes more challenging and higher level grammar.

EXERCISES: The final section of each lesson gives you an opportunity to practice the material covered in that lesson. There are several different types of exercises, including fill-in-the-blanks, multiple choice, translation exercises, and more.

GRAMMAR SUMMARY: The Grammar Summary contains a concise and comprehensive summary of German grammar. This section is an invaluable tool for use either with the course or on its own for independent reference.

LETTER WRITING: This section includes examples of business, formal, and personal letters. There are also forms of salutations and closings, as well as sample envelopes.

E-MAIL AND INTERNET RESOURCES: This section includes sample e-mail correspondence with vocabulary and expressions related to the Internet. There is also a list of Internet resources of interest to the student of German.

THE RECORDINGS

The recordings include the complete dialogues from all twenty lessons in the course book, as well as a number of example sentences taken from the Grammar and Usage sections. Each dialogue is first read at conversational speed without interruption, and then a second time with pauses inserted, allowing you to repeat after the native speakers. By listening to and imitating the native speakers, you'll improve your pronunciation and build your listening comprehension while you reinforce the new vocabulary and structures that you've learned in the book.

HOW TO USE THIS COURSE

Take as much time as you need to work through each lesson. Do not be afraid to look over material that you've already covered if you don't feel confident enough to move ahead. The course is organized so that you can move through it at a pace that is exactly right for you.

Start each lesson by reading through it once to get a sense of what it includes. Don't try to memorize the vocabulary from the dialogue or master the grammar items, and don't attempt to do any of the exercises. Simply familiarize yourself with the lesson in a general sense.

Then start again by reading through the dialogue a first time to get a general sense of it. Then look over the notes to help clarify points that may be confusing. Next, read the dialogue more carefully, focusing on each line and its translation. If you come across new or unfamiliar vocabulary, write it down in a notebook or somewhere else you can return to for practice. Re-read the dialogue until you're comfortable with it.

After you've carefully read the dialogue a few times, turn on the recordings and listen as you read along. The dialogue is first read at normal conversational speed, and then again with pauses inserted for you to repeat. Follow along in your book as you listen, and then again as you repeat, in order to activate two senses—sight and hearing. After you've listened while reading along, close your book and try to follow without any written material. See how much of each sentence and phrase you can successfully repeat. Again, feel free to repeat these steps as many times as you'd like.

After you've finished reading and listening to the dialogue, turn to the Grammar and Usage section. Read each point carefully until it makes sense to you, and take a close look at the example sentences to see how they relate to the point at hand. If you're using a notebook, it's a good idea to take notes on the grammar and try to restate each point in your own words. Try to come up with other examples if you can. After you've completed each point in a similar way, turn on your recordings and listen to the section in the same way as you did for the dialogue. Listening and repeating will serve as an excellent review.

The exercises at the end of each lesson will help you review the material and check your overall progress. If you're unsure of a particular exercise, go back and cover the grammar again. If you're not comfortable moving ahead, make sure you take the time you need.

Turn to the Grammar Summary while you're working through the course to remind yourself of a grammar point you may have forgotten, or to provide yourself with another way of explaining a point you're working on. Also, take a look at the Internet Resources for suggestions on how you can use the Internet as a reference tool or as a way to enhance your studies.

Now, you're ready to begin.

LIVING LANGUAGE®
GERMAN
BEYOND THE BASICS

LESSON 1

EIN STRANDCAFÉ IN DÜSSELDORF?
A BEACH CAFÉ IN DÜSSELDORF?

A. DIALOGUE

1. *Liza und Shawn aus San Diego sind zu Besuch bei ihrem Freund Klaus in Düsseldorf. Das Wetter ist warm und sonnig heute. Sie treffen sich mit Klaus in einem Café.*
   Liza and Shawn from San Diego are visiting their friend Klaus in Düsseldorf. The weather is warm and sunny today. They meet up with Klaus in a café.

2. Liza: **Hallo Klaus. Wie geht's?**
   Hello, Klaus. How are you?

3. Klaus: **Danke, großartig! Und selbst?**
   Great, thanks! And yourself?

4. Liza: **Auch sehr gut!**
   I'm doing great, too.

5. Shawn: **Ausgezeichnet! Aber was für ein Café ist das hier? Strand und Palmen in Düsseldorf? Das ist ja fast wie zu Hause!**
   Excellent! But what kind of café is this here? Beach and palm trees in Düsseldorf? That's really almost like home!

6. Liza: **Ja, Düsseldorf liegt doch gar nicht an der Küste.**
   Yes, Düsseldorf isn't on the coast at all.

7. Klaus lacht: **Das ist einer der neuen Trends in Deutschland. Willkommen im Beach-Club Düs-**

seldorf! Es gibt jetzt Beach-Clubs in sehr vielen deutschen Städten. Natürlich gibt es keinen natürlichen Strand, aber die Ufer an Flüssen oder Seen sind auch gar nicht schlecht. Einige Städte haben Beach-Clubs sogar in den Parks. Sand und Palmen sind importiert.

Klaus laughs: That's one of the new trends in Germany. Welcome to The Beach-Club, Düsseldorf. There are now beach clubs in quite a lot of German cities. Of course, there's no natural beach, but the shores of rivers or lakes are not bad at all either. Some cities even have beach clubs in parks. Sand and palm trees are imported.

8. Shawn: **Es ist sehr angenehm hier, aber es gibt doch so viele nette Straßencafés und Restaurants hier.**
It's very nice here, but there are so many nice sidewalk cafés and restaurants here.

9. Klaus: **Das Lieblingsziel der Deutschen ist der Strand. Leider gibt es in Deutschland nur die Küste im Norden und die Inseln in der Nord- und Ostsee. Und Spanien und Griechenland sind weit.**
The favorite destination for Germans is the beach. Unfortunately, there are only the coast in the north and the islands in the North and the Baltic Seas in Germany. And Spain and Greece are far away.

10. Liza: **Ist es nicht zu kalt hier für die Palmen?**
Isn't it too cold here for the palm trees?

11. Klaus: **Im Winter sind sie unter Glas.**
In winter, they're under glass.

12. Liza: **Sozusagen nach dem Motto: Wenn ich nicht zum Strand komme, bringe ich den Strand in die Stadt?**

Just as the motto goes: If I can't go to the beach, I'll bring the beach to the city?

13. Klaus: **Genau!**
Exactly!

14. *Eine Kellnerin im Bikini kommt an den Tisch:* **Was darf ich Ihnen bringen?**
A waitress in a bikini comes to the table: What can I bring you?

15. Liza: **Ich möchte einen gemischten Salat und eine Tasse Kaffee, bitte.**
I'd like a mixed salad and a cup of coffee, please.

16. Shawn: **Bringen Sie mir bitte ein großes Weizenbier.**
Please bring me a large wheat beer.

17. Klaus: **Und für mich bitte ein Bier und Toast Hawaii.**
And for me a beer and Hawaiian Toast, please.

18. Kellnerin zu Shawn: **Möchten Sie auch etwas essen? Auch einen Toast Hawaii vielleicht? Oder ist das alles?**
Waitress to Shawn: Would you like something to eat as well? Maybe a Hawaiian Toast, too? Or will that be all?

19. Shawn: **Danke.**
Thank you.

20. Kellnerin: **Bitte schön!**
You're welcome!

21. *Nur ein paar Minuten später kommt die Kellnerin mit der Bestellung zurück.*

Just a few minutes later, the waitress comes back with the order.

22. Shawn: **Der Toast sieht ja recht gut aus.**
The toast looks really quite good.

23. Kellnerin: **Möchten Sie doch etwas zu essen?**
Would you like something to eat after all?

24. Shawn: **Oh, Entschuldigung. Ich habe Toast bestellt, oder?**
Oh, I'm sorry. I ordered toast, didn't I?

25. Liza lacht: **'Danke!' bedeutet 'Nein, danke!'**
Liza laughs: Saying 'thank you' means "No, thanks for asking!"

26. Kellnerin: **Kein Problem! Ich bringe gleich noch einen Toast.**
No problem! I'll bring another toast right away.

27. Liza zu Klaus: **Toast Hawaii mit Surfmusik unter Palmen? Morgen möchte ich echte deutsche Gemütlichkeit in einem traditionellen Restaurant.**
Hawaiian Toast with surfer music beneath palm trees? Tomorrow I want a genuine German atmosphere in a traditional restaurant.

28. Klaus: **Dort findest du Toast Hawaii wahrscheinlich auch auf der Karte.**
You'll probably find Hawaiian toast on the menu there as well.

29. Shawn lächelt: **Nun, Frankfurter Würstchen mit Sauerkraut sind auch in San Diego nicht mehr ganz ungewöhnlich. Es ist immer noch besser, das Sauerkraut in die Stadt zu bringen, als die Stadt zum Sauerkraut. Prost!**

Shawn smiles: Well, frankfurters with sauerkraut are not quite so uncommon in San Diego anymore, either. It's still better to bring the sauerkraut to the city than the city to the sauerkraut. Cheers!

B. NOTES

1. *zu Besuch bei* (for a visit at). The preposition *bei* (at) is always followed by the dative case (see Lesson 2).

2. *Wie geht's?* (How is it going?) is neither the formal or polite form of address nor the familiar form, since it avoids addressing somebody directly. It is the short form for *Wie geht es?* (How goes it?)

3. *Und selbst?* (And yourself?) in response to *Wie geht es Ihnen?* (pol.), *Wie geht es dir?* (fam.), or *Wie geht's?* doesn't address the person directly, either. It is commonly used and comes in handy, if you're unsure whether the polite or the familiar form is more appropriate.

5. *Was für ein . . .* What kind of . . . The preposition *für* (for) is always followed by the accusative case (see Lesson 2).
   . . . *wie zu Hause* (lit.: like at home). Remember that *zu Hause* means "at home," but *nach Hause* "to/toward home." The directional preposition *nach* is also used with a city or country. *(nach Boston, nach Amerika,* but: *in die USA).*

7. *Es gibt . . .* (there is, there are) is commonly used. It's also quite easy to use, since the same form addresses singular and plural nouns (lit.: It gives . . .). Remember that the word order changes if the sentence starts with an adverb *(Es gibt heute . . . Heute gibt es . . .).*

Similar to English, *natürlich* can have two meanings, "of course" or "natural(ly)."

8. *angenehm* (pleasant) can also be used in an introduction, meaning "Pleased to meet you!"

9. and 11. *im* (contraction of *in dem*). Another contraction with *in* is *ins (in das)*.

12. *zum* (contraction of *zu dem*). Another contraction with *zu* is *zur (zu der)*.

15. *möchte* (would like) is a subjunctive form of the verb *mögen* (to like). It is commonly used to order in a restaurant or when going shopping.

24. *Ich habe Toast bestellt, oder?* I ordered toast, didn't I? It's a lot easier in German to ask a so-called tag question, since the two parts don't have to agree in tense or negation. Another common form is: *Das Wetter ist schön, nicht wahr?* (The weather is nice, isn't it?).

25. Saying *Danke!* (Thank you!) as a response indicates refusal, meaning "No, but thanks for asking!" This is quite the opposite from English, where a "Thank you!" would indicate acceptance of the offer. To avoid any confusion, you can always say *Ja, bitte!* (Yes, please!) or *Nein, danke!* (No, thank you!).

   Another common mistake when ordering is to use *Ich habe ein Bier* (I'll have a beer). Don't be surprised if a waiter or waitress tells you that this isn't possible, since he or she hasn't brought it yet.

26. *noch ein* (lit.: still a). It is used to order "another one" of what you already have. Never say *Ein anderes*

Bier, bitte! (lit.: Another beer, please!). This would indicate that the one you already have is bad or that you want a different one: *Ich bringe gleich noch einen Toast!* (I'll bring another toast right away!) *Ich bringe gleich einen anderen Toast!* (I'll bring you a different/replacement toast right away!).

29. *Nun* (now) is often used in the beginning of a sentence meaning "well, . . . " *Nun, das habe ich gar nicht gewusst* (Well, I didn't know that at all). Please note that it is mostly used as an adverb: *Nun ist alles gut!* (Now, all is well!). *Nicht mehr* (not anymore), *immer noch* (still [with emphasis]).

Culture Notes

Beach-Clubs have indeed been a very popular trend in Germany in recent years. More than ninety percent of Germans call the beach their favorite vacation spot, but until recently, they could only enjoy the beach during their vacation. Now that's not the case anymore. More than a thousand tons of sand were brought to *Monkey Island*, the beach club in Düsseldorf situated directly on the Rhine river, and as soon as a few rays of sun are out, it is packed with people. Just like bowling alleys sprang up everywhere in the 1970s, these favorite leisure time spots have appeared all over Germany. At Beach-Clubs, people play volleyball or enjoy their piña coladas under palm trees until deep into the night.

A common snack in many moderately priced restaurants and diners is *Toast Hawaii*, consisting of a slice of buttered toast with ham or turkey and a slice of pineapple, topped with melted Swiss or Gouda cheese. *Weizenbier* (wheat beer) is a smooth top-fermented beer, especially popular in the summer.

C. GRAMMAR AND USAGE

1. The German Noun

German nouns have number (singular or plural), gender (masculine, feminine, or neuter) and case (nominative, genitive, dative, and accusative).

> *Der Mann gibt der Frau das Buch.* (The man gives the book to the woman.)

The nouns in the above sentence are:

> *der Mann* (subject): masculine; singular; nominative
>
> *der Frau* (indirect object): feminine; singular; dative
>
> *das Buch* (direct object): neuter; singular; accusative

We'll take a closer look at cases later. Now, we'll cover gender and number. The gender of the noun is easy to determine when it is natural *(der Mann, die Frau, das Kind)*, but in most instances it has to be memorized. There are, however, many guidelines that are helpful in identifying gender. Nouns that refer to a person take the natural gender. Apart from all diminutives ("smaller" forms that have such endings as *-chen* or *-lein*), there are only very rare exceptions to this rule. All diminutives are neuter.

> Masculine: *der Vater* (father), *der Bruder* (brother), *der Lehrer* (teacher, m.).
>
> Feminine: *Die Mutter* (mother), *die Schwester* (sister), *die Lehrerin* (teacher, f.).
>
> Neuter: *das Kind* (child), *das Mädchen* (girl), *das Baby* (baby).

This is also true for most names of animals where the gender is clear: *der Stier* (bull), *der Hengst* (stallion), *die*

Kuh (cow). The most common gender for young animals is neuter: *das Lamm* (lamb), *das Küken* (baby chick). If the term describes the animal species rather than sex, neuter is most common.

All names of the days of the week, months, and seasons are masculine: *der Montag* (Monday), *der Januar* (January), *der Frühling* (spring).

Most kinds of stone, gemstones, weather conditions, currencies, and all names of cars are also masculine: *der Sand* (sand), *der Granit* (granite), *der Diamant* (diamond), *der Regen* (rain), *der Euro* (euro), *der Mercedes* (the Mercedes).

Almost all species of trees, most flowers, names of ships and motorcycles, and all numbers are feminine: *die Eiche* (oak), *die Rose* (rose), *die Titanic* (the Titanic).

All diminutives are neuter. The most common diminutives are built with the suffixes *-chen* and *-lein*: *das Tischlein* (little table), *das Häuschen* (little house). A less common diminutive has the suffix *-le*. It is commonly used in some Southern German dialects: *das Häusle* (little house), *das Männle* (little man).

Almost all countries, cities, and names of metals are neuter as well: *das lebendige Berlin* (the lively Berlin), *das Eisen* (iron).

Verbal nouns (the infinitive of the verb used as a noun) are neuter: *das Schreiben* (writing). Adjectival nouns are neuter, unless they describe a person: *Das Neue und das Alte* (the new and the old), but *der Gute* (the good man). Nouns that derive from English are mostly neuter, unless a gender is clearly visible or has a close relation to another German word: *das Keyboard* (keyboard), *das Feedback* (feedback), *das Internet* (Internet), but *der Computer* (computer), *die Mail* (e-mail).

With most professions, nationalities, and inhabitants of cities or towns, it is easy to adjust the gender: *der Amerikaner / die Amerikanerin* (American), *der Rechtsanwalt / die Rechtsanwältin* (lawyer).

The plural of nouns needs to be memorized. The most common plural form involves the addition of an *-n* or *-en* to the singular: *der See / die Seen* (lake), *der Mensch / die Menschen* (person).

Female nouns that derive from their male counterpart add *-nen* in their plural form: *die Freundin / die Freundinnen* (female friend).

The second most common plural ends with *-e*. Often the stem vowel changes to an umlaut as well: *der Besuch / die Besuche* (visit), *der Freund / die Freunde* (friend), *der Fluss / die Flüsse* (river).

In the third most common plural, *-er* is added to the singular form, and often the stem vowel changes to an umlaut in addition: *das Bild / die Bilder* (picture), *das Glas / die Gläser* (glass).

Nouns that end with *-nis* add *-se* in their plural: *das Erlebnis / die Erlebnisse* (experience), *das Zeugnis / die Zeugnisse* (school report card, testimony).

Some singular and plural forms are identical: *das Ufer / die Ufer* (shore).

The plural form of a diminutive is always the same as the singular: *das Tischlein / die Tischlein* (small table).

Some plurals are formed by changing the stem vowel to an umlaut: *der Vater / die Väter* (father), *die Mutter / die Mütter* (mother).

Most nouns deriving from English add an -s in their plural form. Note that English nouns ending in -y don't change to -ies in German: *das Hobby / die Hobbys* (hobby).

Some nouns do not have a plural form or only exist as plural or mass nouns: *die Leute* (people), *der Sand* (sand).

Singular nouns with Greek or Latin endings may have German plural endings or they may take their original Latin or Greek plurals: *das Antibiotikum / die Antibiotika* (antibiotic), *das Stadion / die Stadien* (stadium).

Case is the third and last way in which a noun changes form. If a noun is the subject of a sentence, it is in the nominative case. Direct objects are in the accusative, indirect objects in the dative, and nouns that show possession or belonging are in the genitive. Objects of prepositions may take different cases. Most nouns only take on a different ending in the genitive masculine and neuter (-s ending), as well as in the dative plural (-n ending). But the articles *der, die, das* and *ein, eine, ein* change much more frequently. Let's examine another sentence where the nouns and articles are in different cases:

> *Die Studentin gibt den Freunden die Bücher des Lehrers.* (The student gives the teacher's books to her [the] friends.)
>
> *die Studentin* (subject): female; singular; nominative
>
> *den Freunden* (indirect object): masculine; plural; dative
>
> *die Bücher* (direct object): neuter; plural; accusative
>
> *des Lehrers* (possessor): masculine; singular; genitive

Notice that there are two examples of nouns changing in certain grammatical cases:

die Freunde became *den Freunden* in the dative plural, and *der Lehrer* became *des Lehrers* in the genitive singular. The only other examples of nouns that take different case endings are the so-called *n*-nouns and the adjectival nouns, both of which will be discussed in Lesson 4.

2. The Nominative Case

The nominative is always easy to determine, because it is the subject of the sentence.

	Definite Articles	Indefinite Articles
masculine	*der Strand* (the beach)	*ein Strand* (a beach)
feminine	*die Palme* (the palm tree)	*eine Palme* (a palm tree)
neuter	*das Land* (the country)	*ein Land* (a country)
plural	*die Städte* (the cities)	—

You can see in the chart above that the form of the noun remains the same whether the definite or indefinite article is used. Only a few nouns (adjectival nouns) change endings in the nominative, depending on whether a definite or indefinite article, or no article at all, is used (see Lesson 4).

All nouns in a simple sentence with *sein* (to be), *werden* (to become) and *bleiben* (to remain), used without any prepositions, have to be in the nominative case.

> *Die Stadt Luxemburg ist auch ein Land.* (The city of Luxembourg is also a country.) *Stadt* is the subject, and *Land* is the predicate that refers back to it.

3. Subject Pronouns

Here are the nominative case pronouns which serve as the subject of a sentence.

I	*ich*	we	*wir*
you	*du*	you (pl.)	*ihr*
he, it	*er*	they	*sie*
she, it	*sie*	You (polite)	*Sie*
it	*es*		

Note that the polite form of "you" is the same as the third person plural "they", even when addressing just one person. The only difference is that formal pronouns are written with a capital letter. Also note that the forms *er* and *sie* (he and she) can be translated as "it" when replacing a non-human noun that has masculine or feminine gender in German.

4. Stress Markers

A stress marker is a particle that is often used in conversation for emphasis. Here are the most common ones in German:

Gar (at all) or *überhaupt* is mostly used in the negative.

Ich habe gar keine Zeit!	I have no time at all!
Der Zahnarzt hat überhaupt nicht gebohrt!	The dentist didn't drill at all!

Ja (yes) or *aber* (but) placed after a verb can add surprise or assurance to a statement.

Das ist ja interessant!	Isn't that interesting!
Das ist aber schön!	That's really beautiful, isn't it?

Doch (but, surely, still) can add extreme emphasis to a statement. If used in an imperative it adds encouragement. As an answer to a negative question it implies disagreement (No, it is so!).

Du weißt doch!	You know that!
Das weißt du doch!	You must know that!
Nehmen Sie doch Platz!	Why don't you have a seat!

5. Word Order When Using Adverbs

In German, an adverb may be placed at the beginning of a sentence, after the verb, or even at the end. If the adverb comes first, then the order of the subject and verb is reversed. There is usually no comma after the adverb, unless the speaker pauses, such as in an imperative.

Heute ist das Wetter sonnig.	Today, the weather is sunny.
Das Wetter ist heute sonnig.	The weather today is sunny.
Das Wetter ist sonnig heute.	The weather is sunny today.
Bitte bringen Sie mir ein Glas!	Please, bring me a glass!
Bitte, bringen Sie mir ein Glas!	(comma adds emphasis)

EXERCISES

A. Give the plural of each noun in the following text:

> *In Deutschland gibt es nur sehr wenige _____ (Strand). Deshalb sind ein paar clevere _____ (Leute) auf die Idee gekommen, tonnenweise _____ (Sand) in die _____ (Stadt) zu bringen. Tatsächlich werden _____ (Berg) von Sand an die _____ (Ufer) deutscher_____ (Fluss) und*

_____ (See) und in die _____ (Park) trans-
portiert. Selbst die kalten deutschen _____ (Winter) halten sie nicht davon ab, _____ (Palme) und
andere exotische _____ (Pflanze) zu importieren.
Und die neuen _____ (Trend) machen sich
bezahlt: Sobald die Sonne herauskommt, sind diese
_____ (Oase) voll von _____ (Mensch).

There are very few beaches in Germany. Therefore,
a few clever people had the idea to bring sand by the
ton into the cities. Indeed, mountains of sand are
being transported to the shores of rivers and lakes
and into parks. Even the cold German winters don't
keep them from importing palm trees and other
exotic plants. And the new trends are paying off. As
soon as the sun comes out, these oases are packed
with people.

B. Change the following nouns and articles as indicated:

  1. *der Architekt* (architect) > female

  2. *die Großmutter* (grandmother) > male

  3. *der Stuhl* (chair) > diminutive

  4. *der Professor* (professor) > female

  5. *die Musiker* (musician, plural) > female

  6. *das Haus* (house) > diminutive

  7. *die Geschäftsfrau* (businesswoman) > male

  8. *das Bett* (bed) > diminutive

C. Add the correct article in the nominative case:

  1. ____ *Aluminium* (aluminum) 2. ____ *Blume*
  (flower) 3. ____ *Hagel* (hail) 4. ____ *Neffe*
  (nephew) 5. ____ *Büchlein* (little book) 6. ____
  Bulle (bull) 7. ____ *Frühling* (spring) 8. ____ *Okto-*

ber (October) 9. ____*Freitag* (Friday) 10. ____
Smaragd (emerald) 11. ____ *Dollar* (Dollar)
12. ____ *Titanic* (the ship Titanic) 13. ____ *Nelke*
(carnation) 14. ____ *Bettchen* (small bed) 15. ____
Messing (brass) 16. ____ *Zahnärztin* (dentist)
17. ____ *Drei* (the three) 18. ____ *Gold* (gold)
19. ____ *Herbst* (autumn) 20. ____ *Mai* (May)

D. Fill in the appropriate stress word. There are at least
   two options in every sentence:

   1. *Das kommt ___ nicht in Frage!* (That's out of the
      question!)

   2. *Nehmen Sie ___ noch einen Kaffee!* (Why don't you
      have another cup of coffee!)

   3. *Das habe ich ___ nicht gewusst!* (I didn't know that
      at all!)

   4. *Daran habe ich ___ kein Interesse!* (I'm not at all
      interested in that!)

   5. *Heute ist ___ schon Donnerstag!* (It's already [!]
      Thursday!)

   6. *Das kann ___ nicht wahr sein!* (That cannot be
      true!)

E. Rewrite the following sentences, beginning with the
   adverb(s) in parentheses:

   1. *Ich gehe ins Theater. (heute Abend)*

   2. *Das Wetter war nicht sehr gut. (gestern)*

   3. *Er arbeitet immer am Computer. (abends)*

   4. *Sie hat Geburtstag. (nächste Woche)*

   5. *Die Sonne scheint wieder. (morgen früh)*

   6. *Bringen Sie mir ein Glas Wein. (bitte)*

7. *Ich gehe früh schlafen. (heute)*

8. *Sie hat keine Zeit. (leider)*

F. Choose the correct translation(s):

1. There are only a few beaches in Germany.
   a) *Es gibt nur wenig Strand in Deutschland.*
   b) *In Deutschland gibt es nur wenige Strände.*
   c) *Es gibt immer weniger Strände in Deutschland.*
   d) *Es gibt weniger Strände als Deutschland.*

2. She is a good teacher.
   a) *Sie ist ein guter Lehrer.*
   b) *Sie sind eine gute Lehrerin.*
   c) *Sie sind gute Lehrerinnen.*
   d) *Sie ist eine gute Lehrerin.*

3. Today, there are beach-clubs in many cities.
   a) *Heute gibt es viele Beach-Clubs in der Stadt.*
   b) *Es gibt heute Beach-Clubs in vielen Städten.*
   c) *Heute haben viele Städte einen Beach-Club.*
   d) *Es gibt heute Beach-Clubs in viele Städte.*

Answer Key

A. *Strände, Leute, Sand, Städte, Berge, Ufer, Flüsse, Seen, Parks, Winter, Palmen, Pflanzen, Trends, Oasen, Menschen.*

B. 1. *die Architektin* 2. *der Großvater* 3. *das Stühlchen* 4. *die Professorin* 5. *die Musikerinnen* 6. *das Häuschen* 7. *der Geschäftsmann* 8. *das Bettchen*

C. 1. *das*; 2. *die*; 3. *der*; 4. *der*; 5. *das*; 6. *der*; 7. *der*; 8. *der*; 9. *der*; 10. *der*; 11. *der*; 12. *die*; 13. *die*; 14. *das*; 15. *das*; 16. *die*; 17. *die*; 18. *das*; 19. *der*; 20. *der*

D. 1. *gar / überhaupt / doch* 2. *doch* 3. *gar / überhaupt* 4. *gar / überhaupt / ja* 5. *ja / doch* 6. *ja / doch*

E. 1. *Heute Abend gehe ich ins Theater.* 2. *Gestern war das Wetter nicht sehr gut.* 3. *Abends arbeitet er immer am Computer.* 4. *Nächste Woche hat sie Geburtstag.* 5. *Morgen früh scheint die Sonne wieder.* 6. *Bitte bringen Sie mir ein Glas Wein.* 7. *Heute gehe ich früh schlafen.* 8. *Leider hat sie keine Zeit.*

F. 1. b; 2. d; 3. b

LESSON 2

DIE ZEITUNG IST VON GESTERN.
THIS IS YESTERDAY'S PAPER.

A. DIALOGUE

1. *Shannon Forman, eine Editorin aus New York, besucht Frankfurt zur Internationalen Buchmesse. Es ist kurz nach acht Uhr am Morgen und Shannon ist im Begriff, die U-Bahn zum Messegelände zu nehmen. Sie macht an einem Kiosk halt, um eine Zeitung zu kaufen.*

 Shannon Forman, an editor from New York, is visiting Frankfurt for the International Book Fair. It is shortly after eight o'clock in the morning, and Shannon is about to take the subway to the fair area. She stops at a newsstand to buy a newspaper.

2. Zeitungsverkäufer: **Schönen guten Morgen.**
 A very good morning to you.

3. Shannon: **Guten Morgen! Ich möchte eine Zeitung, bitte. Haben Sie auch amerikanische Zeitungen?**
 Good morning! I'd like a newspaper, please. Do you also have American newspapers?

4. Zeitungsverkäufer: **Ja, sicherlich. Jetzt für die Messe bekommen wir auch jeden Tag die New York Times und das Wall Street Journal.**
 Yes, of course. Now, for the fair, we're also getting the New York Times and the Wall Street Journal every day.

5. Shannon: **Großartig! Dann nehme ich beide und auch die Frankfurter.**
 Great! Then I'll take both, and also the Frankfurter.

6. Zeitungsverkäufer: **Die Rundschau oder die Allgemeine?**
   The *Rundschau* or the *Allgemeine*?

7. Shannon: **Oh, geben Sie mir bitte auch beide.**
   Oh, give me both, please.

8. Zeitungsverkäufer: **Das macht dann zusammen genau 12 Euro.**
   Then, that comes to exacty 12 euros altogether.

9. *Shannon gibt dem Zeitungsverkäufer einen 20-Euro-Schein.*
   Shannon hands the newspaper salesman a 20 euro bill.

10. Zeitungsverkäufer: **Und acht Euro zurück. Danke schön!**
    And eight euros back. Thank you!

11. Shannon: **Bitte sehr!**
    You're welcome!

12. *Sie wirft einen Blick auf die Times und sagt dann verwundert zum Zeitungsverkäufer:* **Aber das ist ja die Zeitung von gestern!**
    She glances at the Times and then, surprised, says to the salesman: But this is yesterday's paper!

13. Zeitungsverkäufer: **Ja, natürlich! So viel ich weiß, sind die Zeitungen aus Amerika im Moment noch im Druck. Bedenken Sie bitte, es ist doch jetzt erst zwei Uhr morgens in New York.**
    Yes, of course! As far as I know, the newspapers from America are still printing at the moment. Please keep in mind, it is really just two o'clock in the morning in New York.

14. Shannon: **Ja, daran habe ich nicht gedacht. Wann bekommen Sie sie denn?**
Yes, I didn't think of that. When are you getting them then?

15. Zeitungsverkäufer: **Das weiß ich nicht genau, aber fast zur gleichen Zeit wie in New York, in ungefähr fünf oder sechs Stunden.**
I don't know that exactly, but almost at the same time as in New York, in approximately five or six hours.

16. Shannon: **Aber wie ist das denn möglich? Ein Flug von New York nach Frankfurt allein dauert doch fast neun Stunden!**
But how is that possible? A flight from New York to Frankfurt alone takes almost nine hours!

17. Zeitungsverkäufer: **Das ist im Informationszeitalter kein Problem mehr. Sie schicken sie elektronisch mit E-mail und drucken die Zeitungen hier.**
That's no problem anymore in the information age. They send it electronically by e-mail and print the newspapers here.

18. Shannon: **Das ist ja fantastisch.**
That's really fantastic.

19. Zeitungsverkäufer: **Ich nehme die Times und das Journal gerne zurück. Möchten Sie eine andere Zeitung auf Englisch? Kennen Sie die International Herald Tribune aus London? Die ist schon da.**
I'll gladly take the Times and the Journal back. Would you like another newspaper in English? Do you know the International Herald Tribune from London? It's already here.

20. Shannon: **Ja, gern! Vielen Dank!**
    Yes, gladly! Thank you very much!

21. Zeitungsverkäufer: **Dann bekommen Sie noch
    sechs Euro zurück. Bitte sehr! Und einen
    schönen Tag wünsche ich Ihnen.**
    Then you'll still get six euros back. Here we go! And
    I wish you a nice day.

22. Shannon: **Danke, ich Ihnen auch!**
    Thank you, same to you!

B. NOTES

1. An *Editor* (editor) edits books, while a *Redakteur*
   refers mainly to a newpaper editor. *Im Begriff sein*
   (to be about to). Notice that it is used with *etwas zu
   tun,* as in: *Sie ist im Begriff, die Zeitung zu kaufen.*
   She is about to buy the paper.

2. It is common to greet someone with *Schönen guten
   Morgen!* instead of just *Guten Morgen!* It adds
   emphasis to the greeting.

3. Unlike English, country names used as adjectives
   are not written with capital letters.

8. *Das macht . . . Euro.* (lit.: That makes . . .) is commonly used in the sense of "That amounts to . . . "
   or "That comes to . . . " when a salesperson anounces
   the final price for items bought.

10. The same way that it is possible to add emphasis to
    a thank you by adding the adverbs *schön* or *sehr* to
    the word *Danke,* you can add these words to the
    response: *Danke schön!* (lit.: Thank you nicely!),
    Danke sehr! (lit.: Thank you very!), *Bitte sehr!*

(You're very welcome!), *Bitte schön!* (lit.: You're
beautifully welcome!). All of these expressions are
commonly used.

12. *einen Blick werfen auf...* (lit.: to throw a look at ...)
is often used to express a quick glance at something
or somebody.

16. *Wie ist das denn möglich?* (How in the world is that
possible?) The "flavoring" word *denn* rarely indicates doubt, but rather extreme surprise.

19. The adverb *gern* (gladly, with pleasure) is rarely
used at the beginning of a sentence. It usually follows the verb directly, often to describe general liking. *Sie isst gern vegetarisch.* (She likes to eat
vegetarian.)

21. The German verb *bekommen* (to receive) is often
mixed up with the English verb "to become." Please
note that it has a completely different meaning. The
German verb for "to become" is *werden*: *Ich werde
müde*. (I'm becoming/getting tired.)

Culture Notes

The International Book Fair in Frankfurt is the world's
largest trade fair for books, multimedia, and communica-
tions. It is also the largest marketplace for trading in pub-
lishing rights. It takes place yearly in early October and
lasts for five days. Don't plan to visit Frankfurt during this
time unless you have a hotel reservation or other accom-
modation. It is nearly impossible to find one, even in the
suburbs.

It is not unusual for American newspapers to be available in
larger cities almost at the same time as they come to the

newsstands in America. This, of course, is due to modern electronic data transfer possibilities, particularly to the Internet. Newspapers are sent electronically in a printer-ready format and then printed directly on location. Only very large cities with a large American population are served. The demand in smaller cities doesn't justify the costs.

C. GRAMMAR AND USAGE

1. The Accusative and the Dative Cases

The accusative is the case of the direct object, and the dative is the case of the indirect object. Both cases are also used after certain prepositions, which we'll come to later. Most nouns do not change in these cases, but articles do:

	Nominative	Dative	Accusative
masc.	*der Tag* (day)	*dem Tag*	*den Tag*
	ein Tag	*einem Tag*	*einen Tag*
fem.	*die Woche* (week)	*der Woche*	*die Woche*
	eine Woche	*einer Woche*	*eine Woche*
neut.	*das Jahr* (year)	*dem Jahr*	*das Jahr*
	ein Jahr	*einem Jahr*	*ein Jahr*
plural	*die Tage* (days)	*den Tagen*	*die Tage*

In the sentence from the dialogue, *Shannon gibt dem Verkäufer einen 20-Euro-Schein* (Shannon gives the salesman a 20-euro bill), there are examples of all three of these cases. Shannon is the subject and is in the nominative case. The 20-euro bill is the direct object and is in the accusative case *(einen 20-Euro-Schein)*. The salesman is the indirect object and is in the dative case *(dem Verkäufer)*. Other examples are:

Der Lehrer gibt der Studentin ein Buch.
The teacher gives the student (f.) a book.

Die Frau gibt dem Kind das Geschenk.
The woman gives the child the gift.

Die Lehrerin erzählt der Studentin eine Geschichte.
The teacher (f.) tells the student (f.) a story.

2. Accusative and Dative Prepositions

Prepositions in German are used similarly to English prepositions, but they are followed by particular cases. Some prepositions require one specific case; for others, the case following them is determined by their meaning in the sentence.

The prepositions *aus* (out, from), *außer* (except, besides), *bei* (by, at), *mit* (with), *nach* (to, after), *seit* (since), *von* (from) and *zu* (to, for) are always followed by the dative case. Note the following contractions: *beim* (*bei dem*), *zum* (*zu dem*), *vom* (*von dem*) and *zur* (*zu der*).

Shannon besucht Frankfurt zur (zu der) Buchmesse.
Shannon is visiting Frankfurt for the book fair.

Sie fährt mit dem Zug.
She takes the train. ("She travels with the train.")

The prepositions *durch* (through), *für* (for), *gegen* (against, toward), *ohne* (without), and *um* (around) are always followed by the accusative case.

Die Mutter kauft ein Buch für den Jungen.
The mother buys a book for the boy.

Wir gehen durch den Park.
We're walking through the park.

3. Two-Way Prepositions

There are a number of "two-way" prepositions in German that are used with the accusative case in some instances, and the dative case in others. The more common ones are: *an* (on, at), *auf* (on, upon, to), *hinter* (behind), *in* (in, into), *neben* (next to, beside), *über* (over, above), *unter* (below, under), *vor* (in front of), and *zwischen* (between).

As a rule of thumb, if these prepositions express location, they are followed by the dative case.

Das Buch liegt auf dem Tisch.
    The book is (lying) on the table.

Das Bild hängt an der Wand.
    The picture is hanging on the wall.

But if they express the direction of a motion, the accusative case is used.

Er legt das Buch auf den Tisch.
    He lays/puts the book on the table.

Er hängt das Bild an die Wand.
    He hangs the picture on the wall.

It is possible to use the dative case when motion is involved, though. Take a look at these examples:

Sie geht auf die Straße.
    She's walking/going onto the street. (She is moving onto the street from a position off the street.)

Sie geht auf der Straße.
    She's walking/going on the street. (She is moving, but the movement is taking place only on the street.)

4. Object Pronouns

The following are the accusative and dative case pronouns, shown next to the nominative pronouns for comparison:

Nominative	Dative	Accusative
ich (I)	*mir* ([to]me)	*mich* (me)
du (you)	*dir* ([to] you)	*dich* (you)
er (he)	*ihm* ([to] him)	*ihn* (him)
sie (she)	*ihr* ([to] her)	*sie* (her)
es (it)	*ihm* ([to] it)	*es* (it)
wir (we)	*uns* ([to] us)	*uns* (us)
ihr (you)	*euch* ([to] you)	*euch* (you)
sie (they)	*ihnen* ([to] them)	*sie* (them)
Sie (you)	*Ihnen* ([to] you)	*Sie* (you)

Accusative pronouns are used as direct objects and as objects of prepositions requiring the accusative. Dative pronouns are used as indirect objects and as objects of prepositions requiring the dative.

Ich kenne dich.	I know you. (acc.)
Hast du Kaffee für mich?	Do you have coffee for me? (acc. *für*)
Er gibt ihm den Kaffee.	He's giving the coffee to him. (dat.)
Er spricht mit ihr.	He's talking to her. (dat. *mit*)

EXERCISES

A. Add the following preposition and/or the appropriate definite or indefinite articles in the text. Remember that some prepositions are contracted with the article:
Das—zu—der—im—in—die—die—in—ohne—eine—am—zum—den—einen—die—am—Die

Auch in diesem Jahr findet _____ *Oktober* _____ *Frankfurt wieder* _____ *Internationale Buchmesse statt. Nicht nur* _____ *Hotels sind dann voll ausgebucht, auch* _____ _____ *Restaurants gibt es kaum* _____ *freien Tisch.* _____ *U-Bahn und* _____ *Busse sind besonders* _____ *Morgen und* _____ *Mittag bis* _____ *späten Abend überfüllt.* _____ *Touristenbüro rät dringend, Frankfurt nicht* _____ _____ *Zeit zu besuchen* _____ _____ *Hotelreservierung zu haben.*

This year, as usual, the International Book Fair takes place in Frankfurt in October. Not only are the hotels fully booked then, there will be hardly any free tables at a restaurant. The subway and the busses are packed, especially in the morning and at noon until late in the evening. The tourist office is urgently advising (people) not to visit Frankfurt during that time without having a hotel reservation.

B. Change the nouns and/or articles as indicated:

1. *der Hut* (hat) > dative plural

2. *die Großmutter* (grandmother) > accusative plural

3. *die Winter* (winter) > dative singular

4. *der Morgen* (morning) > accusative plural

5. *die Musik* (music) > dative singular

6. *das Gebäude* (building) > accusative singular

7. *die Euro* (euro) > dative singular

8. *das Fenster* (window) > dative plural

C. Choose the correct translation:

1. It is far without a car.
   - a) *Es ist weit für ein Auto.*
   - b) *Es ist weit ohne ein Auto.*
   - c) *Es ist weit ohne kein Auto.*
   - d) *Es ist weit ohne einem Auto.*

2. I hear a bird (masc.) singing.
   - a) *Ich höre den Vogel singen.*
   - b) *Ich höre einem Vogel singen.*
   - c) *Ich höre einen Vogel singen.*
   - d) *Ich höre das Vogel singen.*

3. He reads the paper in the morning.
   - a) *Er liest morgen die Zeitung.*
   - b) *Er liest die Zeitung im Morgen.*
   - c) *Er liest dem Morgen der Zeitung.*
   - d) *Er liest die Zeitung am Morgen.*

D. Replace the underlined phrases with the nouns and articles in parentheses:

1. *Der Student lernt seit einer Woche Deutsch. (ein Jahr)*

2. *Heute bin ich im Kino. (die Oper)*

3. *Er geht morgen ins Theater. (ein Park)*

4. *Wir sind am Nachmittag bei einem Freund. (der Abend/die Tante)*

5. *Das Kino ist direkt neben der Bank. (die Bäckerei/ das Museum)*

6. *Fliegst du mit dem Flugzeug nach Berlin? (die Familie)*

E. Fill in the appropriate articles and/or prepositions:

1. *Ich fahre _____ _____ U-Bahn _____ _____ Stadt.* (with/the/to/the)

2. *Nehmen Sie doch noch _____ Kaffee!* (a)

3. *Ich habe leider keine Zeit _____ _____ Montag.* (on/the)

4. *In _____ Woche habe ich nur _____ Freitag _____ Termin.* (the/on the/a)

5. *Ich möchte _____ Zeitung, bitte!* (a)

F. Add the correct pronouns in parentheses:

1. _____ *fliegt nie ohne* _____ *nach Frankfurt.* (she/him)

2. _____ *gibt* _____ *die Informationen.* (he/her)

3. *Hast* _____ *heute Zeit für* _____? (you, fam./me)

4. _____ *haben wenig Zeit für* _____. (You, pol./them)

5. *Wie geht* _____ _____? (it/you, pol.)

6. *Wie geht* _____ _____? (it/them)

7. *Wie geht* _____ _____? (it/you, plural, fam.)

8. _____ *ist nicht schwer für* _____. (it, us)

9. _____ *gebe* _____ _____ *am Montag!* (I/it/you, fam.)

10. _____ *habt* _____ *auf der Straße gesehen.* (you, plural, fam./us)

Answer Key

A. *im, in, die, die, in den, einen, Die, die, am, am, zum,* ·
Das, zu der, ohne eine

B. 1. *den Hüten;* 2. *die Großmütter;* 3. *dem Winter;* 4. *die
Morgen;* 5. *der Musik;* 6. *das Gebäude;* 7. *dem Euro;*
8. *den Fenstern*

C. 1. b; 2. c; 3. d

D. 1. *einem Jahr;* 2. *in der Oper;* 3. *in einen Park;* 4. *am
Abend / der Tante;* 5. *Die Bäckerei / dem Museum;*
6. *der Familie*

E. 1. *mit der, in die;* 2. *einen;* 3. *an dem;* 4. *der, am, einen;*
5. *eine*

F. 1. *Sie, ihn;* 2. *Er, ihr;* 3. *du, mich;* 4. *Sie, sie;* 5. *es,
Ihnen;* 6. *es, ihnen;* 7. *es, euch;* 8. *Es, uns;* 9. *Ich, es,
dir;* 10. *Ihr, uns*

LESSON 3

ICH GLAUB' MEIN HANDY KLINGELT.
I BELIEVE MY CELL PHONE IS RINGING.

A. DIALOGUE

1. *Nach der Frankfurter Buchmesse fliegt Shannon Forman nach Hannover. Sie besucht dort ihre Freunde Dorothee und Andreas auf ein paar Tage. Dorothee holt Shannon auf Hannovers Flughafen Langenhagen ab, aber Shannon muss sehr lange auf ihr Gepäck warten. Sie ruft Dorothee auf ihrem Handy an:*

   After the Frankfurt Book Fair, Shannon Forman flies to Hannover. She is visiting her friends Dorothee and Andreas there for a few days. Dorothee meets Shannon at Hannover's airport Langenhagen, but Shannon has to wait a long time for her luggage. She calls Dorothee on her cell phone:

2. Shannon: **Hallo Dorothee. Ich bin's, Shannon. Ich hoffe, du wartest noch nicht sehr lange. Das Gepäck des Fluges von Frankfurt ist noch nicht hier.**

   Hello, Dorothee. It's me, Shannon. I hope you haven't been waiting long. The luggage from the Frankfurt flight isn't here yet.

3. Dorothee: **Kein Problem! Andreas sucht ohnehin noch nach einem Parkplatz. Ich warte vor deinem Flugsteig-Ausgang. Das Gate deines Fluges ist A4, oder?**

   No problem! Andreas is still looking for a parking space, anyway. I'm waiting in front of your gate exit. The gate of your flight is A4, isn't it?

4. Shannon: **Richtig! Bis später dann.**
   Right! See you later, then.

5. *Einige Minuten später kommen Shannons Taschen
   auf dem Gepäckband an. Sie nimmt sie und geht zum
   Ausgang. Dorothee begrüßt sie.*
   A few minutes later, Shannon's luggage arrives on
   the conveyor belt. She picks it up and walks to the
   exit. Dorothee greets her.

6. Dorothee: **Hallo, Shannon. Freut mich, dass du da
   bist. Wie war dein Flug?**
   Hello, Shannon. I'm glad that you're here. How was
   your flight?

7. Shannon: **Kurz und schmerzlos. Nur war der
   Motor des Gepäckbandes hier in Hannover
   kaputt. Wo ist dein Mann?**
   Short and painless. But the conveyor belt motor was
   broken here in Hannover. Where's your husband?

8. Dorothee: **Ich habe nicht die geringste Ahnung.
   Ich habe schon zwei Nachrichten auf seinem
   Handy hinterlassen, aber er antwortet nicht.
   Wahrscheinlich sucht er immer noch nach einem
   Parkplatz. Die Parkplätze des Flughafens sind im
   Moment überfüllt.**
   I haven't the slightest idea. I've already left two
   messages on his cell, but he isn't picking up. He's
   probably still looking for a parking space. Parking
   lots at the airport are packed at the moment.

9. Shannon: **Ich könnte sowieso eine Tasse Kaffee
   vertragen und vielleicht einen Becher des
   köstlichen *Mövenpick* Eises dort. Auf dem kurzen
   Flug von Frankfurt haben sie nur eine Tüte Erd-
   nüsse serviert.**
   I could use a cup of coffee anyway, and perhaps a

cup of that delicious *Mövenpick* ice cream over
there. They only served a bag of peanuts on that
short flight from Frankfurt.

10. *Genau in diesem Moment hören sie das Klingeln*
eines Handys.
Just at that moment, they hear the ringing of a cell
phone.

11. Dorothee: **Moment! Ich glaub' mein Handy klin-**
gelt, oder ist es deins?
Just a moment! I believe my cell phone is ringing, or
is it yours?

12. Shannon: **Nein, meins klingelt mit Musik.**
No, mine rings with music.

13. Dorothee beantwortet ihr Handy: **Andreas, wo zum**
Teufel bist du? Wir warten schon auf dich!
Dorothee answers her phone: Andreas, where the
heck are you? We're already waiting for you!

14. Andreas: **Tut mir Leid! Ich bin auf einem Park-**
platz ganz in der Nähe. Jemand hat einen Fernse-
her im Auto neben mir und sie bringen gerade ein
Fußballspiel unserer Mannschaft. Ich bin in fünf
Minuten da.
Sorry! I'm in a parking space nearby. Someone has
a TV in the car next to me, and they're just broadcasting a soccer match of our national team. I'll be
there in five minutes.

15. Dorothee: **Okay, wir essen einen Eisbecher im**
Café vor dem Flugsteig A4. Bis gleich!
Okay, we'll eat a cup of ice cream in the café in front
of gate A4. See you soon.

16. *Während sie im Café sitzen, klingelt Dorothees*
Handy wieder:

While they are sitting in the café, Dorothee's phone rings again:

17. Andreas: **T'schuldigung! Die deutsche Mannschaft hat gerade ein Tor geschossen. Ich komme sofort. Ihr seid nicht böse, oder?**
Sorry! The German team has just scored a goal. I'll be there right away. You (two) aren't angry, are you?

18. Dorothee: **Nein, wir essen unser Eis. Bis dann!**
No, we're eating our ice cream. See you!

19. *Shannon and Dorothee haben ihren Kaffee getrunken und ihr Eis gegessen. Schon wieder klingelt das Handy.*
Shannon and Dorothee have drunk their coffee and eaten their ice cream. The phone rings again.

20. Dorothee: **Andreas, das nächste Mal nehme ich nicht mehr ab. Du kommst besser bald oder wir nehmen ein Taxi.**
Andreas, I'm not picking up the next time. You'd better come soon, or we're taking a cab.

21. *Dorothee drückt die Auflegetaste:*
Dorothee pushes the hang-up button:

22. Dorothee: **Früher habe ich ihm einfach eine halbe Stunde gegeben. Jetzt klingelt das Handy alle fünf Minuten, wenn er nicht pünktlich ist.**
It used to be that I simply gave him half an hour. Now, the cell phone rings every five minutes if he isn't on time.

23. Shannon lächelt: **Zeichen der Zeit. Wir sind jederzeit erreichbar.**
Shannon smiles: Sign of the times. We're reachable all the time.

24. *In diesem Moment hören sie das Klingeln eines Handys am Tisch neben ihnen, aber die Frau telefoniert offensichtlich schon. Sie sagt:* **Entschuldigung, mein anderes Handy klingelt. Bis später!**
At that moment, they hear the ringing of a cell phone at the table next to them, but the woman is obviously already talking on the phone. She says: Sorry, my other cell is ringing. See you later!

25. Dorothee: **Nun, das nenne ich zu viel des Guten!**
Well, I'd call that too much of a good thing!

26. *Plötzlich und ganz unerwartet steht Andreas vor ihnen.*
Suddenly and quite unexpectedly Andreas is standing in front of them.

27. Andreas: **Verzeihung! Es war nur wegen des Fußballspiels ...**
Sorry! It was just because of the soccer game ...

B. NOTES

1. *Ein paar Tage* (a few days) should not be mixed up with *ein Paar Schuhe* (a pair of shoes). While *ein paar* (not written with a capital letter) means simply "a few," *ein Paar* (capitalized) always means "a pair" of something.

3. *Kein Problem!* is a very common expression meaning "No problem!" There are many different ways in German to say "anyway." *Ohnehin* and *sowieso* are used in the middle of a sentence, never in the beginning.

Even though there is a German word for "gate," most people use the English term *das Gate* for airports. The German word is *der Flugsteig* in airports or *der Bahnsteig* (platform) in train stations.

4. *Bis später!* is the most common expression for "See you later" (lit.: Until later). It is not only used when actually expecting to see someone at a later time, but also if you expect to talk to someone soon on the phone. Other expressions with *bis* are: *Bis morgen!* (See you tomorrow!) or *Bis bald!* (See you soon!) or *Bis Montag!* (See you on Monday!).

7. *Kurz und schmerzlos!* Means literally "Short and painless!" It's used much as in English.

8. *Die Nachricht* (message) can have two meanings in its plural form; *die Nachrichten* could mean "messages" but also "the news."

10. *Moment!* is often used to say "Just a moment!" Another common expression meaning the same is *Augenblick!* (lit.: Blink of an eye!)

13. There are two verbs for "to answer" in German. The verb *antworten* requires the preposition *auf*: *Ich antworte auf die Frage* (I answer [to] the question). The prefix *be-* eliminates the need for the preposition: *Ich beantworte die Frage* (I answer the question).

  Wo zum Teufel bist du? (Where the heck are you?) literally means "Where the devil are you?"

14. *Tut mir Leid!* (lit.: It makes sorrow for me!) is a more sincere apology than *"Entschuldigung!"* (Excuse me!), which—of course—could be used if someone is simply standing in your way.

  The verb *bringen* (to bring) is often used colloquially to express radio or TV broadcasting instead of *übertragen* (to broadcast) or *senden* (to send).

16. *Während* (while, during) is not only a preposition. It is often used as a conjunction as well (Lesson 15). Remember that the preposition requires the genitive case (see grammar topic in this lesson).

17. *T'schuldigung!* is a colloquial form of *Entschuldigung!* (My apology! or Excuse me!).
    Note that the adjective *böse* can have two completely different meanings depending on the context and use: *Sie ist böse* (She's angry, or She is mean), *Sie ist eine böse Person* (She is a malevolent/evil person).

22. The adjective *früher* (earlier) has a different meaning if it is used as an adverb: "It used to be that . . . "
    Alle (all) is used here in the sense of "every": *Alle fünf Minuten* (every five minutes).

25. The term *zu viel des Guten* (too much of a good thing) uses the adjectival noun of the adjective and adverb *gut* (good/well). This is described in greater detail in Lesson 4.

27. *Verzeihung!* (Forgive me!) Is another form of apology. It is more sincere than saying *Entschuldigung!* (Excuse me!) but less sincere than *Das tut mir Leid!* (I am sorry!).

Culture Notes

Cell phones are as ubiquitous *(allgegenwärtig)* in the German-speaking countries of Germany, Austria, Switzerland, and Liechtenstein as they are in America. Pretty much the same features are offered by most cell phone service providers *(Handy-Service-Anbieter)*. It's possible to receive e-mail *(E-mail* or simply *Mail)*, and many cell phone manufacturers include a standard PDA or even a digital camera with the phone, where you can take and send pictures right from your cell phone. Even though text messages *(SMS)* are difficult to type on the small keyboard *(die Tastatur* or *das Keyboard)* of a standard cell phone, they are commonly used. Many providers offer a large variety of standard text messages to choose from (i.e., for birthdays or other common occasions), so the user doesn't have to type at all. By the way, the term *Handy* was supposedly invented at a cell phone convention in London, where one person excitedly said, when he saw one of the first cell phones, "That's really handy!" Well, the rest is history.

Mövenpick ice cream (lit.: Seagull's Pick) has been hailed by many as the best ice cream in German-speaking countries. Named after the Swiss hotel/restaurant where it was invented, it quickly made its way to other German countries. If you watch your calories, it might not be for you, at least not on a regular basis, because it is incredibly rich. The ice cream is so popular that children often spell *die Möwe* (seagull) with a "v" instead of the correct "w" in school, much to the dismay of their teachers. The *w* in the name of the Swiss restaurant, and consequently the ice cream that was named after it, was changed to *v,* since the letter symbolized the flight of a seagull much better in the company logo. However, the spelling of the word *Möwe* wasn't changed in the recent German spelling reform (mandatory since January 2005), even though there was a lot of arguing about it.

C. GRAMMAR AND USAGE

1. The Genitive Case

The genitive case describes possession or belonging. Note the changes to the articles below. Also note that masculine and neuter singular nouns take *-s* or *-es.* Nouns that end in *-nis* take *-ses,* and adjectival nouns and *n*-nouns add *-n* or *-en.*

masc.	*des Tages* (of the day)	*eines Tages* (of a day)
fem.	*der Woche* (of the week)	*einer Woche* (of a week)
neut.	*des Jahres* (of the year)	*eines Jahres* (of a year)
plural	*der Monate* (of the months)	

Das Gate des Fluges ist A4, nicht wahr?
   The gate of the flight is A4, isn't it?

Der Motor des Gepäckbandes war kaputt.
   The motor of the conveyor belt was broken.

Der Flughafen der Stadt ist nicht sehr groß.
   The city's airport is not very large.

Das ist ein Zeichen der Zeit.
   That's a sign of the times.

Note that the genitive is <u>not</u> used in the following expressions:

eine Tasse Kaffee	a cup of coffee
ein Glas Bier	a glass of beer
ein Becher Eis	a cup of ice cream

2. Genitive Prepositions

The following prepositions are followed by the genitive case: *anhand* (by means of), *außerhalb* (outside of, beyond), *binnen* (within), *dank* (thanks to), *wegen* (because of), *inmitten* (in the midst of), *innerhalb* (within), *entlang* (along), *jenseits* (beyond), *statt, anstatt* (instead, in place of), *trotz* (in spite of), *während* (during). Note that some of these prepositions can be used as conjunctions as well (Lesson 15).

Anhand dieser Tatsachen traf er seine Entscheidung.
By means of these facts he made his decision.

Während des Fluges ist der Gebrauch von Handys verboten.
During the flight, the use of cell phones is prohibited.

Wegen des Fußballspiels kommt er zu spät.
He is coming late because of the soccer game.

3. Simple Possession

A way to show possession is simply to add an *-s* (without an apostrophe) to a noun:

Shannons Reisetaschen kommen auf dem Gepäckband an.
Shannon's travel bags are arriving on the conveyor belt.

Dorothees Handy klingelt alle fünf Minuten.
Dorothee's cell phone is ringing every five minutes.

4. Possessives

The possessive adjectives (my, your, his . . .) follow the endings of the indefinite articles (*ein, eine,* etc.). They are: *mein* (my), *dein* (your), *sein* (his), *ihr* (her), *sein* (its), *unser* (our), *euer* (your pl.), *ihr* (their), and *Ihr* (your, pol.). Note that, unlike indefinite articles, they do have plural forms.

	Nominative	Dative
masc.	*mein Flug* (my flight)	*meinem Flug*
fem.	*meine Tasche* (my bag)	*meiner Tasche*
neut.	*mein Gepäck* (my luggage)	*meinem Gepäck*
plural	*meine Freunde* (my friends)	*meinen Freunden*

	Accusative	Genitive
masc.	*meinen Flug*	*meines Fluges*
fem.	*meine Tasche*	*meiner Tasche*
neut.	*mein Gepäck*	*meines Gepäcks*
plural	*meine Freunde*	*meiner Freunde*

The other possessives follow the same pattern: *dein, deine, dein,* etc. The only exception is *euer,* which drops its second -*e: euer, eure, euer,* etc. Possessives may also stand on their own, as pronouns or placeholders for a noun, similar to English "mine," "yours," etc. They are the same as the forms above, except in the nominative masculine and neuter, and the accusative neuter, where they add -*r* or -*er* (masc.), and -*s* or -*es* (neut.).

Klingelt mein Handy oder deins?
    Is your cell phone ringing or mine?

Das ist deine Zeitung, nicht meine!
    That's your newspaper, not mine!

Hat unsere Mannschaft ein Tor geschossen oder eure?
    Has our team or yours scored a goal?

Sie telefoniert mit seinem Handy, nicht mit ihrem.
    She is talking on his cell phone, not on hers.

5. Compound Nouns

Nouns can be combined with other nouns or with other parts of speech to form compound nouns. There are many different ways to do this. Note that compound nouns always take the gender of the last part of the compound. (The first part is the qualifier.) Study the following examples:

    das Buch (book) + *die Messe* (fair) = *die Buchmesse* (book fair) *das Gepäck* (luggage) + *das Band* (belt, band) = *das Gepäckband* (conveyor belt)

die Reise (trip, travel) + *die Tasche* (bag) = *die Reisetasche* (travel bag)

auflegen (to hang up) + *die Taste* (key, button) = *die Auflegetaste* (hang-up button)

unter (under) + *die Tasse* (cup) = *die Untertasse* (saucer)

aus (out) + *der Gang* (walk, gait) = *der Ausgang* (exit)

schwer (heavy) + *die Arbeit* (work) = *die Schwerarbeit* (heavy work)

Compound nouns that derive from English or other languages are commonly hyphenated:

das Handy (cell phone) + *der Service* (service) + *der Anbieter* (provider) = *der Handy-Service-Anbieter* (cell phone service provider)

Note that there is a difference between a compound noun and two nouns following each other.

die Kaffeetasse (the coffee cup), but: *die Tasse Kaffee* (cup of coffee)

das Weinglas (the wine glass), but: *das Glas Wein* (the glass of wine)

Also note that an *–s* may be added to the first noun to show possession.

der Liebling (darling) + *das Ziel* (destination, goal) = *das Lieblingsziel* (favorite destination)

der Anwalt (lawyer) + *das Büro* (office) = *das Antwaltsbüro* (lawyer's office)

EXERCISES

A. Add the articles and nouns in parentheses in the genitive case:

1. *Die Farbe* _____ _____ *ist schwarz.* (of the luggage)

2. *Das ist ein Zeichen* _____ _____. (of the time).

3. *Ich warte vor dem Ausgang* _____ _____. (of the flight)

4. *Er ist der Gewinner* _____ _____. (of the game)

5. *Das ist das Ende* _____ _____. (of the day)

6. *Das ist das Handy* _____ _____. (of a friend)

7. *Ich habe die Lösung* _____ _____. (of the problem)

8. *Sie hat das Klingeln* _____ _____ *nicht gehört.* (of the cell phone)

B. Add the genitive prepositions and the correct article as indicated. There are sometimes several possibilities:

1. *Sie ist* _____ _____ *Grenze.* (beyond the)

2. *Ich nehme Tee* _____ _____ *Kaffees.* (instead of the)

3. *Sie kommen* _____ _____ *Woche.* (within a)

4. *Er kommt spät* _____ _____ *Fußballspiels.* (because of a)

5. *Es gibt Weinberge* _____ _____ *Rhein-ufers*. (along the)

6. *Sie hat keine Zeit* _____ _____ *Tages*. (during the)

C. Add the correct nominative possessives:

1. _____ *Straße* (my street) 2. _____ *Tasse Kaffee* (her cup of coffee) 3. _____ *Flug* (their flight) 4. _____ *Neffe* (my nephew) 5. _____ *Büchlein* (her little book) 6. _____ *Handy* (your [sing. fam.] cell phone) 7. _____ *Auto* (your [pol.] car) 8. _____ *Gepäck* (our luggage) 9. _____ *Parkplatz* (your [pl. fam.] parking space) 10. _____ *Problem* (my problem)

D. Fill in the appropriate possessive with the correct case ending:

1. *Das ist die Tasche* _____ *Frau.* (That's my wife's bag.)

2. *Telefonieren Sie doch mit* _____ *Handy?* (Why don't you call on my cell phone?)

3. *Während* _____ *Urlaubs war ich in Amerika.* (I was in America for my vacation.)

4. *Wir nehmen* _____ *Auto.* (We are taking his car.)

5. *Das ist das Spiel* _____ *Mannschaft.* (That's the game of our team.)

6. *Wessen Kaffee ist das,* _____ *oder* _____ ? (Whose coffee is that, mine or yours [sing. fam.]?)

7. *Das Geld ist in* _____ *Tasche.* (The money is in her bag.)

8. *Es ist kein Zucker in* _____ *Tee.* (There's no sugar in my tea.)

9. *Wir haben keinen Fernseher in* _____ *Auto.* (We have no TV in our car.)

10. *Ich warte vor* _____ *Ausgang.* (I'm waiting in front of your [plural fam.] exit.)

E. Combine the following words to compound nouns:

1. *der Flug* (flight) + *der Plan* (schedule) = flight schedule

2. *das Auto* (car) + *die Tür* (door) = car door

3. *rot* (red) + *der Wein* (wine) + *die Flasche* (bottle) = red wine bottle

4. *die Schwierigkeit* (difficulty) + *der Grad* (degree) = degree of (!) difficulty

5. *unter* (under) + *die Schrift* (writing) = signature

6. *die Zeitung* (newspaper) + *die Anzeige* (ad) = newspaper ad (of !)

7. *das Wasser* (water) + *die Leitung* (pipe) = water pipe

8. *das Auto* (car) + *die Bahn* (way, train, lane) + *das Kreuz* (cross, junction) = highway intersection

9. *das Flugzeug* (airplane) + *der Pilot* (pilot) = airplane pilot

10. *der Geschmack* (taste) + *die Richtung* (direction) = flavor (lit.: direction of taste)

Answer Key

A. 1. *des Gepäcks*; 2. *der Zeit*; 3. *des Flug(e)s*; 4. *des Spiels*; 5. *des Tages*; 6. *eines Freundes*; 7. *des Problems*; 8. *des Handys*

B. 1. *jenseits der*; 2. *(an)statt des*; 3. *innerhalb/binnen einer*; 4. *wegen eines*; 5. *entlang des*; 6. *während des*

C. 1. *meine*; 2. *ihre*; 3. *ihr*; 4. *mein*; 5. *ihr*; 6. *dein*; 7. *Ihr*; 8. *unser*; 9. *euer*; 10. *mein*

D. 1. *meiner*; 2. *meinem*; 3. *meines*; 4. *sein*; 5. *unserer*; 6. *meiner, deiner*; 7. *ihrer*; 8. *meinem*; 9. *unserem*; 10. *eurem*

E. 1. *der Flugplan*; 2. *die Autotür*; 3. *die Rotweinflasche*; 4. *der Schwierigkeitsgrad*; 5. *die Unterschrift*; 6. *die Zeitungsanzeige*; 7. *die Wasserleitung*; 8. *das Autobahnkreuz*; 9. *der Flugzeugpilot*; 10. *die Geschmacksrichtung*

LESSON 4

DIE DAME DA FÄHRT SCHWARZ!
THAT LADY THERE IS DODGING THE FARE!

A. DIALOGUE

1. *Shannons Freunde arbeiten am heutigen Montag. Shannon ist allein in der Stadt, aber Hannover hat viel zu bieten. Es gibt keinen Grund zur Langeweile. Shannon hat großes Interesse an orientalischen Teppichen, und sie möchte zuerst ins Orientteppich-Museum. Ja, es gibt tatsächlich ein Museum für orientalische Teppiche in Hannover. Es gibt heute Museen für fast alles. Shannon geht in eine U-Bahnstation und fragt einen Passanten nach dem Weg.*

   Shannon's friends are working this Monday. Shannon is by herself in the city, but Hannover has a lot to offer. There's no reason for boredom. Since Shannon is very interested in Oriental carpets, she wants to go to the Oriental Carpet Museum. Yes, there is indeed a Museum for Oriental carpets in Hannover. There are museums for almost everything today. Shannon enters a subway station and asks a passer-by for directions.

2. Shannon: **Entschuldigen Sie, welche U-Bahn fährt zur Georgstraße?**

   Excuse me, which subway goes to Georgstraße?

3. Passant: **Nehmen Sie die U-Bahn dort. Es sind nur drei Stationen bis zum Steintor.**

   Take the subway over there. It's only three stations to the Steintor.

4. Shannon: **Vielen Dank!**

   Thanks a lot!

5. Passant: **Kein Problem!**
No problem!

6. *Shannon sucht nach einem Fahrkartenschalter, aber es scheint nirgendwo einen zu geben. Sie geht zum Bahnsteig. Das Seltsame ist, es gibt auch kein Drehkreuz. Vielleicht bezahlt man hier <u>in</u> der U-Bahn? Shannon steigt in die gerade angekommene U-Bahn und setzt sich. Dann fragt sie einen jungen Mann neben ihr:*
Shannon looks for a ticket booth, but there seems to be none anywhere. She goes to the platform. The strange thing is, there's no turnstile either. Perhaps one pays <u>in</u> the subway car here? Shannon gets on the train that's just pulling in and sits down. Then she asks a young man next to her:

7. Shannon: **Entschuldigen Sie, aber wo kaufe ich einen Fahrschein für die U-Bahn?**
Excuse me, but where do I buy a ticket for the subway?

8. Junger Mann: **Oh, Sie haben keine Fahrkarte?**
Oh, you don't have a ticket?

9. Shannon: **Nein, ich habe keinen einzigen Fahrkartenschalter gefunden und auch kein Drehkreuz.**
No, I didn't find a single ticket booth, and no turnstile either.

10. Junger Mann, lächelnd: **Dann fahren Sie ja schwarz. Schwarzfahren ist teuer hier. Aber Sie haben eine fünfundneunzigprozentige Chance. Sonst kostet es mindestens 40 Euro.**
Young man, smiling: Then you're dodging the fare. Fare-dodging is expensive here. But you have a

ninety-five-percent chance. Otherwise it costs at least 40 euros.

11. *Die U-Bahn hält an der nächsten Station. Shannon sieht mehrere Beamte mit seriös aussehenden Mützen einsteigen.*
The subway stops at the next station. Shannon sees several officials with serious looking hats entering.

12. *Genau in diesem Moment schreit eine Frau:* **Die Dame da fährt schwarz!**
Just at that moment a woman yells: That lady there is dodging the fare!

13. Junger Mann zu den Beamten: **Das stimmt nicht! Hier ist ihre Fahrkarte und hier ist meine.**
Young man to the officials: That's not true! Here is her ticket and here is mine.

14. *Ein paar Minuten später wendet er sich an die Frau:*
A few minutes later, he turns to the woman.

15. Junger Mann: **Das war wirklich eine Gemeinheit!**
That was really a mean thing!

16. Shannon: **Vielen herzlichen Dank für Ihre freundliche Hilfe. Ich habe gerade mehr als vierzig Euro gespart. Warum haben Sie denn zwei Fahrkarten?**
Many (hearty) thanks for your friendly help. I just saved more than forty euros. Why do you have <u>two</u> tickets?

17. Junger Mann: **Zwei Kollegen haben gerade die U-Bahn verlassen. Ich habe noch ihre Fahrkarten.**

Entschuldigung, aber ignorieren Sie einfach die Hexe dort. Nicht alle Deutschen sind so. Übrigens, ich heiße Klaus.

Two colleagues (of mine) just left the subway. I still have their tickets. Sorry, but just ignore the witch over there. Not all Germans are like that. By the way, my name is Klaus.

18. Shannon: **Ich weiß. Es gibt überall solche Leute. Aber auf jeden Fall möchte ich Sie als Dankeschön zum Essen einladen.**

I know! There are people like that everywhere. But I certainly would like to invite you to dinner as a thank you.

19. Klaus: **Mit Vergnügen! Hier ist meine private Telefonnummer!**

With pleasure! Here's my private phone number!

20. *Die nächste Station ist Am Steintor und Shannon steigt aus:* **Vielen Dank nochmal und hoffentlich bis bald!**

The next station is *Am Steintor* and Shannon gets out: Thanks a lot once again, and hopefully (I'll see you) soon!

21. *Während des Aussteigens bemerkt Shannon den unbefriedigten Ausdruck auf dem Gesicht der Frau. Die Menschen sind doch überall gleich, denkt Shannon. Eigenschaften sind wirklich global, aber die meisten Menschen sind wirklich toll!*

While exiting, Shannon notices the unsatisfied expression on the lady's face. People are really the same everywhere, Shannon thinks. Characteristics are so global, but most people are really great!

B. NOTES

1. *Interesse haben an* . . . (to have an interest in . . .)
   is always used with the preposition *an* (on).

   Be careful with the adjective and adverb *tatsächlich* (indeed) as a response question. It often implies
   sarcasm: *Ich laufe einen Kilometer in zwei Minuten!*
   (I run one kilometer in two minutes!) *Tatsächlich?*
   (Oh, really?! Nobody ever has.)

3. There are two words in German for "there," *da* and
   dort. They are basically interchangeable, but if two
   locations are described in the same context, *da* refers
   to the closer one, *dort* to the one further away. This
   difference might be especially important when calling on the phone: *Tut mir Leid, Frau Forman ist
   nicht da* (Sorry, Mrs. Forman is not there), but: *Sie
   ist nicht dort!* (She isn't over there!).

6. The verb *suchen* (to search) is often followed by the
   preposition *nach* (after, to) meaning "to look for":
   Ich suche nach meinem Schlüssel (I'm looking for
   my key).

   When boarding the subway *(U-Bahn)*, the train
   (der Zug), or the airplane *(das Flugzeug)*, the verb
   steigen (to climb) is used: *Einsteigen, bitte!* (All
   aboard, please!).

7. and 8. *Der Fahrschein* (fare ticket) and *die Fahrkarte*
   are interchangeable and both commonly used. In
   Austria, Switzerland, and Liechtenstein, and in some
   regions of Germany, the word *das Billett* (pronounced "Bill-yet") is more common.

10. *das Schwarzfahren* (fare-dodging) can be used as a
    noun, but also as a separable verb *(Sie fährt
    schwarz)*, where the main verb and the prefix are
    often separated in the sentence. Refer to Lesson 12
    for the rules on separable verbs.

13. *Das stimmt nicht!* (That's not true! That's not correct!) is more emphatic than *Das ist nicht wahr!* (That's not true!). The latter refers more often to an obvious lie, the former to an error.

15. *Die Gemeinheit* (a mean thing to do) should not be mixed up with *die Allgemeinheit* (the general public). The adjective *gemein* (ordinary, general) can also have the meaning of "mean," depending on the context.

18. *Auf jeden Fall* (in any case) could have the meaning of "certainly" or "at least" if used within a sentence. It could also mean "under any circumstance," especially as a response to a question: *Spielst du morgen Tennis?* (Are you playing tennis tomorrow?) *Auf jeden Fall!* (Definitely!).

19. There are several different words for "fun" in German. *Das Vergnügen* (fun, pleasure) implies a little bit of mischief, but never in a negative way, *der Spaß* (fun) implies fun that comes with laughter, *die Freude* refers more to joyous fun. *Viel Vergnügen!* (Have a heck of a good time!) *Viel Spaß!* (Have fun!) *Viel Freude!* (Enjoy yourself!).

21. *Der Ausdruck* can mean "facial expression" as well as "printout."
    The adjective *toll* is often used colloquially meaning "great" or "fantastic."

Culture Notes

You hardly ever find turnstiles *(das Drehkreuz)* and not many ticket booths *(der Fahrkartenschalter)* in the subway stations of the four German-speaking countries. Regular commuters all have monthly passes, but there are controllers

(*Kontrolleure*) more or less frequently checking passengers for tickets within subway cars. *Schwarzfahren* (fare-dodging) is usually quite costly if it's caught. The transit authorities estimate that only every twentieth fare-dodger is caught. However, authorities have not increased the controls, simply because the majority of people caught have been caught repeatedly. It's called the gambler's ruin. It doesn't pay in the long run.

C. GRAMMAR AND USAGE

1. Declension of Adjectives

If an adjective follows a verb, such as *sein*, its form never changes: *Die Lösung ist einfach.* (The solution is simple.) But if an adjective is used right before a noun, it must take a certain ending depending on case, number, and gender: *Das ist eine einfache Lösung.* These endings also depend on what kind of word is used before the adjective (*der, ein, mein,* etc.). Study this pattern of endings, also called a declension pattern.

NOMINATIVE

der neue Lehrer (the new teacher, m.)
ein neuer Lehrer (a new teacher, m.)
die neue Lehrerin (the new teacher, f.)
eine neue Lehrerin (a new teacher, f.)
das neue Buch (the new book, n.)
ein neues Buch (a new book, n.)

Notice that all the adjectives used with the definite article end in *-e* in the nominative case, but if the indefinite article is used, the endings mimic the ending of the matching (and missing) definite article. The pattern becomes even easier in the genitive and the dative case, because all adjectives end in *-en*, regardless of gender:

GENITIVE

des neuen Lehrers (of the new teacher, m.)
eines neuen Lehrers (of a new teacher, m.)
der neuen Lehrerin (of the new teacher, f.)
einer neuen Lehrerin (of a new teacher, f.)
des neuen Buches (of the new book, n.)
eines neuen Buches (of a new book, n.)

DATIVE

dem neuen Lehrer ([to] the new teacher, m.)
einem neuen Lehrer ([to] a new teacher, m.)
der neuen Lehrerin ([to] the new teacher, f.)
einer neuen Lehrerin ([to] a new teacher, f.)
dem neuen Buch ([to] the new book, n.)
einem neuen Buch ([to] a new book, n.)

ACCUSATIVE

Masculine accusative adjectives after both articles have *-en* endings as well, but the feminine and neuter adjectives are the same as in the nominative case, just as the articles are.

den neuen Lehrer (the new teacher, m.)
einen neuen Lehrer (a new teacher, m.)
die neue Lehrerin (the new teacher, f.)
eine neue Lehrerin (a new teacher, f.)
das neue Buch (the new book, n.)
ein neues Buch (a new book, n.)

Adjectives describing definite plural nouns all end in *-en* as well. Naturally, there is no plural form of *ein*.

| Nominative | *die neuen Lehrer, die neuen Lehrerinnen, die neuen Bücher* |
| Genitive | *der neuen Lehrer, der neuen Lehrerinnen, der neuen Bücher* |

| Dative | *den neuen Lehrern, den neuen Lehrerin-nen, den neuen Büchern* |
| Accusative | *die neuen Lehrer, die neuen Lehrerinnen, die neuen Bücher* |

If an adjective is used without an article, it takes the ending of that (missing) definite article: *Die grünen Bäume sind schön.* But: *Grüne Bäume sind schön.* (Green trees are beautiful.) Here are some examples of adjectives and their endings:

Ihre Freunde arbeiten am heutigen Montag.
    Her friends are working today, Monday.

Sie hat großes Interesse an orientalischen Teppichen.
    She has a great interest in oriental rugs.

Das ist guter deutscher Wein.
    That's good German wine.

Sie fragt einen jungen Mann.
    She is asking a young man.

Die U-Bahn hält an der nächsten Station.
    The subway stops at the next station.

Possessives take the same endings as corresponding indefinite articles in the singular, and definite articles in the plural. Notice in the next examples that an adjective can be used along with a possessive to describe a noun, in which case the adjective takes the same ending as if it were following an indefinite article:

Vielen Dank für Ihre freundliche Hilfe.
    Many thanks for your friendly help.

Zwei meiner besten Freunde haben gerade die U-Bahn verlassen.
    Two of my best friends just left the subway.

Hier ist meine private Telefonnummer.
    Here is my private phone number.

Ich telefoniere mit meinem neuen Handy.
　I'm calling with my new cell phone.

Sie trinkt von ihrem guten deutschen Wein.
　She is drinking her good German wine.

2. Adjectival Nouns

Any adjective can also be used as a noun. The adjectives *gut* (good) and *böse* (evil), for example, can change to *das Gute und das Böse* (the good and the evil). If an adjective describes a person, as in *der Alte* (the old [man]) or *die Alte* (the old [woman]), it takes the appropriate article. Adjectival nouns follow the same rules as adjectives in German.

Was gibt es Neues?
　What's new (the new thing)?

Sie mag die Stille im Grünen.
　She likes the quietness in nature (lit.: in the green).

Das Beste kommt zuletzt.
　The best comes last.

Das Seltsame ist, es gibt kein Drehkreuz.
　The strange thing is, there's no turnstile.

3. *N*-Nouns

There are some masculine nouns that always end with *-(e)n* when they are in the genitive, dative, and accusative cases.

Das ist Herr Schulz.
　That's Mr. Schulz.

Ich gebe Herrn Schulz seinen Hut.
　I'm giving Mr. Schulz his hat.

Wo ist das Büro des Präsidenten?
　Where is the president's office?

Die Würde des Menschen ist unantastbar.
   Dignity of humankind is sacred.

Other *n*-nouns are: *der Pilot* (pilot), *der Idiot* (idiot), *der Poet* (poet), *der Bauer* (farmer), *der Bursche* (fellow), *der Architekt* (architect), *der Nachbar* (neighbor), *der Musikant* (minstrel, musician), *der Konsonant* (consonant), *der Informant* (informer), *der Lieferant* (supplier), *der Passant* (passerby), *der Journalist* (journalist), *der Optimist* (optimist), *der Pessimist* (pessimist), *der Diplomat* (diplomat), *der Experte* (expert), *der Drache* (dragon), *der Schwede* (Swede), *der Franzose* (Frenchman), *der Russe* (Russian), *der Schwabe* (Swabian). Many more masculine nouns belonging to countries, regions, or tribes are *n*-nouns as well. Masculine nouns that end in *-ot, -ekt, -ant, -ast, -ent,* or *-ist* are very likely *n*-nouns when they refer to a male representative of the category.

4. Verbal Nouns

The verbal noun is the infinitive of a verb, written with a capital letter. All verbal nouns are neuter:

Das Bewusstsein bestimmt das Sein. (Plato, Hegel)
   Awareness determines being.

Das Schreiben mit dem Computer ist einfach.
   Writing with the computer is easy.

Das Lesen ohne Brille fällt ihm schwer.
   Reading without glasses is difficult for him.

EXERCISES

A. Add the adjectives in parentheses with their correct endings:

   1. *Der _____ Student lernt seit einer Woche Deutsch. (gut)*

2. *Heute bin ich in dem _____ Haus. (schön)*

3. *Er geht morgen in das _____ Theater. (neu)*

4. *Ich kenne ein _____ Café in einer _____ Straße. (nett/ruhig)*

5. *Wir sind bei den _____ Freunden. (amerikanisch)*

6. *Das _____ Theater ist direkt neben der _____ Bank. (alt/groß)*

7. *Fährst du mit _____ Auto an den _____ See? (neu/wundervoll)*

8. *Er möchte das _____ Bier. (deutsch)*

9. *Das ist ein _____ Buch. (interessant)*

10. *Die _____ Debatten sind ermüdend. (lang)*

B. Fill in the correct form of the adjectives and *n*-nouns:

1. *Er gibt dem _____ _____ den Plan. (neu/Architekt)*

2. *Der _____ _____ hat nicht viel Zeit. (nett/Polizist)*

3. *Die Aufgaben des _____ _____ sind schwer. (intelligent/Junge)*

4. *Der Hut des _____ _____ liegt hier. (alt/Herr)*

5. *Die Zeitung hat einen _____ _____. (gut/Journalist)*

C. Choose the correct sentence(s):

1. A nice passerby is giving her the information.
   a) *Ein netter Passant gibt ihr die Information.*
   b) *Einem netten Passanten gibt sie die Information.*

    c) *Einen netten Passanten gibt ihr die Information.*
    d) *Eine netten Passantin gibt ihm die Information.*

2. She is serving a nice customer.
    a) *Sie bedient den netten Kunden.*
    b) *Sie bedient ein netter Kunde.*
    c) *Sie bedient einem netter Kunde.*
    d) *Sie bedient einen netten Kunden.*

3. Shannon sees the official.
    a) *Shannon sieht den Beamten.*
    b) *Shannon sieht den Beamte.*
    c) *Shannon sieht der Beamte.*
    d) *Shannon sieht dem Beamten*

D. Add the correct adjectival noun:

1. *Das _____ ist nicht immer die Grammatik.*
   (interressant)

2. *Die Grammatik ist nicht immer das _____.*
   (schwer)

3. *Bewahre das _____ und schätze das _____. (alt/neu)*

4. *Dem _____ ist das _____ nicht immer willkommen. (alt/neu)*

5. *Das stimmt im _____ und _____.*
   (groß/ganz)

E. Fill in the appropriate adjective or adjectival noun:

1. *Das ist die Essenz des _____. (schön)*

2. *Das ist nicht das _____. (gleich)*

3. *Ich habe das _____ Buch. (gleich)*

4. *Sie hat keinen _____ Fahrkartenschalter gefunden. (einzig)*

5. *Bin ich der _____ hier? (einzig)*

Answer Key

A. 1. *gute*; 2. *schönen*; 3. *neue*; 4. *nettes, ruhigen*;
   5. *amerikanischen*; 6. *alte, großen*; 7. *neuen, wunder-*
   vollen; 8. *deutsche*; 9. *interessantes*; 10. *langen*

B. 1. *neuen Architekten*; 2. *nette Polizist*; 3. *intelligenten*
   Jungen; 4. *alten Herrn*; 5. *guten Journalisten*

C. 1. a; 2. d; 3. a

D. 1. *Interressante*; 2. *Schwere*; 3. *Alte, Neue*; 4. *Alten,*
   Neue; 5. *Großen, Ganzen*

E. 1. *Schönen*; 2. *Gleiche*; 3. *gleiche*; 4. *einzigen*;
   5. *Einzige*

LESSON 5

RECHTS, WO FRÜHER DAS MUSEUM WAR?
TO THE RIGHT, WHERE THE MUSEUM USED TO BE?

A. DIALOGUE

1. *Sie erinnern sich? Shannon möchte ins Museum für Orientteppiche. Gerade hat sie den U-Bahnhof verlassen. Wo in aller Welt ist nur die Georgstraße? Sie fragt einen älteren Herrn nach dem Weg.*
   You remember? Shannon wants to go to the Museum for Oriental Carpets. She just left the subway station. Where in the world is Georgstraße? She asks an older gentleman for directions.

2. Shannon: **Entschuldigen Sie, mein Herr! Können Sie mir vielleicht helfen? Wo finde ich bitte die Georg(e)straße?**
   Excuse me, Sir! Could you perhaps help me? Where can I find Georg(e)straße? (She pronounces it like the English name George.)

3. Älterer Mann: **Ach ja, Moment! Da sind Sie ja ganz falsch hier. Gehen Sie über die große Kreuzung dort rechts in die breite Straße. Das ist die Goethestraße.**
   Oh yes, just a moment! You're completely out of your way here. Go across the large intersection there onto the broad street. That is Goethestraße.

4. Shannon: **Entschuldigen Sie, das ist die Breite Straße oder die Goethestraße?**
   Sorry, that's Broad Street or Goethe Street?

5. **Älterer Mann:** **Oh, ich meine die Goethestraße ist breit, nicht eng. Gehen Sie die Goethestraße immer geradeaus bis zum Hohen Ufer. Dort sehen Sie eine Brücke. Gehen Sie aber nicht über die Brücke, sondern nach links am Ufer entlang und dann die erste Straße wieder links. Augenblick, wie heißt sie noch gleich? Oh, fällt mir im Moment nicht ein! Aber es ist die erste Straße zu Ihrer Linken. Oder ist es die Zweite? Oh, nein! Es ist sicherlich die Erste!**

    Oh, I mean Goethestraße is broad, not narrow. Go straight on Goethestraße until Am Hohen Ufer. You'll see a bridge there. Don't go over the bridge, but left along the riverbank, and then left again on the first street. One second, what is it called again? It doesn't come to me at the moment! But it's the first street on the left. Or is it the second? Oh, no! It is definitely the first one!

6. **Shannon:** **Also noch einmal. Ich gehe die breite Goethestraße bis zum Hohen Ufer. Dort gehe ich nicht über die Brücke, sondern links am Ufer entlang und die erste Straße wieder links? Richtig?**

    So, one more time. I walk on the broad Goethestraße until Am Hohen Ufer. There I turn left along the riverbank, and the first street on the left again? Right?

7. **Älterer Mann:** **Ja ja, genau! Nach ungefähr dreißig Metern gehen Sie in die Allee rechts, wo früher das Museum war.**

    Yes, yes, exactly! After about thirty meters turn right onto the boulevard where the museum used to be.

8. **Shannon:** **Es tut mir sehr Leid, aber ich bin nicht von hier. Ich weiß leider nicht, wo früher das Museum war.**

I'm very sorry, but I'm not from here. Unfortunately, I don't know where the museum used to be.

9. **Älterer Mann: Ach ja! Dann gehen Sie dort einfach rechts.**
Oh yes! Then simply turn to your right there.

10. **Shannon: Nach wie vielen Metern gehe ich rechts und in welche Straße gehe ich dann? Ist das die erste Straße rechts?**
After how many meters do I turn right, and onto which street do I go then? Is that the first street (on the) right?

11. **Älterer Mann: Ja, das ist die einzige Straße rechts. Ich glaube, das ist die Burgstraße. Gehen Sie geradeaus bis zum Holzmarkt. Dort rechts ist dann die Schloßstraße.**
Yes, that's the only street on your right. I think it's Burgstraße. Go straight ahead until Holzmarkt. There on the right is Schloßstraße.

12. **Shannons Kopf raucht: Und wo ist dann die Georg(e)straße?**
Shannon's head is smoking: And then where is Georg(e) Street?

13. **Älterer Mann: Wie bitte? Sie meinen die Ge . . . org . . . straße, nicht die Schloßstraße? Aber wir sind doch schon in der Georgstraße! Ich habe Sie wohl ganz falsch verstanden.**
What? You mean the Geh . . . ork . . . straße, not the Schloßstraße? But we're already on Georgstraße! I must have misunderstood you completely.

14. **Shannon lacht: Kein Problem. Trotzdem vielen Dank für Ihre Hilfe. Wissen Sie vielleicht, wo hier das Orientteppich-Museum ist?**

Shannon laughs: No problem. Many thanks anyway for your help. Do you know perhaps, where the Oriental Carpet Museum is here? (She mispronounces "Teppich.")

15. Älterer Mann: **Entschuldigung, was für ein "Topic"? Ich spreche leider nicht viel Englisch.**
Excuse me, what kind of "topic"? I don't speak much English, unfortunately.

16. *Shannon reißt sich zusammen und lächelt:* **Nein, ich meine "Teppich," nicht "Topic."**
Shannon composes herself and smiles: No, I mean "carpet," not "topic."

17. Älterer Mann: **Oh, Teppichgeschäfte gibt es hier viele. Was für einen Teppich möchten Sie denn? Meine Frau hat gerade einen Teppich im Ausverkauf gekauft. Gehen Sie doch in die Breite Straße, ich meine, die Straße heißt Breite Straße, sie ist gar nicht sehr breit. Sie heißt nur so, weiß der Teufel, warum. Auf jeden Fall, dort hat meine Frau einen sehr schönen neuen Teppich gekauft. Er war recht billig. Gehen Sie einfach die breite Straße dort immer geradeaus, und dann . . .**
Oh, there are many carpet stores around here. What kind of carpet would you like? My wife just bought a carpet on sale. Why don't you go to Breite Straße, I mean, the street is called Breite Straße, it isn't very broad at all. That's just its name, who the heck knows why. Anyway, my wife bought a very beautiful new carpet there. It was very inexpensive. Just take that broad street over there straight ahead, and then . . .

18. Shannon: **Entschuldigen Sie die Unterbrechung, aber ich möchte doch zuerst in die Breite Straße, . . . ähm, . . . ich meine die Georgstraße. Danke**

schön noch einmal und ich wünsche Ihnen noch
einen schönen Tag. Auf Wiedersehen!

Sorry for the interruption, but I would first like to go
to Broad Street, . . . er, . . . I mean Georgstraße. Thank
you again, and I hope you have a nice day. Good bye!

B. NOTES

1. *Erinnern Sie sich?* (Do you remember? lit.: remind
   yourself) uses the verb *erinnern* (remember, remind)
   with the reflexive pronoun *sich* (yourself).

   gerade (just) can have several meanings. It could
   also mean "straight," "even," "direct(ly)," or "at the
   moment": *Er war gerade hier.* (He was just here.)
   Die Sieben ist keine gerade Zahl. (Seven is not an
   even number.) *Das Bild hängt nicht gerade.* (The
   picture isn't hanging straight.) *Ich bin gerade dabei.*
   (I'm at this very moment in the process of doing it.)
   Das ist eine gerade Linie. (That's a straight line.) *Er
   läuft gerade auf das Ziel zu.* (He is running directly
   toward the finish line.)

2. It is not uncommon to address people with *mein
   Herr* (lit.: my gentleman), *meine Dame* (lit.: my
   lady), or even *gnädige Frau* (lit.: merciful, gracious
   woman). It's similar to the English "sir" and
   "ma'am." The use is especially common with service people addressing their customers, in Southern
   Germany and Austria more than in the north.

3. *Da sind Sie falsch* (lit.: There you are wrong) refers
   to the wrong location, never to the correctness of
   what someone said. That would be: *Da haben Sie
   nicht Recht* or *Da haben Sie Unrecht.* (There you are
   not correct.)

5. *Gehen Sie immer geradeaus!* (Walk straight ahead!)
   The *immer* (always) is often added, indicating "all
   the way" or for a longer time.

Even though the street is named *Am Hohen Ufer* (lit.: At the High Bank), going there requires the preposition *zu* followed also by the dative case. The *am* (at the) is left out. There would be a double preposition otherwise, one indicating direction, the other, location. This is a good example of how even the names of streets or other proper names of institutions might change slightly according to a preposition and/or case: *das Rote Kreuz* (the Red Cross), *das Auto des Roten Kreuzes* (the car belonging to the Red Cross).

6. The German word *also* doesn't have the same meaning as "also" in English. It is often used in the beginning of a sentence to mean "so" or "well." *Also, so ist das!* (So, that's the way it is!)

13. In the expression *Ich habe Sie wohl falsch verstanden* (I must have misunderstood you, lit.: I have you well wrongly understood), *wohl* (well) implies an assumption: *Sie sind wohl aus Amerika!* (You must be from America!)

14. *Trotzdem vielen Dank!* (Nevertheless, many thanks!) While *trotz* (despite, in spite of) is a genitive preposition, *trotzdem* (all the same, nevertheless) is used as an adverb here. It is sometimes used as a conjunction, meaning "even though" (see conjunctions, Lesson 15).

16. *Ich meine . . .* (I mean) should not be mixed up with the verb *bedeuten* (to mean). The latter hardly ever refers to people, but rather to the meaning of something. The former refers mostly to what someone thinks about something. The same is true for the corresponding nouns: *die Meinung* (opinion), *die Bedeutung* (the meaning).

The older gentleman in the dialogue misunderstood the word *Teppich*. Remember that the German *ch* is often pronounced similarly to the "h" in the English word "huge."

17. *Weiß der Teufel!* (lit: The devil knows!) is colloquially used to express with emphasis that nobody knows. Any interrogative could be added to refer to the topic of discussion: *Weiß der Teufel, wo!* (Who the heck knows where!).

   Er war recht billig! (It was quite cheap), where *recht* (right) is used to mean "quite."

   Like English, *billig* (cheap) could mean "inexpensive" as well as "cheaply made." The adjective *preiswert* (lit.: priceworthy) is also common.

Culture Notes

You might think that such a confusion over street names as happened to Shannon must be highly fictional, but German street names are not always easy to figure out, and all these names actually exist. Most older cities have street names like *Schloßstraße* (Castle Street), *Burgstraße* (Castle Street), *Bergstraße* (Mountain Street), and then perhaps in addition *Schloßallee* (Castle Avenue), *Schloßgasse* (Castle Lane), and many variations. It's important to get the street name right. Street names are written according to set rules: Single nouns and the word *Straße* are written as one word, and so are single-word names of people, as in *Georgstraße* or *Goethestraße*. If the name consists of more than one word, it is hyphenated, as in *Martin-Luther-Straße* or *John-F-Kennedy-Straße*. Street names that contain a true adjective are always written in two words, as in *Breite Straße* (Broad Street) or *Hohe Straße* (High Street). The confusion comes in—as seen in the dialogue—when an adjective is used to describe a street rather than the street name, as in *die breite Breite Straße* (the broad Broad Street). By the way, street names have not been and will most likely not be updated to the new

German spelling rules mandatory since January 2005. The name *Schloßstraße* will most likely remain unchanged, and not be changed to *Schlossstraße*, but students in school write it that way. Unknown complications might lie ahead!

C. GRAMMAR AND USAGE

1. Basic Interrogatives

As in English, word order is slightly different when asking questions in German. While a simple indicative sentence starts with a subject followed by the verb, a question either starts with the verb followed by the subject, or with an interrogative word followed directly by the verb. The most common interrogatives are *wer* (who), *wessen* (whose), *wem* (to whom), *wen* (whom), *was* (what), *wo* (where), *wann* (when, at what time), *wie* (how), and the interrogative adjectives *welcher* (which)—declined like *der*-words—and *was für ein* (what kind of)—declined like *ein*-words.

Fragt die Frau einen Herrn?
  Does the woman ask a gentleman?

Wo ist die Georgstraße?
  Where is Georgstraße?

Helfen Sie mir? Wer hilft mir?
  Are you helping me? Who is helping me?

Note that the position of an adverb is not as interchangeable with questions. It usually follows after verb and subject.

Wer kommt morgen mit dem Zug?
  Who is coming by train tomorrow?

Verlässt sie gerade den Bahnhof?
  Is she just leaving the train station?

Notice that *welcher* (which) changes to agree with the noun following it:

Welcher Mann hilft ihr?
   Which man is helping her?

Welche Straße ist das?
   Which street is that?

Welches Museum ist in der Georgstraße?
   Which museum is in Georgstraße?

2. Interrogatives with the Dative

Interrogatives referring to the indirect object or another dative noun change to their respective dative form (e.g., *Wer* becomes *Wem*).

Wem hilft der ältere Herr? (dative verb *helfen*)
   Who(m) is the older gentleman helping?

Mit was für einem Herrn spricht sie? (dative preposition *mit*)
   To what kind of gentleman is she talking?

Mit wem spricht sie? (dative preposition *mit*)
   To whom is she talking? / Who is she talking to?

Welchem Studenten gebe ich das Buch? (dative indirect object)
   To which student do I give the book?

In welcher Straße ist sie? (dative location preposition *in*)
   Which street is she on?

3. Interrogatives with the Accusative

Some interrogative pronouns and combinations with prepositions ask specifically about the accusative object of the sentence.

Wen fragt die Frau? (accusative direct object)
   Whom is the woman asking?

Gegen wen spielt die Mannschaft? (accusative preposition *gegen*)
　Against whom is the team playing?

In welche Straße geht sie? (accusative direction preposition *in*)
　Onto which street is she walking? / Which street is she walking onto?

4. Interrogatives with the Genitive

There is only one genitive interrogative pronoun that is commonly used, but prepositional combinations are possible.

Wessen Buch ist das?
　Whose book is that?

Mit wessen Auto fährt sie?
　Whose car is she driving?

5. Asking "Where" in German

In modern English, "where" has replaced older forms such as "whence" (from where) and "whither" (to where). But in German, there are different question words to express location (*wo*), movement from (*woher*), and movement to (*wohin*).

Wo ist Shannon? Sie ist in Hannover.
　Where's Shannon? She's in Hannover.

Woher kommt sie? Sie kommt aus New York.
　Where does she come from? She comes from New York.

Wohin geht sie? Sie geht ins Museum.
　Where is she going? She's going to the museum.

6. Asking "What" with Prepositions

In English, it's possible to use a preposition with the interrogative "what." "<u>What</u> are you talking <u>about</u>?" "<u>What</u> is this made <u>of</u>?" Notice that in conversational English, the preposition and "what" are usually separated. But in German, *was* is replaced by *wo,* and this is combined with the preposition into one word. So, *was + für = wofür.* If the preposition starts with a vowel, then an *-r-* is inserted: *was + aus = woraus.*

Worüber sprechen Sie?
     What are you talking about?

Woneben liegt das Museum?
     Next to what is the museum? / What is the museum next to?

Woran denkst du?
     What are you thinking about?

Worauf können wir uns verlassen?
     On what can we depend? / What can we depend on?

EXERCISES

A. Ask the correct question about the underlined part of the sentences.

1. *Sie geht <u>ins Museum</u> für Moderne Kunst.*

2. *<u>Gestern</u> war das Wetter schön.*

3. *Er fragt <u>nach dem Weg</u>.*

4. *<u>Das Café</u> liegt in einer Seitenstraße.*

5. *Sie ist <u>bei deutschen Freunden</u> zu Besuch.*

6. *<u>Das neue</u> Theater ist in der Schillerstraße.*

7. *Ich fahre am Wochenende <u>in die Berge</u>.*

8. *Die große Kreuzung ist dort rechts.*

9. *Das ist ein langweiliges Buch.*

10. *Wir gehen am Ufer entlang.*

B. Change the following sentences into questions.

1. *Die Frau des älteren Herrn kauft den Teppich in der Breiten Straße.*

2. *An der Straße war früher das Museum.*

3. *Nach ungefähr sieben Stunden war er zu Hause.*

4. *Das neue Auto fährt sehr schnell.*

5. *Heute hat die Zeitung eine gute Reputation.*

C. Translate the following questions into German.

1. Excuse me, could you help me?

2. Where is *Römerplatz*, please?

3. On which street do I turn right?

4. Where do I cross the intersection?

5. Is the post office to my left or to my right?

D. Ask the particular questions for the underlined words in the text:

> *Es ist Freitag heute. Das Wetter ist wundervoll. Viele Menschen sind fürs Wochenende an den Berliner Wannsee gefahren und es gibt fast keinen Parkplatz mehr. Martin hat Glück. Mit einem kleinen Auto findet er fast immer nach kurzer Zeit einen Platz. Das Auto steht jetzt unter schattigen Bäumen in der Nähe des Sees. Die Brücke zum Strand ist auch nicht weit vom Strand entfernt.*

E. Choose the question that relates to each statement:

1. *Wir gehen heute in ein amerikanisches Restaurant essen.*
   a) *Wohin gehen wir heute essen?*
   b) *Womit gehen wir heute essen?*
   c) *Woher gehen wir heute essen?*
   d) *Wozu gehen wir heute essen?*

2. *Sie sucht nach einem Fahrkartenschalter.*
   a) *Wessen Fahrkartenschalter sucht sie?*
   b) *Welchen Fahrkartenschalter sucht sie?*
   c) *Wonach sucht sie?*
   d) *Nach wem sucht sie?*

3. *Sie fragt einen Passanten auf der Straße nach dem Weg.*
   a) *Wonach fragt sie?*
   b) *Auf welchem Weg fragt sie?*
   c) *Wofür fragt sie?*
   d) *Wem fragt sie?*

4. *Er wartet sehr lange auf sein Gepäck.*
   a) *Auf welchem Gepäck wartet er?*
   b) *Womit wartet er?*
   c) *Mit wem wartet er auf?*
   d) *Worauf wartet er?*

5. *Das ist ja zum Glück kein großes Problem.*
   a) *Wozu ist das kein großes Problem?*
   b) *Wem ist das kein großes Problem?*
   c) *Was für ein Problem ist das nicht?*
   d) *Wessen Problem ist das nicht?*

Answer Key

A. 1. *Wohin geht sie?* 2. *Wann war das Wetter schön?*
3. *Wonach fragt er?* 4. *Was liegt in einer Seitenstraße?*
5. *Wo ist sie zu Besuch?* 6. *Welches Theater ist in der
Schillerstraße?* 7. *Wohin fahre ich (fährst du) am Wochenende?* 8. *Welche Kreuzung ist dort rechts?* 9. *Was für
ein Buch ist das? Wie ist das Buch?* 10. *Wo(ran) gehen
wir (geht ihr) entlang?*

B. 1. *Kauft die Frau des älteren Herrn den Teppich in der
Breiten Straße?* 2. *War an der Straße früher das
Museum?* 3. *War er nach ungefähr sieben Stunden zu
Hause?* 4. *Fährt das neue Auto sehr schnell?* 5. *Hat die
Zeitung heute eine gute Reputation?*

C. 1. *Entschuldigung, können Sie mir helfen?/
Entschuldigen Sie, . . . ?* 2. *Wo ist der Römerplatz,
bitte?* 3. *An welcher Straße gehe ich rechts?* 4. *Wo gehe
ich über die Kreuzung? Wo überquere ich die
Kreuzung?* 5. *Ist die Post zu meiner Linken oder zu
meiner Rechten?/Ist die Post links oder rechts von mir?*

D. *Welcher Tag ist heute? Wie ist das Wetter? Wer ist fürs
Wochenende . . . gefahren? Wohin sind viele Menschen
. . . gefahren? Was gibt es fast nicht mehr? Wer hat
Glück? Womit findet man immer . . . einen Platz? Wann
findet man einen Platz? Worunter steht das Auto jetzt?
Welche Brücke ist nicht weit vom Strand entfernt?
Wovon ist die Brücke nicht weit entfernt?*

E. 1. a; 2. c; 3. a; 4. d; 5. c

LESSON 6

IM KAUFHAUS: DIE QUAL DER WAHL!
IN THE DEPARTMENT STORE:
THE TORMENT OF CHOICE!

A. DIALOGUE

1. *Erinnern Sie sich noch an Liza? Sie ist jetzt zum Einkaufen in der berühmten Königsallee in Düsseldorf. Die "Kö" ist als der teuerste Kilometer ganz Deutschlands bekannt, aber es gibt dort nicht nur Luxusartikel zu kaufen; besonders zum Sommer- und Winterschlussverkauf gibt es auch unzählige Gelegenheiten und Schnäppchen. Liza bemerkt eine Ansammlung von Menschen vor einem Kaufhaus. Sie fragt eine Frau:*
   Do you still remember Liza? Now she's going shopping on the famous *Königsallee* in Düsseldorf. The *"Kö"* is known as the most expensive kilometer in all of Germany, but there aren't just luxury items for sale; especially for the end-of-summer and end-of-winter sales there are numerous bargains and great deals. Liza notices a gathering of people in front of a department store. She asks a woman:

2. Liza: **Entschuldigen Sie, warum stehen denn so viele Leute hier vor dem Kaufhaus?**
   Excuse me, why are so many people standing in front of the department store here?

3. Frau: **Oh, das wissen Sie nicht? Heute ist schließlich der erste Tag des Sommerschlussverkaufs. Fast alle Saisonartikel sind um mehr als die Hälfte reduziert. Es ist die beste Zeit zum Einkaufen, doch die Geschäfte sind auch**

recht voll. In fünf Minuten wird dieses Kaufhaus geöffnet, und dann beginnt der Sturm auf die Angebote.
Oh, you don't know? Today is the first day of the end-of-summer sale, after all. Almost all seasonal goods are reduced by more than half. It's the best time for shopping, but the stores are also quite packed. In five minutes, the department store is opening, and then the storm on the sales merchandise begins.

4. Liza: **Danke für die Information.**
Thanks for the information.

5. Frau: **Bitte! Nichts zu danken.**
You're welcome! Don't mention it.

6. Liza: **Kann ja nicht schaden, mal einen Blick hinein zu werfen.**
Can't really hurt to take a look inside.

7. Frau: **Gute Idee! Es ist aber sicher sehr voll.**
Good idea! But it's sure to be crowded.

8. *Wenige Minuten später ist Liza im Kaufhaus und beobachtet, wie zwei Mädchen sich anscheinend um den gleichen Artikel streiten:*
A few minutes later, Liza is inside the department store and watches as two girls apparently argue over the same item.

9. Erstes Mädchen: **Danach suche ich schon so lange.**
I've been looking for that for so long already.

10. Zweites Mädchen: **Tut mir Leid, aber wer zuerst kommt, mahlt zuerst! Oder soll ich sie vielleicht in blau nehmen? Ach ja, wer die Wahl hat hat die Qual.**

I'm really sorry, but first come, first served! Or should I get it in blue, perhaps? Oh well, choice is torment.

11. *Liza ist es hier einfach zu hektisch und sie geht wieder hinaus. Gleich daneben ist ein kleines Designergeschäft und Liza sieht im Fenster genau das, wonach sie sucht. Sie geht hinein. Auch in diesem Geschäft gibt es viele Kunden, aber zumindest auch ausreichendes Personal. Ein Verkäufer kommt auf sie zu:*

    It is simply too hectic for Liza here, and she leaves again. Right next to the department store is a small designer store, and Liza sees just what she is looking for in the window. She goes inside. There are many customers in this store as well, but at least there is sufficient personnel, too. A salesman comes up to her:

12. Verkäufer: **Guten Morgen. Kann ich Ihnen behilflich sein oder möchten Sie sich erst umschauen?**
    Good morning. Can I be of help, or would you first like to take a look around?

13. Liza: **Schönen guten Morgen. Ich interessiere mich für die malvenfarbene Jacke im Schaufenster. Haben Sie sie vielleicht in meiner Größe?**
    Good morning. I'm interested in the mauve jacket in the display window. Do you have it in my size, maybe?

14. Verkäufer: **Ich glaube schon! Ja, diese Größe ist sicher richtig für Sie. Probieren Sie sie doch einmal an!**
    I believe so! Yes, this size is bound to be right for you. Why don't you try it on!

15. *Liza probiert die Jacke an und sie passt tatsächlich wie angegossen.*

Liza tries on the jacket, and indeed it fits like a
glove.

16. Verkäufer: **Sie steht Ihnen ganz ausgezeichnet
    und sie ist sogar um vierzig Prozent reduziert.**
    You look absolutely great in it, and it is even reduced
    by forty percent.

17. Liza lächelt: **Wunderbar, ich nehme sie!**
    Liza smiles: Wonderful, I'll take it!

18. Verkäufer: **Ich möchte Ihnen gern eine Frage
    stellen, wenn ich darf. Sie sind Amerikanerin,
    nicht wahr?**
    There is one question I would like to ask you if I
    may. You're American, aren't you?

19. *Liza nickt mit dem Kopf.*
    Liza nods her head.

20. Verkäufer: **Wie in aller Welt wissen Sie, was mal-
    venfarben ist? Nicht einmal die meisten
    Deutschen kennen den Namen dieser Farbe.**
    How in the world do you know what the color
    mauve is? Even most Germans don't know the name
    of this color.

21. Liza lacht: **Zugegeben, ich habe heute Morgen im
    Wörterbuch nachgesehen. Wenn ich einkaufen
    gehe, bin ich sozusagen auf Schatzsuche!**
    Liza laughs: I admit, I looked it up in a dictionary
    this morning. Whenever I go shopping, I'm on a
    mission!

B. NOTES

1. *Schnäppchen* (bargains) literally means "little
   snaps" or "little catches." *Die Gelegenheit* (bargain)

also could mean "opportunity." By the way, all words ending with the suffix *-heit* are feminine in gender.

3. The adverb s*chließlich* means "finally/at last" as well as "after all," depending on the context. It should not be mixed up with *endlich* (finally!): *Endlich bist du hier!* (Finally, you are here!) *Das ist schließlich eine Gelegenheit.* (That's a bargain, after all.) *Schließlich kommt sie zu Hause an.* (At last, she's arriving home.)

5. *Nichts zu danken!* (lit.: Nothing to thank!) is a common response to a thank you, meaning "Don't mention it!" or "You're welcome!"

8. *anscheinend* (apparently, seemingly)

9. *so lange* (such a long time), not to be mixed up with *solange wie* (as long as).

10. *Wer zuerst kommt, mahlt zuerst!* (lit.: He who comes first, grinds first!) supposedly originated in the old mills, where farmers had to wait in line at the mill with their grain harvest.

   Wer die Wahl hat hat die Qual! (lit.: He who has choice, has the burden of torment!). Of course, it is used ironically in most instances, since most people welcome choice.

11. *Liza ist es einfach zu hektisch hier.* This sentence might have surprised you because there may seem to be two subjects—*Liza* and *es*—but just the singular verb *ist*. The actual subject of the sentence is *es* (it): *Es ist ihr zu hektisch hier* (It is too hectic here for her). Liza is the indirect object.

   The adverb *gleich* can have several meanings: *Das ist gleich neben der Bank.* (That's right next to the bank.) *Sie kommen gleich.* (They'll get here right away.) *Beide Artikel sind gleich.* (Both items are equal.) *Das ist mir gleich.* (It doesn't matter to me. All the same to me!) *Die Menge X ist gleich sieben.* (Quantity X equals seven.)

    zumindest (at least); *auf* (somebody); *zukommen* (to approach somebody)

12. *Ich möchte mich nur umschauen.* (I just want to browse/look around.) *Umschauen* translates exactly as the phrasal verb "look around."

14. *Ich glaube schon!* (I do believe so!) The word *schon* (already) is used here for emphasis.

15. *Es passt wie angegossen* (lit.: It fits as if poured on) is a common idiom to express that a piece of clothing fits perfectly.

16. *sogar* (even) expresses emphasis; *reduziert um* (reduced by)

21. *Zugegeben!* (To be honest, . . . admittedly, . . .) This is the past participle of the verb *zugeben* (to admit).

Culture Notes

Unless a store is going out of business, real sales take place only twice a year for seasonal items. The *Sommerschlussverkauf* and the *Winterschlussverkauf* are, next to the Christmas season, the times when clothing and department stores sell the greatest volume of merchandise. Originally, these events were—of course—meant to free storage space for unsold goods of the season, but each has become such an event that almost every store stocks its warehouse especially for the occasion. Even most designer label stores participate in these sales. By the way, the term *das Warenhaus* doesn't mean what it looks

like. It's just another term for "department store." "Warehouse" is *das Lagerhaus*.

Most department stores in all German-speaking countries
have rather large grocery departments occupying an entire
floor. The flagship department stores in all major cities have
boutique-style counters throughout, where it is possible to
sample international food, go for a wine tasting, or just stop
for a quick snack. The quality is usually excellent. Many
offer American products as well.

Even though shopping malls as they are known in America
are becoming more common, the usual shopping centers are
the so-called *Fußgängerzonen* (pedestrian zones). In most
cities, a large part of the *Altstadt* (old part of town) is closed
to car traffic.

C. GRAMMAR AND USAGE

1. The Simple Present Tense

   The simple present *(Präsens)* is used to express several
   meanings in German.

   Liza kauft eine Jacke.
      Liza buys a jacket.
      Liza is buying a jacket.
      Liza does buy a jacket.

   The difference in meaning is often implied by use of an
   adverb or particle, but the tense remains the same:

   Liza kauft jetzt eine Jacke.
      Liza is buying a jacket now.

   Liza kauft doch eine Jacke!
      Liza does buy a jacket! / Liza is so buying a jacket!

The present tense, combined with an adverb of duration, is the equivalent of the English present perfect, an action that began in the past and has gone on until now.

Danach suche ich schon lange.
  I've been looking for this for a long time.

Even future events can be implied without using the actual future tense. This is more common in spoken language than in writing.

Liza kauft morgen eine Jacke.
  Liza is buying a jacket tomorrow. Liza will buy a jacket tomorrow.

Below is a quick review of the regular verb endings with the verb *denken* (to think):

Heute denke ich an morgen.	*-e*
Heute denkst du an morgen.	*-st*
Heute denkt er an morgen.	*-t*
Heute denken wir an morgen.	*-en*
Heute denkt ihr an morgen.	*-t*
Heute denken sie an morgen.	*-en*
Heute denken Sie an morgen.	*-en*

2. Expressing "Know" with *kennen* and *wissen*

Below is a review of the regular present-tense conjugation of the verb *kennen* (to know, to be familiar with) in comparison to the irregular verb *wissen* (to know, to know about). Remember that the stem vowel of many irregular verbs can change, often to an *Umlaut* or another vowel. But with most irregular verbs, the endings are similar to those of regular verbs in the present tense. For a list of common irregular verbs, refer to the grammar section in the back of this book.

ich kenne	*ich weiß*
du kennst	*du weißt*

er/sie/es kennt	*er/sie/es weiß*
wir kennen	*wir wissen*
ihr kennt	*ihr wisst*
sie kennen	*sie wissen*
Sie kennen	*Sie wissen*

In general, the verb *kennen* means "to know" in the sense of being familiar with something or somebody, while *wissen* usually indicates factual knowledge or know-how. There is an easy grammatical way to tell the two apart. *Kennen* is always followed by a direct object, in other words, by an object in the accusative case:

Die meisten Deutschen kennen den Namen der Farbe nicht.
> Most Germans don't know the name of that color.

If the verb *wissen* refers to an actual noun, it would be most often the object of a preposition or followed by a clause.

Die meisten Deutschen wissen nicht, wie diese Farbe heißt.
> Most Germans don't know what this color is called.

Er weiß nicht viel über die neue Mode.
> He doesn't know much about the new fashion.

Wissen can also be followed by a pronoun or a demonstrative:

Er weiß das nicht.
> He doesn't know that.

It is sometimes used with a noun followed by an infinitive, meaning "to know how to..."

Sie weiß einen schwierigen Kunden zu nehmen.
> She knows how to deal with a difficult customer.

Unlike *kennen*, *wissen* refers only in some rare instances directly to a noun. Compare the meaning of both verbs:

Im Moment weiß ich das Wort nicht, aber ich kenne es.
I don't know (remember) the word at the moment, but I know it.

Er kennt das Wort nicht.
He doesn't know the word. (He's not familiar with the word.)

3. Conjunctions

A conjunction is a word that joins two elements of a sentence, such as words, phrases, or full clauses. The most common conjunctions in German are: *und* (and), *sowie/wie* (like, as well as), *oder* (or), *aber* (but), *doch* (but), *jedoch* (but, however), *sondern* (but instead/rather), *allein* (alone, just), *nur* (only, just), and *denn* (because).

Liza und Shawn kommen aus San Diego.
Liza and Shawn come from San Diego.

Liza und Shawn sowie viele andere Leute stehen vor dem Kaufhaus.
Liza and Shawn, as well as many other people, are standing in front of a department store.

Das Mädchen möchte den Artikel in grün oder in blau kaufen.
The girl would like to buy the article in green or in blue.

Die Verkäuferin ist überrascht, denn Liza kennt die Farbe Malve.
The saleswoman is surprised because Liza knows the color mauve.

Notice that there are a few ways to say "but" in German, with shades of meaning. *Aber* is most neutral, and *sondern* means "but rather" or "instead." *Doch* adds a bit of emphasis, and *jedoch* has an element of narration.

Sie gehen in ein Kaufhaus, aber auch in ein kleines Geschäft daneben.

They go into a department store, but also into a small shop next to it.

Liza kauft die Jacke nicht im Kaufhaus, sondern in dem Geschäft.
Liza doesn't buy the jacket in the department store, but instead in the shop.

Sie gehen ins Kaufhaus, doch es ist dort zu voll.
They go into the department store, but it's too crowded there.

Sie verlassen das Kaufhaus, jedoch gehen sie in ein anderes Geschäft.
They leave the department store, but (however) they go into another store.

4. *da-* Compounds

The concept of *da-* compounds is very similar to the *wo-* compounds in Lesson 5. They combine with prepositions to mean "it" or "that" and are very similar to English constructions using "there" + preposition—therefore, thereafter, therewith, etc. Note however that they're much more common in German.

Danach suche ich schon lange.
I've already looked <u>for it</u> for a long time.

Dort ist ein Kaufhaus. Viele Leute stehen davor.
There is a department store. Many people are standing <u>in front of it.</u>

Gleich daneben ist ein kleines Geschäft.
Right <u>next to it</u> is a small shop.

Was halten Sie davon?
What do you think <u>of it</u>?

Was sagst du dazu?
What do you say <u>about that</u>?

Note that the *da-* compound adds an *-r-* between *da-* and the preposition if the preposition starts with a vowel, just like the *wo-* compounds.

Wo ist meine Brieftasche? Mein Geld ist darin.
   Where is my wallet? My money is <u>in it</u>.

Darin besteht der Unterschied.
   <u>Therein</u> lies the difference.

Da- compounds can be used with most prepositions, but they are not possible with prepositions followed by the genitive, or with *seit* (since), *bis* (until), or *ohne* (without).

EXERCISES

A. Add the correctly conjugated verb (present tense) in parentheses.

1. *Ich _____ mich gut an die Freunde von Klaus.* (erinnern)

2. *Heute _____ Liza und Shawn zum Einkaufen in die Stadt. (gehen)*

3. *_____ Sie das nicht in meiner Größe?* (haben)

4. *Du _____ sicher ein nettes Restaurant in der Nähe! (kennen)*

5. *Es _____ im Sommer und im Winter Ausverkäufe. (geben)*

6. *Viele Geschäfte _____ am Sonntag nicht offen. (sein)*

7. *_____ du immer mit dem Zug nach Berlin? (fahren)*

8. *Wir _____ immer viele Leute in der Altstadt. (sehen)*

9. *Du* _____ *ja immer noch nicht zu Hause! (sein)*

10. *Im Geschäft* _____ *drei Verkäuferinnen auf mich zu. (kommen)*

B. Choose between *wissen* or *kennen* (conjugated form):

1. *Ich* _____, *wo die Stadt ist, aber ich* _____ *sie nicht.*

2. *Sie* _____ *alle ihre Studenten beim Namen.*

3. *Er* _____ *viel über Physik.*

4. *Das* _____ *ich leider nicht.*

5. *Er* _____ *fast alle Journalisten bei der Zeitung.*

C. Choose the correct sentence(s):

1. I've been waiting such a long time for them already.
   a) *Ich warte schon so lange darauf.*
   b) *Ich warte schon so lange auf ihnen.*
   c) *Ich warte schon so lange auf sie.*
   d) *Ich warte schon so lange dafür.*

2. You can depend on it!
   a) *Sie können sich damit verlassen!*
   b) *Du kannst dich darauf verlassen!*
   c) *Sie kann sich darauf verlassen!*
   d) *Du kannst dich danach verlassen!*

3. What do you think about it?
   a) *Was denkst du darüber?*
   b) *Was denken Sie dabei?*
   c) *Was denken sie darüber?*
   d) *Was halten Sie dazu?*

D. Add the appropriate conjunction:

1. *Gehst du heute ins Theater* _____ *bleibst du zu Hause?*

2. *Heute bleiben wir nicht zu Hause, _____ wir gehen ins Kino.*

3. *Die Jacke ist nicht blau _____ rot.*

4. *Liza kauft keine Bluse _____ eine Jacke.* (two possibilities)

5. *Sie verlassen das Kaufhaus, _____ es ist zu voll.*

6. *Die Jacke im Fenster passt nicht, _____ es gibt sie in Lisas Größe.* (two possibilities)

7. *Die Verkäuferin ist überrascht, _____ Liza kennt die Farbe.*

8. *Die Jacke passt gut _____ sie ist sogar reduziert.*

9. *Stehen Leute vor dem Kaufhaus _____ vor dem kleinen Geschäft?*

10. *Schatzsuche _____ Einkaufen sind für Liza identisch.*

E. Translate the following sentences using *da-* compounds:

1. My book is here. I'm reading something in it.

2. I'm visiting friends, and after that I go to Berlin.

3. I wouldn't (don't) think of it!

4. Next to it is a department store.

Answer Key

A. 1. *erinnere*; 2. *gehen*; 3. *Haben*; 4. *kennst*; 5. *gibt*;
   6. *sind*; 7. *Fährst*; 8. *sehen*; 9. *bist*; 10. *kommen*

B. 1. *weiß, kenne*; 2. *kennt (kennen)*; 3. *weiß*; 4. *weiß*;
   5. *kennt*

C. 1. c; 2. b; 3. a

D. 1. *oder*; 2. *sondern*; 3. *sondern*; 4. *sondern, aber*;
   5. *denn*; 6. *doch, aber*; 7. *denn*; 8. *und*; 9. *oder*; 10. *und*

E. 1. *Mein Buch ist hier. Ich lese etwas darin.* 2. *Ich
   besuche Freunde und danach fahre ich nach Berlin.*
   3. *Ich denke nicht daran!* 4. *Daneben ist ein Kaufhaus.*

LESSON 7

HAPPY-HOUR: AN DER BAR ZAHLEN SIE BAR!
HAPPY HOUR: ONLY CASH AT THE BAR!

A. DIALOGUE

1. *Sie erinnern sich sicher an Shannon und ihren Besuch in Hannover, aber wer war Klaus nochmal? Klaus war mit Freunden im Beach-Club in Düsseldorf, und es handelte sich auch um einen gewissen Klaus in der U-Bahn in Hannover. Ja, es war tatsächlich der gleiche Klaus, denn er ist im Moment ein- oder zweimal pro Woche beruflich in Hannover. Shannon und ihre Freunde Dorothee und Andreas gehen heute in ein Restaurant. Das ist eine gute Gelegenheit für Shannon, sich bei Klaus zu revanchieren. Sie ruft Klaus an und er antwortete gleich.*

   Most likely you remember Shannon and her visit to Hannover, but who was Klaus again? Klaus was in a beach club in Düsseldorf with his friends, and it was also a certain Klaus in the Hannover subway. Yes, it was indeed the same Klaus, because these days he's in Hannover once or twice a week for work. Shannon and her friends, Dorothee and Andreas, are going to a restaurant today. It's a good opportunity for Shannon to return the favor to Klaus. She calls Klaus, and he answers right away.

2. Shannon: **Guten Tag, Klaus. Hier ist Shannon.**
   Hello, Klaus. This is Shannon.

3. Klaus: **Entschuldigung, wer ist dort?**
   Excuse me, who is it?

4. Shannon: **Erinnern Sie sich? Ich hatte keinen Fahrschein in der U-Bahn. Ich schulde Ihnen noch das versprochene Essen.**
   You remember? I didn't have a ticket in the subway. I still owe you the promised dinner.

5. Klaus: **Oh ja, natürlich! Ich wusste Ihren Namen nicht sofort.**
   Oh yes, of course! I didn't remember your name right away.

6. Shannon: **Ich möchte mich gern für die freundliche Hilfe bedanken. Haben Sie heute Abend Zeit?**
   I would like to thank you for the kind help. Do you have time tonight?

7. Klaus: **Ja, passt mir ausgezeichnet. Ich wollte sowieso über Nacht in der Stadt bleiben und ich freue mich auch auf ein Wiedersehen mit Ihnen.**
   Yes, that suits me perfectly. I wanted to stay overnight in the city anyway, and I'm also looking forward to seeing you again.

8. *Wenige Stunden später trifft Klaus sich mit Shannon in einem Restaurant mit Bar. Happy-Hour ist in vollem Schwung. Shannon und ihre Freunde warten bereits an der Bar als Klaus eintrifft.*
   A few hours later, Klaus meets Shannon in a restaurant with a bar. Happy hour is in full swing. Shannon and her friends are already waiting at the bar when Klaus arrives.

9. Klaus: **Hallo. Entschuldigung, ich wusste Ihren Namen vorher nicht mehr.**
   Hi! Sorry I didn't remember your name anymore earlier.

10. Shannon: **Kein Wunder! Ich hatte ja auch nur Ihren Namen.**
    Not surprising! Only I had your name after all.

11. Klaus: **Ach natürlich!**
    Oh, of course!

12. *Shannon stellt ihm ihre Freunde vor. Sie begrüßen sich und dann holt Shannon Getränke von der Bar. Sie schaut in ihr Portemonnaie:* **Oh, nur zehn Euro?**
    Shannon introduces her friends to him. They greet one another, and then Shannon gets drinks from the bar. She looks into her wallet: Oh, only ten euros?

13. Shannon zum Barkeeper: **Entschuldigung, kann ich mit Kreditkarte zahlen?**
    Shannon to the bartender: Excuse me, can I pay by credit card?

14. Barkeeper: **Tut mir Leid, an der Bar nur in bar!**
    I'm sorry, at the bar, cash only!

15. *Glücklicherweise steht Klaus bereits neben ihr und zahlt.*
    Luckily, Klaus is standing right beside her and pays.

16. Shannon: **Mein Schwarzfahren scheint immer teurer für Sie zu werden.**
    My fare-dodging seems to become more and more expensive for you.

17. *Klaus lacht:* **Das ist überhaupt kein Problem! Zum Wohl!**
    Klaus laughs: That's no problem at all! Cheers!

18. Dorothee: **So, Sie kommen aus Düsseldorf?**
    So, you're from Düsseldorf?

19. Klaus: **Ja, aber zur Zeit arbeite ich ein- bis zweimal die Woche hier. Aber duzen wir uns doch! Auf der Arbeit ist es schon formell genug.**
Yes, but for the time being I'm working here once or twice a week. But why don't we use the familiar form? It's already formal enough at work.

20. Shannon: **Gern! Fliegst du jedesmal hierher?**
Gladly! Do you fly here every time?

21. Klaus: **Eigentlich selten. Ich brauche nur zweieinhalb Stunden mit dem Zug, aber Fliegen dauert mit An- und Abfahrt zu den Flughäfen fast sechs Stunden. Ich fliege gern, aber ich komme selten zum Lesen. Im Zug ist das anders. Ich nutze die Zeit mehr.**
Rarely, actually. I just need two and a half hours by train, but flying takes almost six hours with going to and coming from the airports. I like to fly, but then I seldom get to read. That's different on the train. I use the time more.

22. Andreas: **Ah, es gibt endlich einen freien Tisch für uns. Jetzt hab' ich wirklich einen Riesenhunger. Gefällt euch der Tisch dort am Fenster?**
Ah, there's finally a free table for us. Now I'm really extremely hungry. Do you like the table there at the window?

23. *Beim Essen lernen sich die Vier besser kennen, besonders Shannon und Klaus. Sie scheinen sich zu mögen. Selbst Dorothee und Andreas bemerken die offensichtliche Sympathie.*
Over dinner, the four get to know one another better, especially Shannon and Klaus. They do seem to like each other. Even Dorothee and Andreas notice the obvious connection.

24. Klaus: **Wirklich schade! Ich fahre morgen schon wieder zurück nach Hause und komme erst nächsten Monat zurück. Wie lange bleibst du denn in Deutschland?**
Really too bad! I'm going back home tomorrow already, and I won't come back before next month. How long are you staying in Germany?

25. Shannon: **Ja, zu schade! Ich bleibe nur noch drei Wochen.**
Yes, too bad! I'll only stay another three weeks.

26. *Aus der Musikbox hören sie plötzlich einen Schlager aus den sechziger Jahren: Wärst du doch in Düsseldorf geblieben . . . Du wirst nie ein Cowboy sein.*
Suddenly, they hear a hit from the Sixties coming from the jukebox: If only you had stayed in Düsseldorf . . . You will never be a cowboy.

27. Klaus: **Na, ich hoffe das war kein Wink mit dem Zaunpfahl.**
Well, I hope that wasn't an attempt to give me a really subtle hint.

28. Dorothee: **Ach komm! Die alten Schlager sind nun mal wieder modern.**
Oh come on! The old hits are simply in style again.

29. *Andreas lacht:* **Aber es passte ja mal wieder wie die Faust aufs Auge.**
Andreas laughs: But it really fits again just perfectly.

30. *Klaus sieht auf seine Uhr:* **Oh verflixt! Ist es wirklich schon so spät? Ich komme in Teufels Küche, wenn ich morgen früh nicht pünktlich bin. Nun, eine Stunde mehr macht jetzt den**

Kohl auch nicht fett. Ich kann ja morgen im Zug schlafen.

Klaus takes a look at his watch: Oh damn! Is it already that late? I'll be in hot water if I'm late tomorrow morning. Well, an hour more wouldn't make much difference now. I can sleep on the train tomorrow.

B. NOTES

1. *Gelegenheit* doesn't mean "bargain" here, but "opportunity" or "chance."

7. The verb *passen* is used here reflexively, meaning "to suit." *Das passt mir gut!* (That suits me fine!) The exact same sentence could be used to express that a piece of clothing fits well.

8. *bereits* (already) is often interchangeable with *schon*. This is not the case, though, when *schon* is combined with other adverbs: *immer schon* (always [in the past]). *Als* (when) always refers to the past. It is also used in comparisons, meaning "than."

10. *Kein Wunder!* (No wonder!) That doesn't come as a surprise.

12. The French word *das Portemonnaie* (wallet, purse) is commonly used. There is also a German version, *das Portmonee*. Another common word for wallet is *die Geldbörse*. A larger wallet is called *die Brieftasche*.

14. *Ich zahle bar.* (I'm paying cash.), *die Bar* (the bar).

16. See Lesson 8 for more on the verb *werden* (to become).

17. *Zum Wohl!* (To your health!) is commonly used when raising your glass.

18. There is a difference between *Ich komme aus Berlin* and *Ich komme von Berlin*. While *aus* indicates origin or at least permanent residence, *von* might indicate that you are just coming from there.

19. *ein- bis zweimal* (once or twice). Note that both *ein* and *zwei* are compounded with *mal*, and a hyphen is used in the written language to show this. You'll see this a lot with nouns, as in: *die Haupt- und die Nebenstraße* (the main and the side street).

    There are verbs for using the familiar or the polite form of address: *Sie können mich duzen.* (You can use the familiar form.) *Wir siezen uns immer noch.* (We are still using the formal form of "you.")

21. The expression *zu etwas kommen* (lit.: to come to something) actually means "to be able to find time for something" (to get to something): *Ich komme nicht dazu.* (I'm not finding time for it.)

22. *Ich habe einen Riesenhunger.* (lit.: I'm hungry as a giant.), *riesig* (gigantic)

24. *Wie schade!* (lit.: What a pity!) This should not be mixed up with the verb *schaden* (to damage, do harm).

27. *Ist das ein Wink mit dem Zaunpfahl?* (lit.: Is that a wave with a fence pole?) This is a German saying often used jokingly when someone is trying to give a discreet hint that is not discreet at all, but rather obvious. It's something like "Oh, real subtle!"

28. *Schlager* (music hit). It only refers to hits sung in German. For songs in English, the term *der Hit* is used.

29. *Das passt wie die Faust aufs Auge!* (lit.: That fits like the fist on the eye!) This expression originally meant that something didn't suit a situation at all, but it has been used ironically so much that today it describes something that suits a situation surprisingly well.

30. *Ich komme in Teufels Küche.* (lit.: I'll get into the devil's kitchen.) I'll get into hot water.
      Das macht den Kohl auch nicht fett. (lit.: That doesn't enrich the cabbage either.) It isn't of any help. It makes no difference.

Culture Notes

Even though the formal form of address is common in business and between adults who don't know each other, it is rather unusual for people who socialize privately to use the polite form of address for long. Whenever you are unsure which form of address is more appropriate, start out using the polite form. The native speaker will certainly invite you to use the familiar form if the situation is more suited for it. Colleagues at work might never switch to the familiar form in order to keep professional distance, but this isn't the case in a personal friendship.

The song *Wärst du doch in Düsseldorf geblieben* is one of the most famous songs from the mid 1960s, which has enjoyed—along with many others from that period of time—a very big comeback. There is hardly a German who doesn't know it. The topic of the song is a man from Düsseldorf who falls in love with a woman from Texas. He moves to Texas, but fails utterly as a cowboy. Anyway, love prevails.

C. GRAMMAR AND USAGE

1. The Simple Past Tense

The simple past tense *(das Imperfekt)* is often called the written past or the narrative past, because it is usually used in writing. The German language mostly uses the present perfect tense to express the past—in spoken language, that is (see Lesson 9). There are a few verbs that are an exception. The simple past forms of the auxiliary verbs *sein* (to be) and *haben* (to have) are frequently used in conversations, as well as the modal verbs *können* (can), *müssen* (must, have to), *dürfen* (be allowed to, may), *sollen* (shall, should), *wollen* (want), *mögen* (to like), the half-modal *brauchen* (to need), and the verbs *wissen* (to know), *kennen* (to know), *sagen* (to say), *erzählen* (to tell), and *glauben* (to believe). Otherwise, in spoken German, the simple past is used mostly in narratives—when you're telling a story about yourself or someone else.

Look at the conjugation of the four verbs below in the simple past. Note that even irregular verbs show more regularity than in the present tense. Please refer to the grammar section for other conjugation examples.

sein (to be)	*haben* (to have)	*können* (can)	*glauben* (to believe)
ich war	*ich hatte*	*ich konnte*	*ich glaubte*
du warst	*du hattest*	*du konntest*	*du glaubtest*
er war	*sie hatte*	*es konnte*	*er glaubte*
wir waren	*wir hatten*	*wir konnten*	*wir glaubten*
ihr wart	*ihr hattet*	*ihr konntet*	*ihr glaubtet*
sie (Sie) waren	*sie (Sie) hatten*	*sie (Sie) konnten*	*sie (Sie) glaubten*

To see how the simple past might be used in conversation, let's pretend Klaus is back in Düsseldorf, and his visitors are asking him about the trip to Hannover. Notice that this is essentially a piece of narration, the telling of a story.

Was war los in Hannover?
   What was going on in Hannover?

Ich war in der U-Bahn und eine junge Amerikanerin hatte keine Fahrkarte.
   I was in the subway, and a young American woman had no ticket!

Gab es eine Kontrolle? (past tense of: *es gibt*)
   Was there a ticket check?

Ja, aber ich hatte noch eine gültige Karte extra. Sie war sehr dankbar und versprach mir ein Essen.
   Yes, but I still had another valid ticket. She was very thankful and promised me a dinner.

Und wart ihr zusammen in einem Restaurant?
   And were you together in a restaurant?

Ja, und es passte mir recht gut. Ich wollte sowieso dort übernachten. Der Abend wurde aber sehr spät und heute Morgen konnte ich kaum meine Augen aufhalten.
   Yes, and it suited me quite well. I wanted to stay overnight anyway. But it got quite late, and this morning, I could hardly keep my eyes open.

2. Reflexive Pronouns

Reflexive pronouns are used to reflect back to the person who is acting: *Sie setzt sich auf den Stuhl.* (She sits down/sits herself down in the chair.) They can also indicate reciprocal action with plural subjects: *Sie mögen sich.* (They like each other.) Many verbs can be used reflexively. Others are reflexive verbs altogether or take on a different meaning if used reflexively. In German, the reflexive pronouns are identical to the object pronouns in the first and second person, but they are different in the third person *(sich)*. The accusative and the dative reflexive pronouns are also identical, except in the first and second person singular:

subject pronoun	reflexive pronoun
ich	*mich/mir* (myself)
du	*dich/dir* (yourself)
er	*sich* (himself)
sie	*sich* (herself)
es	*sich* (itself)
wir	*uns* (ourselves)
ihr	*euch* (yourselves)
sie (Sie)	*sich* (themselves, yourself/ yourselves, pol.)

Sie begrüßen sich.
They greet each other.

Ich wasche mich und kämme mir das Haar.
I wash myself and comb my hair.

Fragst du dich, wer das ist?
Are you asking yourself who that is?

The reflexive pronoun of the polite form is not written with a capital letter, since it doesn't address the person, it simply refers back.

Bitte nehmen Sie sich Zeit!
Please take your time!

Notice that the reflexive pronouns may express a truly reflexive relationship, or an indirect relationship. True reflexives are accusative, and indirect reflexives are dative.

Du siehst dich im Spiegel an. (accusative)
  You are looking at yourself in the mirror.

Du siehst dir die Augen im Spiegel an. (dative)
  You are looking at your eyes in the mirror.

3. Reflexive Verbs

Certain verbs called reflexive verbs always require the use of a reflexive pronoun. True reflexive verbs can only be used with the accusative reflexive pronoun, the direct object.

Ich bedanke mich für die freundliche Hilfe.
  I am obliged for the friendly help.

Shannon revanchiert sich mit einem Essen.
  Shannon is returning the favor with a dinner.

Klaus freut sich auf das Treffen mit Shannon.
  Klaus is looking forward to the meeting with Shannon.

Sie freut sich sehr über das nette Geschenk.
  She is happy about the nice present.

Ich erinnere mich noch gut an die Reise nach Liechtenstein.
  I remember the trip to Liechtenstein well.

Note that there is a difference between *sich erinnern* (to remember) and *erinnern* (to remind), which is not reflexive. A reflexive verb has to refer back to the subject. *Ich erinnere ihn an den Termin!* (I remind him of the appointment.) is not reflexive. A similar difference exists between *sich unterhalten* (to have a conversation) and the non-reflexive *unterhalten* (to entertain, maintain, support):

Klaus und seine Freunde unterhalten sich über einen neuen Film. (reflexive verb)
    Klaus and his friends are talking about a new movie.

Er unterhält seine Gäste sehr gut. (non-reflexive verb)
    He entertains his guests very well.

4. Expressing Likes and Dislikes

There are several different ways in German to express likes and dislikes. The verb *mögen* is frequently used in the subjunctive form *möchte* (would like) to express a desire to purchase or to have something, and also to express an intention.

Ich möchte die Jacke dort im Schaufenster.
    I would like the jacket over there in the display window.

Shannon möchte auch noch in den Süden.
    Shannon would still like to go to the South as well.

The indicative of *mögen* is often used to express liking with food and people.

Er mag deutsches Bier.
    He likes German beer.

Ungeduldige Leute mögen wir nicht.
    We don't like impatient people.

Klaus mochte das Essen in dem Restaurant nicht.
    Klaus didn't like the food in the restaurant.

Another way to express liking is with the verb *gefallen*. Remember that *gefallen* literally means "to please," so the thing or person that is liked is the subject, and the person to whom it is pleasing is the indirect object in the dative case.

Die Jacke gefällt ihr sehr gut.
    She likes the jacket very much. (The jacket is very pleasing to her.)

Die Berge im Süden gefallen ihm.
> He likes the mountains in the South.

Gefallen mostly refers to things that are visual, never to the taste of food. If it is used with people, it most likely refers to their visual appearance, rarely their character or other attributes.

Das Essen gefällt ihm, aber er mag es nicht.
> He likes how the food looks, but he doesn't like the taste.

Das Wetter gefällt uns ganz und gar nicht, aber die Leute mögen wir sehr.
> We don't like the weather at all, but the people we like very much.

The adverb *gern* (gladly, with liking) is another common option to convey liking or the opposite. An exact translation of the word by itself is difficult, but its use is easy. *Gern* can follow almost any verb, and it expresses that someone likes to perform that action. It is often combinded with *sehr* (very) or *so* (so).

Dorothee geht gern in ein Restaurant und sie fährt sehr gern ans Meer.
> Dorothee likes to go to a restaurant, and she very much likes to go to the ocean.

Sie möchte Hannover sehr gern wieder einmal besuchen.
> She very much would like to visit Hannover again.

EXERCISES

A. Add the conjugated verb (simple past tense) in parentheses:

1. *Er* _____ _____ *an den Urlaub in der Schweiz. (sich erinnern)*

2. *Gestern* _____ *wir nicht zu Hause. (sein)*

3. _____ *du gestern keine Zeit? (haben)*

4. *Da _____ auch viele Museen in der Nähe!*
   (sein)

5. *Es _____ in der Stadt keinen Parkplatz.*
   (geben)

6. *Was _____ denn die Frau von dir?(wollen)*

7. *Der Zug _____ nur drei Minuten zu spät an.*
   (kommen)

8. *Ihr _____ doch ein Haus in der Altstadt.*
   (haben)

9. *Um 12 Uhr _____ er immer noch nicht zu*
   Hause! (sein)

10. *Im Geschäft _____ gleich drei Verkäuferin-*
    nen. (kommen)

B. Choose the correct translation:

1. Would you like a coffee?
   a) *Brauchen sie einen Kaffee?*
   b) *Möchten Sie einen Kaffee?*
   c) *Haben Sie Kaffee gern?*
   d) *Gefällt ihnen ein Kaffee?*

2. With pleasure, thanks!
   a) *Sehr gern, danke!*
   b) *Gefällt mir, danke!*
   c) *Mit mögen, danke!*
   d) *Ich bin vergnügt, danke!*

3. He is very fond of her.
   a) *Er mag ihr sehr.*
   b) *Er hat sie sehr.*
   c) *Er hat sie sehr gern.*
   d) *Ihm gefällt sie sehr.*

C. Insert the correct reflexive pronoun:

1. *Ich freue _____ schon sehr auf den Urlaub.*

2. *Darauf können Sie _____ garantiert verlassen.*

3. *Wir stellen _____ immer erst vor.*

4. *Du stellst _____ schon im Winter den Sommer vor.*

5. *Ich freue _____ sehr über das interessante Buch.*

D. Translate the sentences using the simple past tense:

1. I didn't have time this morning.

2. Were they in a restaurant?

3. Whose car did you have? (fam. sing.)

4. She didn't know that.

5. He believed her.

E. Match the German sentences to the translations:

1. *Sie gefallen ihr.*   a. She likes him.

2. *Ihr gefällt das.*   b. She likes how he looks.

3. *Sie mag ihn.*   c. She likes how you look.

4. *Er hat sie gern.*   d. That may be.

5. *Das mag sein.*   e. She likes that.

6. *Er gefällt ihr.*   f. He likes her.

Answer Key

A. 1. *erinnerte sich*; 2. *waren*; 3. *Hattest*; 4. *waren*, 5. *gab*; 6. *wollte*; 7. *kam*; 8. *hattet*; 9. *war*; 10. *kamen*

B. 1. b; 2. a; 3. c.

C. 1. *mich*; 2. *sich*; 3. *uns*; 4. *dir*; 5. *mich*

D. 1. *Ich hatte heute Morgen keine Zeit.* 2. *Waren sie in einem Restaurant?* 3. *Wessen Auto hattest du?* 4. *Das wusste sie nicht. Sie wusste das nicht.* 5. *Er glaubte ihr.*

E. 1. c; 2. e; 3. a; 4. f; 5. d; 6. b

LESSON 8

IM THEATER: VON NUN AN KOMME ICH IMMER ZU SPÄT.
AT THE THEATER: FROM NOW ON, I'LL ALWAYS BE LATE.

A. DIALOGUE

1. *Während ihr Gastgeber Klaus beruflich in Hannover zu tun hat, möchten Liza und Shawn ins Theater. Es gibt eine Neuinszenierung der Drei-Groschen-Oper. Es ist ein bisschen spät, um Karten zu kaufen, aber Liza und Shawn versuchen ihr Glück. Sie stehen vor der Theaterkasse.*

   While their host, Klaus, is in Hannover for business, Liza and Shawn would like to go to the theater. There is a new production of the Threepenny Opera. It's a little late to buy tickets, but Liza and Shawn are trying their luck. They're standing in front of the theater ticket booth.

2. Liza: **Guten Tag. Haben Sie noch Karten für die Drei-Groschen-Oper heute Abend?**

   Good afternoon. Do you still have tickets for the Threepenny Opera tonight?

3. Kartenverkäufer: **Da haben Sie wirklich Glück. Ich habe gerade noch zwei zurückgegebene Karten in der Platzgruppe fünf. Möchten Sie die Karten?**

   You're really lucky there. I just have two returned tickets in seating area five. Would you like those tickets?

4. Liza: **Ja, sehr gern! Wie viel macht das zusammen?**

   Yes, gladly! How much does it come to?

5. Kartenverkäufer: **Das macht zusammen vierund-
zwanzig Euro.**
That comes to twenty-four euros together.

6. Shawn: **Nur zwölf Euro pro Karte? Sind diese
Plätze einigermaßen okay?**
Only twelve euros per ticket? Are these seats any
good?

7. Kartenverkäufer: **Um ehrlich zu sein, sie sind in
der letzen Reihe im zweiten Rang, aber es sind,
wie gesagt, die allerletzten freien Plätze.**
To be honest, they are in the last row of the upper
circle, but they are, as I said, the very last free
seats.

8. Shawn: **Werden wir von diesen Plätzen aus überhaupt etwas sehen?**
Will we see anything at all from these seats?

9. Kartenverkäufer: **Etwas werden Sie sicher sehen.
Aber die Plätze sind weder in der Mitte, noch ist
die Akustik dort sehr gut.**
You certainly will see something. But the seats
aren't in the middle, and the acoustics there aren't
very good either.

10. Liza: **Jetzt sind wir schon mal hier. Da werden
wir wohl mal in den sauren Apfel beißen müssen.
Es wird schon nicht so schlimm sein.**
Now we're here already, after all. We'll just have to
grin and bear it. It won't be all that bad.

11. *Einige Stunden später kommen Liza und Shawn
zur Vorstellung zurück zum Theater. Es ist neun
Minuten nach acht. Sie hasten die Stufen des Theaters hinauf und zeigen dem Platzanweiser ihre
Karten.*

A few hours later, Liza and Shawn come back to the theater for the performance. It's nine minutes past eight. They hurry up the stairs of the theater and show their tickets to the usher.

12. Platzanweiser: **Tut mir wirklich sehr Leid, doch Sie werden bis zum nächsten großen Applaus warten müssen. Der Beginn der Vorstellung war um acht Uhr, aber gehen Sie doch dort zum Monitor hinüber. Dann werden Sie den Anfang nicht verpassen.**

    I'm really very sorry, but you'll have to wait until the next big applause. The beginning of the performance was at eight o'clock, but why don't you go over there to the monitor. Then you won't miss the beginning.

13. *Liza und Shawn gehen zu einer Nische mit einem sehr großen Monitor. Mehrere andere Nachzügler stehen in der Nähe. Ein Mädchen kommt herüber und sagt:*

    Lisa and Shawn walk over to a niche with a very large monitor. Several other latecomers are standing near. A girl comes over and says:

14. Mädchen: **Wir werden nicht lange warten müssen. Der nächste Applaus ist in fast zehn Minuten. Ich habe sowieso keine gute Karte. Wahrscheinlich sehe ich hier auf dem riesigen Monitor besser als auf meinem Platz.**

    We won't have to wait long. The next applause is in almost ten minutes. I don't have a good ticket anyway. I'll probably see better on this huge monitor than from my seat.

15. Liza mitfühlend: **Ich fürchte wir haben auch schlechte Karten.**

    Liza, sympathetically: I'm afraid we have very bad tickets as well.

16. *In diesem Moment hastet ein Mann an Ihnen vorbei; dann scheint er es sich anders zu überlegen und kommt zurück.*

    At this moment, a man hurries past them; then he seems to change his mind, and returns.

17. Der Mann: **Ich habe eine Loge mit drei leeren Plätzen. Freunde von mir stecken hoffnungslos im Stau weit von hier. Also, wenn sie möchten . . . ?**

    I have a theater box with three empty seats. Friends of mine are hopelessly stuck in a traffic jam far from here. So, if you would like . . . ?

18. Mädchen: **Mit größtem Vergnügen!**

    With the greatest pleasure!

19. *Bevor Liza und Shawn sich versehen, zieht das Mädchen Shawn am Ärmel den Gang hinunter.*

    Before Liza and Shawn can turn round, the girl pulls Shawn by his sleeve down the hallway.

20. Liza: **Ist das wirklich kein Problem? Wir möchten uns nicht aufdrängen.**

    Is this really no problem? We don't want to impose.

21. Der Mann: **Ganz und gar kein Problem. Mein Name ist übrigens Michael Stern, aber bitte nennen Sie mich einfach Michael.**

    Absolutely no problem. My name, by the way, is Michael Stern, but please call me just Michael.

22. Shawn: **Freut mich! Ich bin Shawn Stern und das ist meine Frau Liza. Was für ein Zufall, wir haben den gleichen Familiennamen.**

    Glad to meet you! I'm Shawn Stern and that's my wife Liza. What a coincidence that we have the same last name.

23. Michael: **Ach ja, das Leben ist eine Reihe von Zufällen. Aber es freut mich auch. Und wie heißt Ihre hübsche Tochter?**
Oh well, life is a series of coincidences. But glad to meet you, too. And what's the name of your pretty daughter?

24. Mädchen: **Iris, und ich bin nicht die Tochter. Ich bin nicht nur viel zu alt, sondern ich habe auch ihren netten Akzent nicht. Nächste Woche werde ich vierzehn.**
Iris, and I'm not the daughter. I'm not only much too old, but I don't have their nice accent, either. I'll be fourteen next week.

25. *Iris sagt das mit einem leicht hochnäsigen Unterton, und keiner kann sich ein Lächeln verkneifen. Jetzt öffnen sie die Tür zur Loge und setzen sich in die komfortablen Sessel. Die Drei-Groschen-Oper kann beginnen.*
Iris says this with a slightly haughty undertone, and nobody can suppress a smile. Now, they open the door to the theater box, and sit down in the comfortable seats. The Threepenny Opera can begin.

26. Iris: **Je später der Abend, desto besser die Chancen. Von nun an komme ich immer zu spät.**
The later the evening, the better the chances. From now on, I'll always be late.

B. NOTES

1. The expression *zu tun haben in* (lit.: to have to do in) mostly refers to work.

   Er hat in Berlin zu tun. (He is on business in Berlin.)

   sein Glück versuchen (to try one's luck)

6. *einigermaßen* (lit.: in some kind of measure, some-what)

7. *es sind:* Notice that this is a "placeholder" similar to "there is/are" or "it is" in English. *Es sind Keine Plätze mehr frei.* (There are no more free seats.) *Es sind die Kühle Nächte, die ich mag.* (It's the chilly nights that I like.)
der/die/das allerletzte (lit.: last of all) is an adjective meaning the very last of something.

10. The idiom *in den sauren Apfel beißen müssen* (lit.: to have to bite into the sour apple) is used in situations that are apparently unchangeable (to grin and bear, to bite the bullet, etc.).

13. *Nachzügler* (latecomers) is a slightly friendlier term than *Zuspätkommer* (latecomer). While the latter indicates tardiness in regards to time, the former refers to the last people dropping in.

16. The term *sich etwas anders überlegen* (to change one's mind) uses the dative reflexive pronoun. This is only visible in the first and second person singular (Lesson 7): *Ich habe es mir anders überlegt.* (I changed my mind.)

18. *Mit größtem Vergnügen!* (With the greatest plea-sure!) The adjective here is the superlative. This is one of the rare examples where an adjective refers to a singular noun without an article. Since the adjective replaces the article, it takes the ending of that "missing" article *dem* (see Lesson 2).

19. The idiom *bevor man sich versieht* (before one could turn around) uses the accusative reflexive pronoun (true reflexive). *Bevor ich mich versah, war ich hoffnungslos verliebt.* (Before I knew what was happening, I had hopelessly fallen in love.)

20. The phrase *sich nicht aufdrängen wollen* (to not want to impose) uses the accusative reflexive pronoun here. *Du drängst dich ganz und gar nicht auf!* (You're absolutely not imposing!)

25. The idiom *sich etwas nicht verkneifen können* (unable to suppress the urge) can also be used positively (without *nicht*) and with other modal verbs (see Lesson 12). It uses the dative reflexive pronoun. *Das wirst du dir verkneifen müssen!* (You'll have to restrain yourself from that!)

Culture Notes

It is well known that punctuality is of great importance to Germans, as well as to the people of the other German-speaking countries, but it is more a cultural aspect than anything else. Most people simply feel disrespected if another person doesn't seem to value their time. There are some regional differences. For instance, the people in Swabia (where many German cars are built) are known to be exactly on time for any occasion, and the Bavarians are a little less time-conscious. In most theater or opera performances, as well as in classical concerts, people might have to wait a little, if they are more than five minutes late and the curtain has already risen. This is of course to avoid any distractions for the audience trying to enjoy the show without anyone trying to squeeze by to get to his or her seat. What many people don't know is that latecomers have the right to get their money back, if not let into the performance right away. This might require a letter from the *Verbraucherschutz* (Consumer Protection Agency), though.

Many theaters don't have the old seating categories *das Parkett* (orchestra), *Erster Rang* (dress circle), *Zweiter Rang* (upper circle), or *Oberster Rang* (balcony) anymore. They now just categorize by *Sitzgruppe* (seating group), with the lowest number referring to the best seats in the house.

C. GRAMMAR AND USAGE

1. The Simple Future Tense

The simple future tense *(das Futur)* is not difficult to use in German. The auxiliary *werden* (will) is conjugated, and the verb to which it refers remains in the infinitive at the end of the clause: *Sie werden heute Abend ins Theater gehen.* (They will go to the theater tonight.)

ich werde sehen	I will see
du wirst sehen	you will see
er/sie/es wird sehen	he/she/it will see
wir werden sehen	we will see
ihr werdet sehen	you (pl.) will see
sie/Sie werden sehen	they (you pol.) will see

Es wird heute Abend regnen.
　　It will rain this evening.

Werden wir von diesen Plätzen gut sehen?
　　Will we see well from these seats?

Especially in spoken language, the grammatical future is often replaced by the present tense, using an adverb to indicate future.

Klaus kommt morgen von Hannover zurück.
　　Klaus is coming back from Hannover tomorrow.

In fact, it sometimes sounds a little stilted if the grammatical future is used in conversations.

Klaus wird morgen von Hannover zurückkommen.
　　Klaus will come back from Hannover tomorrow.

2. Uses of the Verb *werden*

Not only can *werden* be used with another main verb to express the future, it can also be used on its own as a main verb meaning "to become" or "to get."

Es wird morgen regnen.
> It's going to rain tomorrow.

Das Wetter wird schön.
> The weather is getting nice.

It also possible to confuse the modal verb *wollen* (to want, to insist) with *werden*, simply because of the similarity to the English verb "will."

Er will seine Suppe nicht essen.
> He doesn't want to eat his soup.

Er wird seine Suppe nicht essen.
> He will not eat his soup.

The verb *werden* is also used in the passive voice, but we'll come back to that in Lesson 17.

3. Two-Part Conjunctions (Coordinating)

These conjunctions connect two parts of a sentence, where the parts of the conjunction relate to each other. This is in many instances similar to English:

> *nicht nur . . . sondern auch* (not only . . . but also)

Ich bin nicht nur zu alt, sondern ich habe auch nicht den netten Akzent.
> Not only am I too old, but I also don't have that nice accent.

The next two-part conjunction is similar to the one above, but the first part of the sentence is not negative:

> *Sowohl . . . als auch* (not only/such . . . but even, but . . . as well . . .)

Sie haben sowohl Glück noch Theaterkarten zu bekommen, als auch später im Theater.
> They're having such luck to still get theater tickets, and even later on in the theater.

entweder . . . oder (either . . . or)

Sie müssen entweder in den sauren Apfel beißen oder ganz auf das Theater verzichten.
> They either have to bite the bullet, or completely do without the theater.

weder . . . noch (neither . . . nor)

Sie kommen weder rechtzeitig für gute Karten, noch sind sie zur Vorstellung pünktlich.
> They neither come in time for good tickets, nor are they on time for the performance.

Je . . . desto (the . . . the)

Je mehr unglückliche Zufälle es gab, desto mehr Glück hatten sie am Ende.
> The more unlucky coincidences there were, the more luck they had in the end.

je . . . umso (the . . . even)

Je später der Abend, umso schöner die Gäste. (adage, often ironic)
> The later the evening, the (even) more beautiful the guests.

4. Negation: *Nicht* and *Kein*

In general, the negation of the definite article or of possessives uses *nicht* (not), while the negation of the indefinite article (or lack of an article) uses *kein* (no, not any). Verbs are only negated with *nicht*. The placement of the negation is often different from English, mostly due to the fact that German doesn't use "do" in negations. *Kein* is usually placed before the noun. As a rule of thumb, if *nicht* negates a verb, it is often placed after that verb or at the end of the sentence.

Er wartet nicht.
> He isn't waiting.

Sie benutzen ihre Sitzplätze nicht.
They're not using their seats.

If *nicht* specifically negates another element of the sentence, it is placed before that element.

Sie benutzen nicht ihre Sitzplätze.
They're not using <u>their</u> seats. (But they're using someone else's.)

Nicht sie benutzen ihre Sitzplätze.
<u>They're</u> not using their seats. (But someone else is.)

Sie benutzen nicht die Sitzplätze.
They're not using <u>the seats</u>. (They are using something else, a bench perhaps.)

Remember that *kein* is used to negate indefinite nouns or nouns that have no article at all.

Sie haben keine guten Karten.
They don't have (any) good tickets.

Sie haben nicht die besten Karten. (negating noun and adjective)
They don't have the best tickets.

Er spricht kein Französisch.
He speaks no French. / He doesn't speak any French.

Ich sehe kein blaues Auto.
I don't see any blue car. / I see no blue car.

5. *hin* vs. *her*

Similar to *da-* and *wo-* in compunds, *hin* and *her* can be combined with many prepositions to communicate movement toward or away from the speaker. The *wo-* compounds *woher?* (from where?) and *wohin?* (where to?) clearly demonstrate the meaning.

In the following paragraph, everything is narrated from the perspective of the speaker:

Ich gehe die Straße hinunter, dann einen Hügel hinauf und bis hinüber zu meinem Haus. In diesem Augenblick kommt meine Tante heraus. Sie steigt die Treppe herunter und ich die Treppe hinauf. Sie geht zu einem Kiosk hinüber. Sie nimmt ihre Geldbörse heraus und kauft eine Zeitung, doch die Zeitung fällt ihr hinunter. Ein junger Mann eilt herbei und hebt die Zeitung auf. Dann kommt sie wieder zu mir herüber. Sie steigt die Treppe zu mir herauf und wir gehen ins Haus hinein.

I walk down the street, then up a hill and over to my house. At this moment, my aunt comes outside. She goes down the stairs while I walk up. She walks over to a newsstand. She takes out her wallet and buys a newspaper, but the paper falls down. A young man hurries to her side and picks up the paper. Then she comes back toward me. She walks up the stairs toward me, and we go inside.

EXERCISES

A. Write the following sentences in the negative by negating the underlined word or phrase.

    1. *Er hat <u>beruflich</u> in Hannover zu tun.*

    2. *Es gibt <u>Karten</u> für die nächste Vorstellung.*

    3. *Ich werde <u>am Montag</u> ins Theater gehen.*

    4. *Sie hat <u>immer</u> Glück mit einem Parkplatz.*

    5. *Er wird morgen einen <u>Brief</u> schreiben.*

    6. *Der Beginn der Vorstellung war <u>um acht Uhr</u>.*

    7. *<u>Wir</u> werden jetzt die besten Plätze haben.*

8. *Sie werden <u>morgen</u> ins Museum gehen.*

9. *Ich sehe die Vorstellung <u>sehr gut</u> auf dem Monitor.*

10. *Er gibt einem Besucher <u>Karten</u>.*

B. Combine or change the following sentences by using the two-part conjunctions given.

1. *Die Arbeit wird ihm Spaß machen. Sie ist interessant. (nicht nur . . . sondern auch)*

2. *Wir verzichten auf die Karten und auf das Geld. (sowohl . . . als auch)*

3. *Das Wetter wird morgen gut werden. Wir gehen ins Theater. (entweder . . . oder)*

4. *Sie fährt nicht mit der U-Bahn. Sie geht nicht zu Fuß. (weder . . . noch)*

5. *Er spricht darüber mehr. Er freut sich mehr auf den Urlaub. (je . . . desto)*

C. Rewrite the following text into the future tense:

Am Montag kommt Klaus wieder nach Hause. Er erzählt Liza und Shawn von seinen Erlebnissen in Hannover, und sie berichten ihm von ihrem doppelten Glück im Theater. Dann planen sie die Woche. Klaus arbeitet am Dienstag nicht. Sie fahren nach Köln, gehen in das berühmte Museum Ludwig und besuchen viele andere interessante Gebäude in der Stadt. Liza macht eine Liste. Es wird* sicher ein großes Vergnügen für alle.

D. Choose *hin* or *her*:

1. *Kommen Sie doch bitte _____! (hinein/ herein)*

*Note that *werden* is not future tense here, but "to become"!

2. *Sie geht die Treppe* _____. *(hinauf/herauf)*

3. *Er kommt den Hügel* _____. *(hinauf/herauf)*

4. *Sie schwimmt zum anderen Ufer* _____. *(hinüber/herüber)*

5. *Hinauf war nicht schwer, aber wie kommt er wieder* _____. *(hinunter/herunter)*

E. Translate the following sentences:

1. I will write the letter today.

2. It won't be all that bad.

3. They hurry up the stairs.

4. You'll have to wait.

5. I won't be late.

Answer Key

A. 1. *Er hat nicht beruflich in Hannover zu tun.* 2. *Es gibt keine Karten für die nächste Vorstellung.* 3. *Ich werde nicht am Montag ins Theater gehen.* 4. *Sie hat nicht immer Glück mit einem Parkplatz.* 5. *Er wird morgen keinen Brief schreiben.* 6. *Der Beginn der Vorstellung war nicht um acht Uhr.* 7. *Nicht wir werden jetzt die besten Plätze haben.* 8. *Sie werden nicht morgen ins Museum gehen.* 9. *Ich sehe die Vorstellung nicht sehr gut auf dem Monitor.* 10. *Er gibt einem Besucher keine Karten.*

B. 1. *Die Arbeit wird ihm nicht nur Spaß machen, sondern sie ist auch interessant.* 2. *Wir verzichten sowohl auf die Karten als auch auf das Geld.* 3. *Das Wetter wird morgen entweder gut werden oder wir gehen ins Theater.* 4. *Sie fährt weder mit der U-Bahn noch geht sie zu Fuß.* 5. *Je mehr er darüber spricht, desto mehr freut er sich auf den Urlaub.*

C. *Am Montag wird Klaus wieder nach Hause kommen. Er wird Liza und Shawn von seinen Erlebnissen in Hannover erzählen, und sie werden ihm von ihrem doppelten Glück im Theater berichten. Dann werden sie die Woche planen. Klaus wird am Dienstag nicht arbeiten. Sie werden nach Köln fahren, in das berühmte Museum Ludwig gehen und viele andere interessante Gebäude in der Stadt besuchen. Liza wird eine Liste machen. Es wird sicher ein großes Vergnügen für alle werden.*

D. 1. *herein;* 2. *hinauf;* 3. *herauf;* 4. *hinüber;* 5. *herunter*

E. 1. *Ich werde den Brief heute schreiben.* 2. *Es wird schon nicht so schlimm sein.* 3. *Sie hasten die Stufen hinauf.* 4. *Sie werden (Du wirst) warten müssen.* 5. *Ich werde nicht zu spät kommen.*

LESSON 9

IM MUSEUM: WO IST NUR MEIN MANN GEBLIEBEN?
IN THE MUSEUM: WHAT ON EARTH HAPPENED TO MY HUSBAND?

A. DIALOGUE

1. *Klaus und seine amerikanischen Gäste haben heute ein volles Programm. Köln liegt nur einen Katzensprung entfert, und es gibt auch dort viel zu sehen. Liza hat einen detaillierten Plan gemacht, denn das Angebot ist einfach überwältigend. Gestern hatte es geregnet, aber heute zeigt sich kein Wölkchen am strahlend blauen Himmel. Auf Lizas Plan steht zunächst das Museum Ludwig. Nach der kurzen Fahrt stehen sie jetzt vor dem Museum.*

   Klaus and his American guests have a full day ahead of them. Cologne is just a stone's throw away, and there is a lot to see there as well. Liza has made a detailed schedule, because the choices are simply overwhelming. Yesterday it rained, but today not a single small cloud is visible in the bright blue sky. The *Museum Ludwig* is first on Liza's itinerary. After the short drive there, they're standing in front of the Museum.

2. Shawn: **Eigentlich ist das Wetter ja fast zu schön.**

   Actually, the weather is almost too nice.

3. Klaus: **Dann ist es vielleicht nicht so voll im Museum.**

   Maybe the museum isn't so crowded then.

4. Shawn: **Viele Leute haben mich eigentlich nie gestört.**
   A lot of people actually never bothered me.

5. Klaus lacht: **Warum habe ich das dumpfe Gefühl, du bist nicht gerade scharf auf's Museum?**
   Klaus laughs: Why do I get a vague feeling you're not really keen on going to the museum?

6. Liza: **Ich habe ihn vielleicht zu oft ins Museum geschleppt, aber hinterher hat es ihm immer gefallen.**
   Perhaps I've dragged him to a museum too often, but afterwards he always liked it.

7. Shawn: **Ich hab' mich nicht beklagt!**
   I didn't complain!

8. *Aber bevor jemand noch etwas sagen kann, hat Liza die Eintrittskarten bereits gekauft.*
   But before anybody can say anything, Liza has already bought the admission tickets.

9. Liza: **Interessiert ihr euch für die Sonderausstellung in der Videolounge?**
   Are you interested in the special exhibit in the video lounge?

10. Shawn: **Oh ja, selbstvertändlich! Gehen wir doch da zuerst hin!**
    Oh yes, of course! Why don't we go there first!

11. *Sie haben das Museum betreten. Auf dem Weg zur Videoausstellung sieht Liza plötzlich einen Raum mit Aquarellen und anderen Gemälden.*
    They've entered the museum. On the way to the video exhibit, Liza suddenly sees a room with watercolors and other paintings.

12. Liza: **Nicht so schnell! Nun wartet doch mal! Dort hängt das berühmte Picasso-Portrait von Max Jacob.**

Not so fast. Now wait already! The famous Picasso portrait of Max Jacob is hanging over there.

13. Shawn: **Großmutter was hast du für große Augen?**

Grandmother, what big eyes you have!

14. Liza zu Klaus: **Shawn nimmt heute mal wieder überhaupt nichts ernst. Das ist wirklich ein fantastisches Bild. Picasso hat es vor ungefähr hundert Jahren gemalt. Damals ist er erst fünfundzwanzig Jahre alt gewesen.**

Liza to Klaus: Once again, Shawn is taking nothing seriously today. That's really a fantastic picture. Picasso painted it about a hundred years ago. At the time, he was just twenty-five years old.

15. Klaus: **Freilich hat Shawn nicht ganz Unrecht. Die Augen auf dem Bild sind ziemlich groß. Schließlich sind sie fast so breit wie der ganze Kopf.**

Frankly, Shawn isn't totally wrong. The eyes are pretty big in this picture. After all, they're almost as wide as the entire head.

16. Liza: **Das ist ja gerade der Punkt. Er hat die Augen absichtlich so groß gemalt. Besonders die Augen haben für Picasso Charisma gezeigt. Er war wie ein Kind im Spielzeugladen. Alles Visuelle hat ihn sein ganzes Leben lang fasziniert, und er hat bis in seine Neunziger gelebt.**

That's just the point. He painted the eyes that big on purpose. The eyes especially showed charisma for Picasso. He was like a kid in a toy store. He was fascinated by everything visual all his life, and he lived into his nineties.

17. Klaus: **Das ist ja wirklich interessant!**
    That's really interesting!

18. Shawn: **Charisma? Was ist das? Kann man das essen?**
    Charisma? What's that? Can you eat that?

19. Liza seufzend: **Okay! Gehen wir in die Video-lounge!**
    Liza sighing: Okay! Let's go into the video-lounge!

20. *Ein paar Minuten später stehen sie vor dem in blaues Licht getauchten Raum . . .*
    A few minutes later, they're standing in front of the room, bathed in blue light . . .

21. Shawn: **Einfach großartig! Willkommen in meinem Wohnzimmer!**
    Simply great! Welcome to my living room!

22. *Danach gehen sie durch die Hauptausstellung und Liza unterhält sich mit Klaus über viele der Kunst-werke. Mehrmals ist Liza freudig überrascht, denn bisher hat sie einige nur in Büchern gesehen. Nach mehr als einer Stunde bemerken sie es plötzlich: Shawn ist verschwunden.*
    Afterwards, they walk through the main exhibit, and Liza talks to Klaus about many of the pieces of art. Several times, Liza is happily surprised, because up until now, she has seen some of them just in books. After more than an hour, they suddenly realize it: Shawn has disappeared.

23. Liza: **Wo ist denn mein Mann geblieben? Ach, er ist wahrscheinlich in der Cafeteria.**
    Where has my husband disappeared to? Oh, he's probably in the cafeteria.

24. *Klaus und Lisa betreten die Cafeteria. Schließlich sehen sie ihn an einem Tisch sitzen und ein Bier trinken. Shawn hatte schon eine halbe Stunde auf sie gewartet.*

Klaus and Liza go into the cafeteria. Finally, they see him sitting at a table and drinking a beer. Shawn had already been waiting for them for half an hour.

25. Klaus: **Warum hast du denn nichts gesagt?**

Why didn't you say anything?

26. Shawn: **Tut mir Leid! Ich hatte euch unabsichtlich verloren. Es ist alles so schön bunt hier. Ich konnte mich gar nicht entscheiden!**

I'm sorry! I'd lost you unintentionally. It's all so colorful around here. I couldn't make up my mind at all!

B. NOTES

1. The idiom *nur einen Katzensprung entfernt* (lit.: just the jump of a cat away) is used when something is not very far at all (just a stone's throw away).

    The expression *es zeigt sich kein Wölkchen am Himmel* (lit.: not a little cloud is showing itself in the sky) uses the diminutive *-chen*.

5. The term *ein dumpfes Gefühl haben, dass* . . . (lit.: muffled feeling) is mostly used with another clause (Lesson 15) to express an inkling or a vague, unspecified belief about something.

6. *schleppen* (to drag, labor something or somebody along), regular verb, past participle: *geschleppt*. You may recognize this verb from American slang.

13. The saying *Großmutter, was hast du für große Augen!* (Grandmother, what big eyes you've got!) is

taken from the fairy tale *Rotkäppchen* (Little Red Riding Hood) by the Brothers Grimm. It is said jokingly when someone is staring with big eyes, like the big bad wolf in the tale.

14. *etwas ernst nehmen* (to take something seriously)

16. *Das ist gerade der Punkt!* (That's just the point!); *Das ist genau der Punkt!* (That's exactly the point!); *Bitte kommen Sie auf den Punkt!* (Please, get to the point!)

20. Adjectival phrases that come right before the noun they describe can be quite long in German: *der in blaues Licht getauchte Raum* (the in-blue-light-bathed room). Notice that English prefers to put such phrases after the noun: the room, bathed in blue light.

22. *Haupt-* (main) is always part of a compound noun: *die Hauptstraße* (the main street); *der Haupteingang* (the main entrance).

Culture Notes

The phrase *Es ist alles so schön bunt hier! Ich kann mich gar nicht entscheiden!* (It's all so colorful around here. I cannot make up my mind at all!) has become an idiom. It originated in the early 1980s, a quote from a song by the former East German artist Nina Hagen who was almost dumbfounded when she came to the West for the first time. Whether people like her music or not, the saying has become an intrinsic part of the German language. Of course, it is never meant seriously.

C. GRAMMAR AND USAGE

1. The Present Perfect Tense

The present perfect tense *(das Perfekt)* is the primary tense used to communicate past events in German. It is often referred to as conversational past. Similar to English, for most verbs the tense is built with the auxiliary verb *haben* (to have) and the past participle. Some verbs, mostly verbs of motion, use *sein* (to be) as the conjugated auxiliary. Please refer to the grammar section for a list of verbs that use *sein*. Note that in the conjugation examples below, the German *ich habe gesehen* may be translated as "I saw," "I have seen," or "I did see," depending on the context. "I saw" is the most common meaning, however.

ich habe gesehen	I have seen / I saw / I did see
du hast gesehen	you have seen / you saw / you did see
er/sie/es hat gesehen	he/she/it has seen / he/she/it saw / he/she/it did see
wir haben gesehen	we have seen / we saw / we did see
ihr habt gesehen	you (pl.) have seen / you saw / you did see
sie/Sie haben gesehen	they (you pol.) have seen / they saw / they did see

A verb such as *gehen* (to go, to walk) which expresses a change of position or state, uses *sein* as a past auxiliary:

ich bin gegangen	I have gone / I went / I did go
du bist gegangen	you have gone / you went / you did go
er/sie/es ist gegangen	he/she/it has gone / he/she/it went / he/she/it did go
wir sind gegangen	we have gone / we went / we did go

| *ihr seit gegangen* | you (pl.) have gone / you went / you did go |
| *sie/Sie sind gegangen* | they (you pol.) have gone / they went / they did go |

The perfect tense of *sein* (to be) also uses *sein* as an auxiliary verb:

ich bin gewesen	I have been / I was
du bist gewesen	you have been / you were
er/sie/es ist gewesen	he/she/it has been / he/she/it was
wir sind gewesen	we have been / we were
ihr seit gewesen	you (pl.) have been / you were
sie/Sie sind gewesen	they (you pol.) have been / they were

It is best to memorize each verb in its basic forms: infinitive, simple past, and present perfect. For example: *gehen* (to go), *ging* (went), *ist gegangen* (have gone); *bleiben* (to stay), *blieb* (stayed), *ist geblieben* (have stayed); *sein* (to be), *war* (was), *ist gewesen* (have been); *haben* (to have), *hatte* (had), *hat gehabt* (have had).

In English, the past participle follows the auxiliary immediately, or at least comes before any object (I have seen . . ., I have rarely seen . . .) But in a German sentence, the past participle is placed after the object(s) at the end of the clause.

Liza hat einen detaillierten Plan gemacht.
    Liza made a detailed plan.

Er hat das Bild vor ungefähr hundert Jahren gemalt.
    He painted the picture about a hundred years ago.

Picasso ist damals erst fünfundzwanzig Jahre alt gewesen.
    Picasso was only twenty-five years old at the time.

Some verbs can take either *haben* or *sein* in the perfect tenses, but there will be a slight change of meaning. For example, *ist gefahren* means "drove" in a general sense, but *hat etwas gefahren* means "drove something." If such verbs are used transitively, i.e., with a direct object, they take *haben* as their auxiliary; if they are used intransitively, i.e. without a direct object, they take *sein*.

Sie sind mit dem Auto nach Köln gefahren.
> They went to Cologne by car.

Er hat das Auto nach Köln gefahren.
> He drove the car to Cologne. (Note the direct object "the car.")

But some verbs e.g., *sein, werden, bleiben,* can only use *sein* as auxiliary.

Sie sind drei Stunden im Museum geblieben.
> They stayed in the museum for three hours.

Sie sind durch das ganze Gebäude gegangen.
> They went through the entire building.

2. The Past Perfect Tense

The past perfect tense *(das Plusquamperfekt)* is formed the same way as the present perfect, but with the auxiliary *haben* or *sein* in its simple past form. This again is exactly like English. The use is also similar to English. It expresses a completed action or event in the past. It can also be used to express two past events, one of which is even further in the past than the other one.

Ich war dreimal in Deutschland gewesen, bevor ich Deutsch studiert habe.
> I had been to Germany three times before I studied German.

Als Klaus und Liza in die Cafeteria kamen, hatte Shawn schon auf sie gewartet.
> When Klaus and Liza came into the cafeteria, Shawn had already waited for them.

Bevor sie ins Theater gingen, hatten sie die Karten schon gekauft.
> Before they went to the theater, they already had bought the tickets.

But German uses the past perfect more often than English, mostly because German restricts use of the simple past (as opposed to the present perfect) to the written language.

Es hatte geregnet.
> It (had) rained. (indicating that there is no visible sign of the rain anymore)

Es hat geregnet.
> It rained. (the streets might still be wet)

3. Adverbs of Time

Remember that adverbs of time are used as any other adverbs regarding word order. Most can be used at the beginning of a sentence followed by a verb, or following the verb directly. Many could end a sentence or a clause as well. The following is a list of the most common adverbs of time: *heute* (today), *früh* (early), *gestern* (yesterday), *früher* (before, as it used to be), *morgen* (tomorrow), *frühestens* (at the earliest possible), *morgens* (in the morning), *spätestens* (at the latest), *vormittags* (before noon), *spät* (late), *abends* (in the evening), *später* (later), *schließlich* (finally/after all), *seitdem* (since then), *bald* (soon), *jemals* (ever), *selten* (seldom), *ewig* (eternally), *noch* (still), *nun* (now), *einmal/mal* (once), *zunächst* (next, first that follows), *plötzlich* (suddenly), *schon* (already), *dann* (then), *bereits* (already), *hinterher* (afterwards), *zuerst* (first), *mittags* (at noon), *nachmittags* (in the afternoon), *tagsüber* (during the day), *damals* (at the time, long ago), *werktags* (on working days), *feiertags* (on holidays), *montags* (Mondays [same with other days]), *(so)eben* (just), *vorgestern* (on the day before yesterday), *gerade* (just), *übermorgen* (on the day after tomorrow), *inzwischen* (in the meantime), *manchmal* (sometimes), *vorher* (before [not conj.]), *nachher* (afterwards), *kürzlich* (recently), *immer* (always), *mitunter* (now and then), *nie/niemals* (never), *unlängst* (not too long ago), *jetzt* (now), *einst* (once upon a time), *seinerzeit* (at that particular time).

Zunächst gehen sie ins Museum. Sie gehen zunächst ins Museum.
First (next) they go to the museum.

Danach essen sie in einem netten Restaurant. Sie essen danach in einem netten Restaurant.
Afterwards they eat in a nice restaurant.

It's also possible to combine adverbs, for such expressions as: *immer dann* (always then), *spät abends* (late evenings), *morgen früh* (tomorrow morning/early). Some combinations are used idiomatically: *immer schon* (always/forever), *immer wieder* (again and again), *immer noch* (still after a long time). A combination with *bis* (until) is also possible: *bis später* (until later), *bis kürzlich* (until recently), *bis dann* (up until then).

4. Adverbs of Mode

Some adverbs of mode are more restricted in their placement and word order. Their area of usage is more specific as well. (Note that adverbs with the prefix *irgend-* are explained separately in Lesson 12.) Some of the common ones are: *gern* (gladly), *ohnehin** (anyway), *genau* (exactly), *genug** (enough), *besonders* (especially), *sehr** (very), *mehr** (more), *eigentlich* (actually), *wirklich** (really), *natürlich* (naturally/of course), *geradezu** (downright), *überhaupt* (above all), *übrigens* (by the way), *ziemlich** (rather), *teils* (partly), *wenigstens* (at

least), *etwa** (about), *bis** (up to/until [also time]), *sogar**
(even), *auch* (also), *allein* (alone), *freilich* (of course/
admittedly/however), *eben** (even/just/exactly), *ausgerechnet* (of all things), *allerdings* (however/indeed),
jedoch (however), *vielleicht* (perhaps), *wahrscheinlich*
(probably), *sicher* (surely), *möglicherweise* (possibly),
sicherlich (certainly), *glücklicherweise* (luckily), *bestimmt* (certainly), *hoffentlich* (hopefully), *zweifellos*
(doubtlessly), *leider* (unfortunately).

The adverbs that are marked * are not very common at
the beginning of a sentence or they may require a different word order, but all of them are possible right after
the conjugated verb. Note that some of the above
adverbs can also be used as adjectives, conjunctions, or
particles.

*Zweifellos hatten Klaus und seine Freunde einen langen
Tag.*
   Klaus and his friends doubtlessly had a long day.

*Vielleicht werden sie wirklich noch einmal genau die
selbe Stadt besuchen.*
   Maybe they'll visit exactly that same city another
   time.

EXERCISES

A. Change the following sentences to the present perfect
   tense.

   1. *Sie fahren mit dem Auto nach Köln.*

   2. *Das Wetter ist sehr gut.*

   3. *Er entscheidet sich für den Besuch.*

   4. *Sie findet sofort einen Parkplatz.*

   5. *Wir bleiben den ganzen Tag in der Stadt.*

6. *Das Museum ist nicht sehr voll.*

7. *Drei Stunden im Museum sind genug.*

8. *Nicht das kleinste Wölkchen ist am Himmel.*

9. *Er wartet schon drei Stunden auf sein Gepäck.*

10. *Es ist alles hier so schön bunt.*

B. Rewrite the following text into the present perfect tense.
   Am Montag kommt Klaus wieder nach Hause. Er erzählt Liza und Shawn von seinen Erlebnissen in Hannover, und sie berichten ihm von ihrem doppelten Glück im Theater. Sie planen die Woche. Klaus arbeitet am Dienstag nicht. Sie fahren mit dem Auto nach Köln, gehen in das berühmte Museum Ludwig und besuchen viele andere interessante Gebäude in der Stadt. Liza macht eine Liste.

C. Rewrite the text in exercise B in the past perfect tense, and add the following adverbs in the same order as listed: *früh, gern, später, danach, glücklicherweise, morgens, zuerst, dann, übrigens gern.*

D. Add the adverb in its correct place without changing the word order.

   1. *Wir besuchen Köln noch einmal.* (probably)

   2. *Sie haben nicht genug Zeit.* (perhaps)

   3. *Morgen werden sie sich die Stadt ansehen.* (certainly)

   4. *Shawn wird in der Cafeteria sein.* (surely)

   5. *Es wird heute noch regnen.* (possibly)

E. Rewrite the short paragraph, so that all the adverbs are

in a different place, but without changing the meaning of the sentence.

> *Zweifellos hatten Klaus und seine amerikanischen Freunde einen langen Tag. Freilich war es auch sehr interressant. Vielleicht werden sie noch einmal die Stadt besuchen, allerdings nicht in diesem Jahr, denn leider fahren sie bald schon nach Süddeutschland, aber natürlich kommen sie gern zurück.*

Answer Key

A. 1. *Sie sind mit dem Auto nach Köln gefahren.* 2. *Das Wetter ist sehr gut gewesen.* 3. *Er hat sich für den Besuch entschieden.* 4. *Sie hat sofort einen Parkplatz gefunden.* 5. *Wir sind den ganzen Tag in der Stadt geblieben.* 6. *Das Museum ist nicht sehr voll gewesen.* 7. *Drei Stunden im Museum sind genug gewesen.* 8. *Nicht das kleinste Wölkchen ist am Himmel gewesen.* 9. *Er hat schon drei Stunden auf sein Gepäck gewartet.* 10. *Es ist alles hier so schön bunt gewesen.*

B. *Am Montag ist Klaus wieder nach Hause gekommen. Er hat Liza und Shawn von seinen Erlebnissen in Hannover erzählt, und sie haben ihm von ihrem doppelten Glück im Theater berichtet. Sie haben die Woche geplant. Klaus hat am Dienstag nicht gearbeitet. Sie sind mit dem Auto nach Köln gefahren, sind in das berühmte Museum Ludwig gegangen und haben viele andere interessante Gebäude in der Stadt besucht. Liza hat eine Liste gemacht.*

C. *Am Montag war Klaus früh wieder nach Hause gekommen. Er hatte Liza und Shawn gern von seinen Erlebnissen in Hannover erzählt, und später hatten sie ihm von ihrem doppelten Glück im Theater berichtet. Danach hatten sie die Woche geplant. Gücklicherweise hatte Klaus am Dienstag nicht gearbeitet. Sie waren morgens mit dem Auto nach Köln gefahren, waren zuerst in das berühmte Museum Ludwig gegangen und hatten dann viele andere interessante Gebäude in der Stadt besucht. Liza hatte übrigens gern eine Liste gemacht.*

D. 1. *Wir besuchen wahrscheinlich Köln noch einmal.* 2. *Sie haben vielleicht nicht genug Zeit.* 3. *Morgen werden sie sich sicherlich die Stadt ansehen.* 4. *Shawn wird sicher in der Cafeteria sein. 5. Es wird vielleicht heute noch regnen.*

E. *Klaus und seine amerikanischen Freunde hatten zweifellos einen langen Tag. Es war freilich auch sehr interressant. Sie werden vielleicht noch einmal die Stadt besuchen, allerdings nicht in diesem Jahr, denn sie fahren leider schon bald nach Süddeutschland, aber sie kommen natürlich gern zurück.*

LESSON 10

DIE RHEINFAHRT: ABER BITTE HÖR' MIT DEM SINGEN AUF!
TOUR ON THE RHINE RIVER: BUT PLEASE STOP THE SINGING!

A. DIALOGUE

1. *Auf dem heutigen Programm steht eine Schifffahrt auf dem Rhein. Liza und Shawn freuen sich auf die abenteuerliche Tour. Am späten Nachmittag werden sie sie beendet haben, und dann sind sie bei jemandem zum Essen eingeladen. Doch das ist eine ganz andere Geschichte. In der kleinen Stadt Rüdesheim, idyllisch zwischen den Weinbergen des Ufers gelegen, haben Liza, Shawn und Klaus gerade den Dampfer betreten.*
   A boat ride on the Rhine River is on today's agenda. Liza and Shawn are looking forward to the adventurous tour. They will have finished it by late afternoon, and then they are invited for dinner at someone's house. But that's quite another story. Liza, Shawn, and Klaus have just boarded the boat in the small town of *Rüdesheim*, quaintly nestled among vineyards on the river's shore.

2. Shawn: **Wirklich schön hier, aber warum sind wir denn eigentlich mit dem Zug hierher gekommen? Düsseldorf ist doch schließlich auch am Rhein.**
   Really beautiful here but, anyway, why did we come here by train? After all, Düsseldorf is on the Rhine as well.

3. Klaus: **Wir werden den Dampfer in Königswinter verlassen, gar nicht weit von Zuhause. Dann wer-**

**den wir lange genug auf einem Schiff gewesen
sein und sicherlich genug gesehen haben. Eine
Hin- und Rückfahrt mit dem Dampfer dauert
einfach zu lange. Die Aussicht ist flussabwärts
auch ein bisschen besser.**

We'll leave the boat in Königswinter, not far from
home at all. By then, we'll have been on a boat long
enough, and we'll certainly have seen enough. A
round trip by boat simply takes too long. The view
is also a little better downstream.

4. *Nach einer Weile öffnet sich der Fluss zu einer
   weiten Schlucht. Oben an den Hängen links und
   rechts sehen sie mehrere Burgen und Schlösser.*

   After a while, the river opens up into a wide gorge.
   Up on the slopes, they see several castles left and
   right.

5. Liza: **Wahnsinnig schön! Es ist so wie die Bilder
   in meinen alten Märchenbüchern. Shawn, du
   musst sie mir unbedingt fotografieren.**

   Incredibly beautiful! It's just like the pictures in my
   old fairy tale books. Shawn, you have to take a photo
   for me.

6. Klaus lacht: **Das ist noch gar nichts. Allein im
   mittleren Rheinland gibt es mehr als 500 Burgen
   und Schlösser. Einige sind mehr als tausend
   Jahre alt. Natürlich spinnen sich darum unzählige Legenden und Geschichten. Aber Shawn, du
   bist ja heute so ruhig. Geht es dir nicht gut?**

   Klaus laughs: Oh, that's nothing. In the middle
   region of the Rhine, there are more than 500 castles.
   Some are more than a thousand years old. Naturally,
   countless legends and stories revolve around them.
   But Shawn, you're so quiet today. Are you not feeling well?

7. Shawn: **Ich bin nur beeindruckt! Kein Wunder, dass es so viele deutsche Geschichten über Drachen und Burgen gibt. Hier hat man die perfekte Szenerie dafür.**

I'm just impressed! No wonder there are so many German stories about dragons and castles. Here you have the perfect scenery for it.

8. Klaus: **Ja, viele der deutschen Märchen beziehen sich nämlich auf dieses Gebiet, aber mehr noch auf das Siebengebirge. Dort werden wir am Nachmittag ankommen, aber erst essen wir zu Mittag in einer alten Ritterburg nicht weit von hier.**

Yes, many of the German fairy tales are specifically about this area, but even more so about the area of the Seven Mountains. We'll get there in the afternoon, but first we'll eat lunch in an old knight's castle not far from here.

9. *Vom Oberdeck hören sie plötzlich ein Violinenspiel. Klaus beginnt mitzusingen.*

From the upper deck, they suddenly hear a violin playing. Klaus starts singing along.

10. Klaus: **Ich weiß nicht was soll es bedeuten, dass ich so traurig bin . . .**

I don't know what it could mean, that I am so sad . . .

11. Shawn lächelt: **Erzähl' uns doch mehr, aber bitte hör' mit dem Singen auf!**

Why don't you tell us more, but please stop the singing!

12. Klaus lacht: **Okay, schon gut! Ich weiß, ich kann nicht singen. Also, dort drüben ist die berühmte Loreley. Der Legende nach hat ein wunderschönes Mädchen dort oben auf dem steilen**

Felsen gesessen. Die Schiffer waren von ihrem Gesang verzaubert, und deshalb stießen sie auf die Felsen und ertranken.

Klaus laughs: Alright already! I know I can't sing. Well, over there is the famous *Lorelei*. Legend has it, that a beautiful girl sat up there on the steep rock. The sailors were enchanted by her singing, and so they hit the cliffs and drowned.

13. Shawn: **Hast du das mit deinem Gesang auch versucht? Vielleicht wird es ja klappen, aber bestimmt nicht wegen der Verzauberung.**

    Did you try that with your singing as well? Perhaps, it'll work, but certainly not because of enchantment.

14. Liza: **Guckt doch mal, ihr beiden. Wir werden gleich angelegt haben. Seht ihr sie, die Ritterburg da? Unser Mittagessen wartet auf uns dort oben.**

    Look over there, both of you. We'll have landed in a moment. Do you see it, the knight's castle there? Our lunch is waiting for us up there.

15. *Klaus beginnt wieder zu singen:* **Dort droben auf dem Berg, gleich unter den silbernen Sternen . . .** *aber es scheint seinen Zuhörern keinerlei Freude zu machen. Er macht eine tiefe Verbeugung vor Liza.*

    Klaus starts singing again: Up there, on the mountain, right underneath the silver stars . . . but it doesn't seem to bring any joy to his listeners whatsoever. He bows deeply before Liza.

16. Klaus: *Holde Maid,* **darf ich** *Euch* **zum Bankett bitten?**

    My fair maiden, may I ask thee to the banquet?

17. Shawn: **Ich bestehe auf einem Duell. Die holde Maid ist vergeben.**
I insist on a duel. The fair maiden is spoken for.

18. Liza: **Nun, ich kann euch eins sagen! Die Maid ist nicht immer so hold und kann auch ohne Ritter. Die Maid hat nämlich Kreditkarten. Oh, seht nur da drüben, ein Glasbläser! Und viel anderes Kunsthandwerk. Die Maid will einkaufen . . .**
Well, I can tell you one thing! The maiden is not always that fair, and she can manage without a knight. The maiden has credit cards. Oh, look over there, a glassblower! And lots of other handicrafts. The maiden wants to go shopping . . .

19. Klaus lacht: **Kreditkarten sind nutzlos hier. Nur bare Münze, bitte.**
Klaus laughs: Credit cards are useless here. Hard cash only, please.

B. NOTES

1. The adverb *heute* (today) is used here as adjective changing to *heutig* (today's). Several adverbs of time can be changed this way to become adjectives: *gestern: gestrig* (yesterday's)*; morgen: morgig* (tomorrow's).

   The adjective *gelegen* (situated, nestled) should not be mixed up with the past participle of *legen* (to lay, to put down): *habe gelegt* (have laid).

2. *hierher* (to here, over here) is only used to express movement toward the speaker.

3. *das Zuhause* (the home), *zu Hause* (at home), *nach Hause* (to home, toward home). Note that it has a different meaning without the *–e: das Haus* (the house).

4. There are several words for "castle" in German. While *das Schloss* mostly refers to a castle with many little turrets, large windows, and often numerous roof louvers, *die Burg* is a little more like a fortress *(die Festung)*, often with a moat around it. *Burgen* are usually older than *Schlösser.*

6. *Das ist doch gar nichts!* (lit.: That's nothing at all!) You haven't seen anything yet!

8. *aber mehr noch* (even more so)
   zu Mittag essen (lit.: to eat for noon) means to have lunch.

11. People often drop the *-e* of a verb with an informal imperative: *Hör' auf!* (Stop!)

12. The phrase *der Legende nach* (lit.: after the legend) is used idiomatically to mean "legend has it." There are a few other idiomatic uses in which the preposition *nach* (after, according to, to) follows the noun to which it refers: *meiner Meinung nach* (in my opinion).
    Note the spelling of the word *Loreley*. The original German spelling is *Loreley,* because the modern German *ei* was written *ey* in the Middle Ages. However, the legend most likely was invented by Clemens Brentano in the early 19th century in the 1802 ballad *Die Lore Lay*. The name was put together from the Middle High German words *lur*, meaning "elf" or "fairy," and *lei* (with an "i"), meaning "rock" or "cliff." The common English spelling reflects the modern German spelling of that sound.

13. The verb *klappen* (to work out) is a common colloquialism: *Es hat sehr gut geklappt.* (It has worked out very well.)

wegen (because of) is always followed by the genitive case.

15. *keinerlei* (none/any whatsoever)

16. The adjective *hold* (fair) is outdated, but sometimes used jokingly to refer to times long gone. The same is true for *die Maid* (maiden), and for using *Euch* (you), a plural form, with a single individual. *Euch* can also be used with a little bit of sarcasm when talking to a person who might be acting like a bit of a prima donna.

17. *auf etwas bestehen* (to insist on something) *Ich bestehe darauf!* (I insist on it!)

Culture Notes

The middle section of the Rhine *(der Mittelrhein)* is indeed the source of many legends and tales. The beautiful landscape and the abundance of castles and ruins have inspired many writers. This is the area where many of the well known fairy tales collected by the Brothers Grimm originated. It is also one of Germany's main wine regions, and many people like to attribute the vivid imagination of the region's inhabitants to that fact, as well. Whatever it may be, the people of the *Mittelrhein* are most hospitable, the food is among Germany's best, and the scenery is simply breathtaking.

C. GRAMMAR AND USAGE.

1. The Future Perfect Tense

The construction of the future perfect, as well as its use, is very similar to English. It can be used to speak of an action or event that is completed in the future. But most often it is used to express probability in past time: *Er wird es (wohl) getan haben*. (He probably did it.), Just like the simple future, the future perfect uses the auxiliary *werden*, but it combines it with the past infinitive, i.e., the past participle of a verb along with *haben* or *sein*. Compare:

Ich werde eine Dampferfahrt auf dem Rhein machen. (simple future)
   I <u>will take</u> a boat trip on the Rhine.

Ich werde eine Dampferfahrt auf dem Rhein gemacht haben. (future perfect)
   I <u>will have taken</u> a boat trip on the Rhine.

The future perfect can be used to compare two events in the future: By the time this or that happens, I <u>will</u> already <u>have done</u> something else.

In wenigen Minuten werden wir schon angelegt haben.
   In a few minutes, we <u>will have landed</u> already.

Dann werden wir lange genug auf dem Boot gewesen sein.
   Then, we'<u>ll have been</u> on the boat long enough.

Bevor wir nach Hause kommen, werden wir die Tour beendet haben.
   Before we get home, we <u>will have finished</u> the tour.

Wenn sie wieder auf dem Schiff sind, werden sie bereits in der Ritterburg gegessen haben.
   When they are back on the boat, they <u>will</u> already <u>have eaten</u> inside the knight's castle.

Notice that in the last two examples the future perfect is compared to another future action, but that other action is expressed in the present tense *(kommen, sind)*. This is exactly like English.

2. Double Pronouns

As in English, it's possible to have two object pronouns in a German sentence. Word order depends on which object is replaced by a pronoun. As we have seen before, in sentences with two noun objects the indirect object comes before the direct object. In sentences with both a noun and a pronoun object, the pronoun will always come first. Take a look at these examples with both nouns and pronouns.

Liza gibt Shawn und Klaus die Eintrittskarten.
    Liza gives the admission tickets to Shawn and Klaus.

Sie gibt ihnen die Eintrittskarten.
    She gives them the tickets.

If the indirect object is replaced by a pronoun, the word order is still the usual one. But as soon as the direct object is replaced by a pronoun, the word order changes, with the direct object pronoun preceding the indirect object. Remember that it is always the direct object that causes the change. The indirect object, whether it's a pronoun or an actual noun, has no effect on the word order: To summarize, with noun objects, the indirect object comes first. With one pronoun object, the pronoun comes first, regardless of case. With two pronoun objects, word order is reversed, i.e., the direct object comes first.

Sie gibt sie Shawn und Klaus.
    She gives them to Shawn und Klaus.

Sie gibt sie ihnen.
    She gives them to them.

The change in word order applies also to the reflexive pronouns:

Morgen kaufe ich mir ein Buch.
    Tomorrow, I'll buy myself a book.

Morgen kaufe ich es mir.
Tomorrow, I'll buy it for myself.

3. Adverbs of Location and Movement

You've already seen the most common adverbs of location, *hier* (here), *da* (there), and *dort* (over there). When they refer to movement, they are often combined with *hin* and *her*.

Er fährt morgen dahin. Da fährt er morgen hin. Dahin fährt er morgen.
He is going there tomorrow.

Kommt sie wirklich heute hierher?
Is she really coming here today?

Other common combinations can describe location with the prepositions *da* (there), *nach* (to), or *hin* and *her*. They are not separated in a sentence, but they are written as two words: *da unten* (down there), *da oben* (up there), *da drüben* (over on the other side).

Da oben steht ein Schloss auf dem Berg.
Up there is a castle on the mountain.

Gehen Sie bitte nach oben!
Please, go upstairs!

Note that *da oben* may also be said as *droben*.

Other common adverbs of location or movement are: *aufwärts* (upward), *abwärts* (downward), *überall* (everywhere), *weg* (away), *fort* (away), *herum* (around something), *innen, drinnen* (inside), *außen, draußen* (outside), *irgendwo* (somewhere), and *nirgendwo* (nowhere).

Jetzt fahren wir stromabwärts.
Now we're going downstream.

Am Rhein stehen überall Burgen.
There are castles everywhere at the Rhine river.

4. Other Common Adverbs

Other common adverbs describe a cause, reason, or some other kind of relationship. These adverbs mostly stand at the beginning of a sentence or after the conjugated verb. The most comon ones are: *nämlich* (namely), *deswegen* (therefore), *folglich* (consequently), *dadurch* (through that), *trotzdem, dennoch* (despite the fact), *nichtsdestoweniger* (nevertheless), and all combinations with the possessives and *wegen*: *meinetwegen* (as for me, for my sake).

Deshalb stießen sie auf die Felsen.
Therefore they hit the cliffs.

Meinetwegen könnt ihr weiter Unsinn machen.
As far as I'm concerned, you can continue with the nonsense.

Nichtsdestoweniger ist auch das Mittagessen keine schlechte Idee.
Nevertheless, lunch is not a bad idea either.

Sie sind dennoch nicht müde.
They are not tired despite that fact.

EXERCISES

A. Change the following sentences to the future perfect tense.

1. *Sie machen eine Tour auf dem Rhein.*

2. *Auf der Ritterburg gibt es guten Wein.*

3. *Sie haben viel Vergnügen.*

4. *Sie sehen die Loreley.*

5. *Wir bleiben den ganzen Tag am Rhein.*

6. *Das Wetter ist ausgezeichnet.*

7. *Er singt nicht sehr gut.*

8. *Am Abend gehen sie wieder essen.*

9. *Sie fahren zuerst mit dem Zug.*

10. *Er ist sehr beeindruckt.*

B. Choose the correct translation:

1. Are you giving the card (it) to her?
   a) *Geben Sie sie sie?*
   b) *Geben ihr sie sie?*
   c) *Geben Sie sie ihr?*
   d) *Geben Sie ihr sie?*

2. Are you interested in music (it)?
   a) *Interessierst du dir dafür?*
   b) *Interessieren Sie sich dafür?*
   c) *Interessieren Sie sie dafür?*
   d) *Interessierst du dich für sie?*

3. I will buy myself the book (it) today.
   a) *Heute werde ich mir es kaufen.*
   b) *Heute werde ihn mir es kaufen.*
   c) *Heute werde ich es mir kaufen.*
   d) *Heute werde ich es ihm kaufen.*

C. Add the adverb in its correct place(s) without changing the word order:

1. *Wir kommen immer wieder.* (to here)

2. *Die Ritterburg ist auf dem Berg.* (up)

3. *Sie steigen auf den Berg.* (up)

4. *Wir gehen nach . . .* (downstairs)

5. *Sie fahren auf dem Rhein.* (downstream)

D. Translate the following sentences:

1. I will have done that by eight o'clock.

2. Therefore, they are going downstream.

3. He is just imagining it.

4. I insist on it!

5. He is buying it (for) her.

Answer Key

A. 1. *Sie werden eine Tour auf dem Rhein gemacht haben.*
2. *Auf der Ritterburg wird es guten Wein gegeben
haben.* 3. *Sie werden viel Vergnügen gehabt haben.*
4. *Sie werden die Loreley gesehen haben.* 5. *Wir werden den ganzen Tag am Rhein geblieben sein.* 6. *Das
Wetter wird ausgezeichnet gewesen sein.* 7. *Er wird
nicht sehr gut gesungen haben.* 8. *Am Abend werden
sie wieder gegessen haben.* 9. *Sie werden zuerst mit
dem Zug gefahren sein.* 10. *Er wird sehr beeindruckt
gewesen sein.*

B. 1. c; 2. b; 3. c

C. 1. *Wir kommen immer wieder hierher.* 2. *Die Ritterburg
ist oben auf dem Berg.* 3. *Sie steigen auf den Berg hinauf.* 4. *Wir gehen nach unten.* 5. *Sie fahren flussabwärts auf dem Rhein.*

D. 1. *Das werde ich um acht Uhr gemacht haben.*
2. *Deshalb fahren sie stromabwärts.* 3. *Er stellt es sich
nur vor.* 4. *Ich bestehe darauf!* 5. *Er kauft es ihr.*

LESSON 11

EIN LANGER, SICH WINDENDER WEG
A LONG AND WINDING ROAD

A. DIALOGUE

1. *Erinnern sie sich noch an Michael? Er hatte Liza
   und Shawn im Theater in seine Loge eingeladen.
   Nach der heutigen Dampferfahrt gehen Liza, Shawn
   und Klaus zu ihm zum Essen, und sie werden auch
   ein Schloss gleich neben Michaels kleinem Haus
   besuchen. In der kleinen Stadt Königswinter, mitten
   im Siebengebirge, legt der Dampfer an. Michael
   wartet bereits am Landungssteg auf sie.*
   Do you remember Michael? He had invited Liza and
   Shawn to his box at the theater. After today's boat
   ride, Liza, Shawn and Klaus are going to dinner at
   his house, and they will also visit a castle right next
   to Michael's little house. The boat is landing in the
   small town of *Königswinter* in the middle of the
   Seven Mountains. Michael is already waiting at the
   dock.

2. Michael: **Hallo, freut mich euch wiederzusehen.
   Wie war die Dampferfahrt?**
   Hi, I'm happy to see you again. How was the boat
   trip?

3. Shawn: **Fantastisch! Das ist übrigens unser Freund
   Klaus.**
   Fantastic! This is our friend Klaus by the way.

4. *Sie begrüßen sich und gehen ein kurzes Stück.
   Dann kommen sie plötzlich an einen sich steil
   bergauf windenden Weg. Es ist der Weg auf den
   Drachenfels.*

They greet one another, and walk a short distance. Then, they suddenly get to a steep winding road leading up. It's the way up the Dragon Mountain.

5. Michael: **Der Drachenfels ist einer der sieben Berge. Leider haben wir nicht die Zeit für das atemberaubende Nachtigallental dort. Aber ihr müsst wiederkommen.**
The Dragon Rock is one of the Seven Mountains. Unfortunately, we don't have time for the breathtaking Nightingale Valley over there. But you must come back.

6. Liza: **Es ist hier sicher unmöglich für Autos.**
It must be impossible here for cars.

7. Michael: **Im Sommer geht es schon, aber man braucht ein starkes Auto. Im Winter müssen wir natürlich zu Fuß gehen. Deshalb wohnen nicht viele Leute oben auf dem Berg. Außerdem ist fast das ganze Siebengebirge Naturschutzgebiet, und man darf keine neuen Häuser bauen.**
It's okay in the summer, but you need a strong car. In the winter, we naturally have to walk. That's why not many people live up the mountain. Aside from that, almost the entire area of the Seven Mountains is a nature preserve, and you are not allowed to build any new houses.

8. *Auf halber Höhe kommen sie endlich an ein großes eisernes Tor. Michael öffnet es. Dahinter können sie ein Schloss mit vielen Türmchen und Spitzen erkennen.*
Halfway up the mountain, they finally reach a large iron gate. Michael opens it. Behind it they can see a castle with many small turrets and spires.

9. Shawn: **Sind wir noch in Deutschland und im gleichen Jahrhundert?**
Are we still in Germany and in the same century?

10. Michael: **Ich wohne in einem der wenigen Häuser im Schlosspark. Es ist klein und bescheiden, aber von meinem Garten habe ich einen wunderschönen Blick auf das Rheintal. Lasst uns aber erst eine Schlossbesichtigung machen.**
I live in one of the few houses within the castle's park. It's small and humble, but I have a very beautiful view down to the Rhine valley from my garden. But let's tour the castle first.

11. Klaus: **Schloss Drachenburg ist nicht so alt wie die meisten anderen Schlösser, nicht wahr?**
The Dragon Castle isn't as old as most of the other castles, is it?

12. Michael: **Richtig. Angeblich hatte ein Baron es für seine Geliebte gebaut, doch die besagte Dame soll andere Pläne gehabt haben. Nun kommen wir in die Festhalle.**
Right. Supposedly, a baron built it for his beloved, but the lady in question was said to have had a different agenda. Now, we'll get to the ballroom.

13. *Plötzlich hören sie einen schimpfenden Papagei in einem Erker am Fenster.*
Suddenly, they hear the voice of a scolding parrot sitting in one of the bay windows.

14. Michael: **Der Papagei soll über hundert Jahre alt sein und hat seine eigene Geschichte. Angeblich erscheint er manchmal nicht auf Fotos. Das hat natürlich mit Lichtreflektionen des Erkerfensters zu tun, aber die Leute lieben Rätsel. Leider**

sagt er selten etwas Nettes. Einige Besucher werden fürchterlich verärgert.

The parrot is supposed to be more than a hundred years old, and it has its own story. Supposedly, it sometimes doesn't appear in photographs. It has something to do with light reflections from the bay window, of course, but people love mysteries. Unfortunately, it rarely says anything nice. Some visitors get terribly upset.

15. Klaus lächelt: **Wie kann man sich über etwas ärgern, was ein Vogel sagt? Man sollte vielleicht als erstes immer die Quelle der Kritik in Betracht ziehen.**

    Klaus smiles: How can they get angry about what a bird says? Perhaps they should consider the source of the criticism first.

16. Shawn: **Aber ein Foto ist eine gute Idee. Könnt ihr euch zusammen dort in den Erker stellen?**

    But a photo is a good idea. Could you stand together over there in the bay window?

17. Michael: **Aber dann ist es Zeit zum Essen. Es gibt heute Abend unten am Rhein eine Feuer-Show. Und wir haben die besten Plätze in meinem Garten.**

    But then it's time for dinner. There is a fireworks show down at the Rhine tonight. And from up here in my garden we'll have the best seats.

18. Liza: **Großartig! Es sieht so aus, als ob wir mit dir immer die besten Plätze bekommen.**

    Great! Looks like we always get the best seats with you.

19. *Später, während des Essens in Michaels Garten mit Blick auf das Rheintal . . .*

Later during dinner in Michael's garden overlooking
the Rhine valley . . .

20. Liza: **Zu schade, wir haben bereits ein Auto
    gemietet. Wir fahren Dienstag nach Süddeutsch-
    land.**
    Too bad we've already rented a car. We're going to
    Southern Germany on Tuesday.

21. Michael: **Fahrt ihr auch nach Österreich?**
    Are you going to Austria as well?

22. Klaus: **Wir haben es nicht geplant, aber . . .**
    We didn't plan it, but . . .

23. Michael: **Warum kommt ihr morgen nicht in die
    Stadt? Ich habe ein Reisebüro in der Stadt, und
    ich kann euch ein fantastisches Hotel in Wien
    empfehlen.**
    Why don't you come into town tomorrow? I own a
    travel agency in town, and I can recommend a fan-
    tastic hotel in Vienna.

24. Liza: **Nach diesem sagenhaften Erlebnis hier
    braucht man wohl nicht daran zu zweifeln.
    Ziehen wir Wien in Betracht!**
    After this terrific experience here, we don't need to
    doubt it. Let's consider Vienna!

B. NOTES

1. *mitten* (in the midst of)

3. *übrigens* (by the way)

4. The phrase *sich steil bergauf windend* (lit.: winding
   itself steeply uphill) is used to describe a long and
   winding road or a path up the mountain.

7. The idiomatic expression *Es geht schon* (lit.: It goes already) is used to convey that something is working out just fine.
   zu Fuß gehen (to go on foot)

8. *auf halber Höhe* (lit.: at half height) means "halfway up."

12. The adjective *besagt* (lit.: bespoken) means "aforementioned" or "in question."

14. *das Rätsel* (mystery, enigma, puzzle). *Das Rätsel ist gelöst.* (The mystery is solved.)
   Numerous German mystery stories are named *Das Rätsel um . . .* (Mystery of the . . .).

15. *sich ärgern über . . .* (to get angry or annoyed about . . .)

16. *Der Erker* is a large bay window, almost like a nook that extends outwards. Many older houses and castles have *Erker* in Germany.

24. *in Betracht ziehen* (to take into consideration)

Culture Notes

Beware! You're entering the land of fairy tales! The area of the Seven Mountains (*das Siebengebirge*) is in fact one of the most preserved areas in Germany. Many writers have been inspired by its natural beauty, but this is also the area most intricately connected to the Brothers Grimm and the many centuries-old fairy tales that they collected, such as *Dornröschen* (Sleeping Beauty), *Schneewittchen und die sieben Zwerge* (Snow White and the Seven Dwarfs), or *Aschenputtel* (Cinderella), to name just a few. Even today, a tourist hiking through the area can be transported to a different time (disregarding the occasional candy wrapper, that is). The *Drachenfels* (Dragon Rock) is one of the Seven Mountains, with *Schloss Drachenburg* (Dragon Castle) half-way up, and a much older castle ruin on top. From the city of *Bonn* across the Rhine river, the small city of *Königswinter* at the foot of the mountain can be reached by boat in just ten minutes. A ride by car from Cologne takes about half an hour, or about forty-five minutes from Düsseldorf.

C. GRAMMAR AND USAGE

1. Modal Verbs in the Present Tense

Modal verbs are mostly used to add a certain condition to another verb. They are: *können* (can, be able to), *dürfen* (may, be allowed to), *müssen* (have to, must), *sollen* (shall, be supposed to, be said to), *wollen* (want), and *mögen* (like, may). The modal verb is conjugated and the main verb is placed at the end of the clause in its infinitive form.

Ihr müsst nächste Woche wiederkommen.
    You have to come back next week.

Man soll die Quelle der Kritik zuerst bewerten.
    One is supposed to / should evaluate the source of the criticism first.

Das mag die Wahrheit sein.
    That may be the truth.

Note that *müssen* in the negative doesn't mean "must not," but rather "doesn't have to".

Klaus muss heute nicht arbeiten.
    Klaus doesn't have to work today.

To express "must not," *nicht dürfen* (lit.: not allowed to) is used.

Das dürfen wir nicht vergessen.
> We must not forget that.

Wir wollen am Montag nach Süddeutschland.
> We want (to go) to Southern Germany on Monday.

Note that *wollen* (want) means "to insist" if used for something you really want to have.

Ich will das Auto.
> I insist on having that car.

Note that a subjunctive form of *mögen* is used to mean "would like."

Ich möchte eine Tasse Kaffee.
> I'd like a cup of coffee.

2. Use of Modals in Perfect Tenses

The past participle of modal verbs is only used when a modal verb is used on its own, without another verb.

Sie haben das Essen sehr gern gemocht.
> They liked (have liked) the food very much.

Otherwise the infinitive replaces the past participle. Note the placement of modal verbs in the perfect tenses.

Sie haben zu Fuß gehen müssen.
> They had to go on foot.

Sie haben auch ein Schloss besuchen können.
> They were able to visit a castle as well.

3. The Half-Modals *brauchen* and *lassen*.

The verbs *brauchen* (to need) and *lassen* (to let, to leave, to have done) are called half-modals, because they are often used by themselves, but they can also be used in combination with other infinitives, just like modals.

Er lässt seine Kleidung reinigen.
> He has his clothing cleaned. / He gets his clothing cleaned.

Sie lassen sich das Schloss von Michael zeigen.
> They let Michael show them the castle.

Brauchen is used as a modal verb only in the negative, and then always with the preposition *zu*. In an affirmative sentence, it always relates to a direct object meaning simply "to need":

Ich brauche ein neues Auto, aber ich brauche mich nicht gleich zu entscheiden.
> I need a new car, but I don't need to decide right away.

Sie brauchen an Michaels Rat nicht zu zweifeln.
> They don't have to doubt Michael's advice.

4. Indefinite Pronouns

The most common indefinite pronouns are: *etwas* (something, some, anything), *man* (one), and *nichts* (nothing). Note that *etwas* is often abbreviated as *was* in conversations.

Hat er etwas gesagt?
> Did he say anything?

Es ist Zeit, was zu essen. Wir haben seit fünf Stunden nichts gegessen.
> It's time to eat something. We haven't eaten anything for five hours.

Das kann man wohl sagen!
> You (one) could certainly say that!

Other indefinite pronouns change according to case, number and gender: *keiner* (no, none, not any), *einer* (one), *jeder* (every, each), *jemand* (somebody), *niemand* (anybody), *einige* (some), and *alle* (all). All follow the pattern of the definite articles. If the person or the people are of non-specific gender, the masculine article determines the ending (except *alle* and *einige*).

Keiner langweilte sich, und jeder war vergnügt.
　　Nobody was bored, and everyone was in a good mood.

It is acceptable to use *jemand* and *niemand* without the proper case endings, but it sounds better with them:

Ich habe keinen gesehen aber jemand(en) gehört.
　　I didn't see anyone, but I heard somebody.

Alle (all) and *einige* (some) take an *-s* ending when not referring to people:

Alles ist in Ordnung, doch eins muss ich dir sagen.
　　It's all okay, but one thing I have to tell you.

Einiges hat ihnen besonders gefallen.
　　Some (things) they liked especially well.

Alle and *einige* follow the pattern of the plural definite article for people:

Alle waren vergnügt, und allen hat der Besuch gefallen.
　　All (people) were in a good mood, and all liked the visit.

Note that *alle* (all) and *jeder* (every) are easily mixed up. They are not as interchangeable as they are in English. While *alle* refers more to the "whole of people or all within a group," jeder refers to "each individual," as in each and every one.

EXERCISES

A.　Add the modal verb in parentheses to the following sentences.

1. *Sie gehen zu Fuß auf den Berg. (müssen)*

2. *Das Wetter wird sehr gut. (sollen)*

3. *Sie werden ein Schloss besuchen. (können)*

4. *Wir haben die Quelle der Kritik bewertet. (können)*

5. *Die Sicht auf den Rhein ist sehr schön. (müssen)*

6. *Man ist sehr zufrieden über diesen Besuch. (dürfen)*

7. *Das ist sicher richtig. (mögen)*

8. *Wir kommen nächste Woche wieder. (sollen)*

9. *Er hat lange auf den Zug gewartet. (müssen)*

10. *Niemand weiß die Antwort. (können)*

B. Choose the correct translation. More than one answer choice might be correct.

1. We don't need to walk.
   a) *Wir müssen nicht zu Fuß gehen.*
   b) *Wir brauchen nicht zu Fuß gehen.*
   c) *Wir lassen uns nicht zu Fuß gehen.*
   d) *Wir brauchen nicht zu Fuß zu gehen.*

2. I have my car repaired.
   a) *Ich brauche mein Auto repariert.*
   b) *Ich lasse mein Auto reparieren.*
   c) *Ich lasse mein Auto zu reparieren.*
   d) *Ich muss mein Auto reparieren.*

3. It can be done by tomorrow.
   a) *Das lässt sich morgen machen.*
   b) *Das lässt sich bis morgen machen.*
   c) *Das kann bis morgen machen.*
   d) *Das lässt bis morgen gemacht.*

C. Replace the underlined word(s) with the indefinite pronoun.

1. *Ein Mann wartet auf sie.* (somebody)

2. *Sie haben das Schloss gesehen.* (something)

3. *Den Freunden hat es viel Vergnügen gemacht.* (to all)

4. *Sie hören ihn sprechen.* (somebody)

5. *Die Erlebnisse waren phantastisch.* (all)

D. Translate the following sentences.

1. You don't need to write the letter.

2. I didn't hear anything.

3. That must be true.

4. I can hardly believe that.

5. You (one) can go by car.

E. Rewrite the following sentences in the negative.

1. *Klaus muss heute arbeiten.*

2. *Er hat etwas gehört.*

3. *Sie müssen zu Fuß gehen.* (use: *brauchen*)

4. *Wir wollen nach Süddeutschland fahren.*

5. *Jemand hat etwas gesagt.*

Answer Key

A. 1. *Sie müssen zu Fuß auf den Berg gehen.* 2. *Das Wetter soll sehr gut werden.* 3. *Sie werden ein Schloss
besuchen können.* 4. *Wir haben die Quelle der Kritik
bewerten können.* 5. *Die Sicht auf den Rhein muss sehr
schön sein.* 6. *Man darf sehr zufrieden über diesen
Besuch sein.* 7. *Das mag sicher richtig sein.* 8. *Wir
sollen nächste Woche wiederkommen.* 9. *Er hat lange
auf den Zug warten müssen.* 10. *Niemand kann die
Antwort wissen.*

B. 1. a and d; 2. b; 3. b

C. 1. *Jemand*; 2. *etwas*; 3. *Allen*; 4. *jemand(en)*; 5. *Alle*

D. 1. *Du brauchst (Sie brauchen) den Brief nicht zu
schreiben.* 2. *Ich habe nichts gehört.* 3. *Das muss wahr
sein.* 4. *Das kann ich kaum glauben.* 5. *Man kann mit
dem Auto fahren.*

E. 1. *Klaus muss heute nicht arbeiten.* 2. *Er hat nichts
gehört.* 3. *Sie brauchen nicht zu Fuß zu gehen.* 4. *Wir
wollen nicht nach Süddeutschland fahren.* 5. *Niemand
hat etwas gesagt.*

LESSON 12

IM REISEBÜRO: REISEN IST TÖDLICH?
AT THE TRAVEL AGENCY: TRAVEL IS FATAL?

A. DIALOGUE

1. *Es ist Montagmorgen und unsere drei Freunde sind gerade in Michaels kleinem Reisebüro angekommen. Mit einer frischen Tasse Kaffee sitzen sie vor Michaels Schreibtisch.*
   It's Monday morning, and our three friends just arrived at Michael's small travel agency. They are sitting in front of Michael's desk with a fresh cup of coffee.

2. Michael: **Ausgerechnet heute ist mit der Internetverbindung etwas nicht in Ordnung, aber ich habe den Serviceprovider schon angerufen. Also, was steht denn bereits auf eurer Liste, und wie viel Zeit habt ihr?**
   Today of all days there's something wrong with the Internet connection, but I've already called the service provider. So, what's on your agenda so far and how much time do you have?

3. Shawn: **Eigentlich bisher nur München. Wir haben zwei Wochen geplant, aber schon ein Auto gemietet, denn wir wollen auch etwas von der Landschaft sehen. Wir geben das Auto dann später in München ab und fliegen zurück. Aber den Flug haben wir noch nicht gebucht.**
   Actually, up until now only Munich. We've planned for two weeks, but we've already rented a car, since we want to see a little of the surrounding area as well. In Munich, we'll turn the car in and then fly back. But we haven't booked the flight yet.

4. Michael: **Warum macht ihr nicht einen kleinen Abstecher in die Alpen? Schließlich habt ihr schon das Auto. Der Grimselpass in der Schweiz ist zum Beispiel ein unvergessliches Erlebnis. Dort könnt ihr in einem Alpenhotel übernachten, dann nach Wien fahren, und zurück nach München. So habt ihr von allem das Beste.**
Why don't you make a little detour into the Alps? After all, you already have the car. The Grimsel Pass in Switzerland, for example, is an unforgettable experience. There you could stay overnight in an alpine hotel, then drive to Vienna, and from there go back to Munich. That way, you'll get the best of everything.

5. Liza: **Du hast mich bereits überzeugt. Ich habe keine Zweifel! Du scheinst dich auszukennen.**
You've already convinced me. I have no doubt! You seem to know your way around.

6. *Shawn und Klaus nicken.*
Shawn and Klaus nod.

7. Michael: **Nun, wollt ihr dann von Wien nach München fliegen oder mit dem Auto fahren, und soll ich euch das Alpenhotel und ein Hotel in München und Wien buchen?**
Well, do you want to fly to Vienna then or drive, and should I book the hotel in the Alps, and a hotel in Munich and Vienna for you?

8. Klaus: **Ich denke, jeder stimmt deinen Empfehlungen zu, und keiner hat irgendwelche Einwände. Offensichtlich weißt du, was gut ist.**
I think everyone agrees to your suggestions, and no one has any kind of objections. Obviously, you know what's good.

9. Michael: **Reisen ist meine Leidenschaft! Ah, und da ist auch die Computerverbindung wieder hergestellt. Gerade im richtigen Moment.**
Traveling is a passion of mine! Ah, and there's the computer connection restored again. Just at the right moment.

10. *Michael ist jetzt für ein paar Minuten mit dem Computer beschäftigt. Dann lädt er die Daten herunter und druckt die Reiseroute aus.*
Michael is occupied on the computer for a few minutes. Then he downloads the data and prints out the itinerary.

11. Michael: **Alles gebucht. Ich hoffe, die Reise wird euch gefallen. Vergesst nicht, eure Pässe mitzunehmen. An der österreichischen Grenze checken sie vielleicht den Pass nicht, aber sicher in der Schweiz. Hier ist euer Computer-Ausdruck mit E-Ticket für den Flug.**
Everything is booked. I hope you'll like the trip. Don't forget to bring your passports. They might not check your passport at the Austrian border, but they certainly will in Switzerland. Here's your computer printout with e-ticket for the flight.

12. Liza: **Das kann doch nicht dein Ernst sein. Für zwei Wochen Hotel und den Flug berechnest du uns so wenig?**
You can't be serious. For two weeks of hotels and the flight, you charge us that little?

13. Michael: **Das ist mein Job. Ich kenne die besten Angebote.**
That's my job. I know the best deals.

14. *Plötzlich fällt Shawn etwas auf. Der Bildschirm von Michaels Computer ist schwarz geworden. Eine*

Schrift erscheint: "Reisen ist tödlich!" Und einige Sekunden später: "Für Vorurteile!"

Suddenly Shawn notices something. The screen of Michael's computer has turned black. A message appears: "Travel is fatal!" And a few seconds later: "For prejudice!"

15. Shawn: **Reisen ist tödlich für Vorurteile? Nichts kann der Wahrheit näher kommen! Wer hat das gesagt?**

    Travel is fatal for prejudice? Nothing could come closer to the truth! Who said that?

16. Michael: **Einer eurer Landsleute, Mark Twain!**

    One of your fellow countrymen, Mark Twain!

B. NOTES

2. *ausgerechnet* (of all things) is commonly used with things, but also with people, places, or time: *Ihr wollt ausgerechnet dorthin?* Of all places, you want to go there?

   in Ordnung (lit.: in order) has a variety of meanings: *Alles in Ordnung!* Everything is okay! *Etwas ist nicht in Ordnung!* Something isn't working! *Das ist nicht in Ordnung!* That is not all right!

   Even though there are German words for many computer terms, the English words are more commonly used: *Der Serviceprovider* or *der Internetanbieter* (Internet service provider), *das Keyboard* or *die Tastatur* (keyboard), *downloaden* or *herunterladen* (to download), *browsen* (to browse), *mailen* (to e-mail). Verbs taken from English are conjugated as regular verbs and have an *-en* infinitive.

   also (so, well) is easily mixed up with the English word "also," which is *auch* in German: *Das ist also deine Frau!* So, that's your wife!

4. *zum Beispiel* (for instance) is also commonly abbreviated: *z. B.* (e.g.)

    When *der Pass* (pass) refers to a road, it is only
an alpine road. But this word also means passport.

10. *laden* (to load) and *herunterladen* (to download)
have an irregular conjugation. They change the stem
vowel to an Umlaut in the second and third person
singular: *Ich lade, du lädst er lädt, wir laden* . . .
(*lädst* and *lädt* are contractions of the older forms
ladest and *ladet* which are still used sometimes as
well.)

11. *checken* (to check), *einchecken* (to check in), and
auschecken (to check out) are verbs taken from
English. The conjugation is regular: *Ich checke, du
checkst, er checkt, wir checken, ihr checkt, sie
checken. Ich habe gecheckt.*

12. *Das kann doch nicht dein Ernst sein.* (lit.: That cannot be your seriousness.) This is used idiomatically
to mean: You must be joking!

14. *auffallen* (to notice) is a verb used with the dative
case: *Ihm (Shawn) fällt etwas auf.* He is noticing
something (lit.: something "falls" into his con-
sciousness, i.e., suddenly becomes noticeable to
him).

Culture Notes

Mark Twain is one of the most celebrated American writers
in all four of the German-speaking countries, partly due to
the fact that he visited several times, but mostly because of
his sense of humor. His essay, called "The Awful German
Language," is about German grammar, which seemed to him
to have more exceptions to the rules than instances of the

rules themselves. But he wasn't the kind of person to give up on anything, and eventually, he even gave speeches in German. You can look up his German speeches on the Internet (Google: "The Awful German Language"). You won't stop laughing.

You won't get a paper ticket anymore in Europe for your flight. There are machines in every airport that print out your boarding pass when you insert a credit or debit card *(die Eurokarte)*. If you don't have a credit card or *Eurokarte*, you can show your passport or ID at the check-in counter. Travel agencies print out an itinerary including the electronic ticket, which is nothing more than a number.

C. GRAMMAR AND USAGE

1. Separable Verbs

A number of German verbs are separated from their prefix in the present tense and the simple past tense. For example, the infinitive of the verb *ankommen* (to arrive) is separated as follows: *Sie kommen um 9 Uhr in München an* (They arrive in Munich at 9 o'clock). The prefix is usually placed at the end of the sentence. Here are some more examples.

anrufen (to call on the phone, to call up)

Er ruft den Serviceprovider an.
He calls the service provider.

abfliegen (to depart by plane)

Sie fliegen am Dienstag ab.
They depart on Tuesday.

abgeben (to turn in)

Sie geben das Auto in München ab.
They turn in the car in Munich.

2. Future Tense of Separable Verbs.

In the future tense, separable verbs are used in their infinitive form, just like any other verb:

Wir werden von dort zurückfliegen.
We'll fly back from there.

Sie werden ihm sicher zustimmen.
You will certainly agree with him.

Es wird ihr sicher auffallen.
She will certainly notice it.

3. Perfect Tenses of Separable Verbs

Separable verbs are written as one word in all perfect tenses as well, but the common prefix for past participles, *ge-*, is placed between the prefix and the verb:

Er hat den Reiseplan downgeloadet.
He downloaded the itinerary.

Sie sind gerade im Reisebüro angekommen.
They just arrived at the travel agency.

Hast du ihn noch nicht angerufen?
You haven't called him yet?

4. *irgend-* Compounds

The *irgend-* and *nirgend-* prefixes are similar to the English "some-" and "any-" compounds. The common ones are: *irgendein* (any, some kind of), *irgendwelche* (any), *igendwer* (someone, anyone), *irgendwem* (to anyone), *irgend(et)was* (anything, something), *irgendjemand* (anybody, somebody), *irgendwie* (somehow), *irgendwann* (anytime, sometime), *irgendwo* (anywhere, somewhere), and *nirgendwo* (nowhere):

Keiner hat irgendwelche Einwände!
Nobody has any objections!

Hast du irgendetwas gesagt?
  Did you say something (anything)?

Irgendwie werden wir das Problem lösen.
  We'll somehow solve the problem.

Note that *irgend-* is never used in a negative sense, as in "not any." *Ich möchte irgendetwas lesen.* (I want to read something.) But: *Ich möchte nichts lesen.* (I don't want to read anything.) *Nirgend-*, on the other hand, is always a negation:

Ich finde meinen Pass nirgendwo. Irgendwo muss er doch sein.
  I can't find my passport anywhere. It has to be somewhere, after all.

Die Straße mit dem Namen "Irgendwann" führt in die Stadt "Nirgendwo."
  The street called "Sometime" leads to a town called "Nowhere." (proverb)

Notice that "sometimes" is *manchmal* in German:

Manchmal hat man einfach Glück.
  Sometimes, you are simply lucky.

EXERCISES

A. Rewrite the following sentences in the present. Watch out for the separable prefixes!

  1. *Nichts hat ihn von seinem Plan abgebracht.*

  2. *Wir sind erst am Nachmittag angekommen.*

  3. *Ich werde das Fenster aufmachen.*

  4. *Sie haben sich einen Film angesehen.*

  5. *Wir werden noch heute abfahren.*

  6. *Wann wirst du zurückfliegen?*

7. *Ich habe mir die Nachrichten angehört.*

8. *Die Bank hat um 4 Uhr zugemacht.*

9. *Er hat sich gut ausgekannt.*

10. *Wir werden von München abfliegen.*

B. Rewrite the following text with separable verbs in the future tense:

> *Schon am Morgen kommen die Freunde in Michaels Reisebüro an. Sie hören seinen Vorschlägen gut zu. Dann lädt Michael den Reiseplan vom Computer herunter. Liza sieht sich den Ausdruck an und ist sehr überrascht. Es ist gar nicht teuer.*

C. Rewrite the text in exercise B in the present perfect tense.

D. Choose the correct sentence(s). Several answers might be correct.

1. Is anybody here?
   a) *Ist jemand hier?*
   b) *Ist irgendwer hier?*
   c) *Ist irgendjemand hier?*
   d) *Ist nirgends hier?*

2. I forgot something!
   a) *Ich habe irgendwas vergessen!*
   b) *Ich habe etwas vergessen!*
   c) *Ich habe irgendetwas vergessen!*
   d) *Ich habe nirgends was vergessen!*

3. Somewhere over the rainbow, skies are blue.
   a) *Nirgendwo über dem Regenbogen ist der Himmel blau.*
   b) *Irgendwie über dem Regenbogen ist der Himmel blau.*

    c) *Irgendwelche Regenbögen sind am Himmel blau.*

    d) *Irgendwo über dem Regenbogen ist der Himmel blau.*

E. Translate the following sentences using –*(n)irgend* prefixes:

  1. Sometime we have to visit Liechtenstein, too.

  2. I searched for it, but it isn't anywhere.

  3. I have heard something.

  4. She will give the book to someone.

  5. Somehow we'll get there.

Answer Key

A. 1. *Nichts bringt ihn von seinem Plan ab.* 2. *Wir kommen erst am Nachmittag an.* 3. *Ich mache das Fenster auf.* 4. *Sie sehen sich einen Film an.* 5. *Wir fahren noch heute ab.* 6. *Wann fliegst du zurück?* 7. *Ich höre mir die Nachrichten an.* 8. *Die Bank macht um 4 Uhr zu.* 9. *Er kennt sich gut aus.* 10. *Wir fliegen von München ab.*

B. *Schon am Morgen werden die Freunde in Michaels Reisebüro ankommen. Sie werden seinen Vorschlägen gut zuhören. Dann wird Michael den Reiseplan vom Computer herunterladen. Liza wird sich den Ausdruck ansehen und sehr überrascht sein. Es wird gar nicht teuer sein.*

C. *Schon am Morgen sind die Freunde in Michaels Reisebüro angekommen. Sie haben seinen Vorschlägen gut zugehört. Dann hat Michael den Reiseplan vom Computer heruntergeladen. Liza hat sich den Ausdruck angesehen und ist sehr überrascht gewesen. Es ist gar nicht teuer gewesen.*

D. 1. a, b, c; 2. a, b, c; 3. d

E. 1. *Irgendwann müssen wir auch Liechtenstein besuchen.* 2. *Ich habe danach gesucht, aber es war nirgendwo (nirgends).* 3. *Ich habe irgend(et)was gehört.* 4. *Sie wird irgendwem (irgendjemandem) das Buch geben.* 5. *Irgendwie kommen wir dahin (dorthin).*

LESSON 13

SIE KÖNNEN NICHT MIT KUPPLUNG FAHREN?
YOU CAN'T DRIVE STICK?

A. DIALOGUE

1. *Es ist Dienstag. Shawn ist am Computer beschäftigt,
   und Klaus muss noch ein paar Dinge im Büro erledi-
   gen. Liza ist bei der Autovermietung und holt den
   Wagen für ihre Reise ab.*
   It is Tuesday. Shawn is busy on the computer, and
   Klaus has to take care of a few things at the office.
   Liza is at the car rental and picks up the car for their
   trip.

2. Angestellter: **Ich empfehle Ihnen doch ein Auto
   mit Vierradantrieb in Ihrem Fall. Schließlich
   fahren Sie ja durch die Alpen. Ich kann das ohne
   Probleme ändern.**
   I really recommend a car with four-wheel drive in
   your case. You're driving through the Alps after all.
   It's no problem to change it.

3. Liza: **Kostet das wesentlich mehr?**
   Is that considerably more expensive?

4. Angestellter: **Es ist natürlich etwas teurer, aber
   dann sind Sie auch am besten ausgerüstet. Die
   meisten Probleme haben wir mit Zweiradantrieb
   in den Bergen, das zweite Mal schon in dieser
   Woche und trotz des Sommers. Es hat dieses Jahr
   in den Alpen viel mehr geschneit als gewöhnlich.**
   Of course it's a little more expensive, but then you'll
   be better equipped too. Most of the problems we
   have in the mountains are with two-wheel drive,
   twice already this week even though it's summer.

It's snowed in the Alps a lot more than usual this year.

5. Liza: **Ist ein Auto mit Vierradantrieb nicht weniger angenehm auf der Autobahn?**
Isn't a car with four-wheel drive less comfortable on the highway?

6. Angestellter: **Manche Autos sicherlich, besonders einige Geländewagen, aber unsere Leihwagen nicht. Sie sind optimal für Straßenverhältnisse.**
Some cars certainly, especially several off-road vehicles, but not our rental cars. They're optimal for road conditions.

7. Liza: **Brauchen wir denn auch Winterreifen in den Alpen?**
Do we need winter tires for the Alps too?

8. Angestellter: **Nein, breitere Reifen mit besserem Profil sind sicher gut genug.**
No, broader tires with better tread are good enough.

9. Liza: **Nun, dann ist die Sache entschieden. Aber eine Frage habe ich noch. Ist das Auto voll versichert?**
Well, then the matter has been decided. But I still have one more question. Is the car fully insured?

10. Angestellter: **Absolut! Das ist Standard bei uns. Und Sie geben das Auto dann am einundzwanzigsten des Monats in unserer Filiale in München ab. Auf einen Tag mehr oder weniger kommt es natürlich nicht an.**
Absolutely! That's standard with us. And you'll hand in the car on the twenty-first of the month at our branch in Munich. One day more or less wouldn't matter, of course.

11. *Der Angestellte füllt ein paar Formulare aus. Liza
    liest die Bedingungen. Zum Glück gibt es nichts
    Kleingedrucktes. Sie unterschreibt den Vertrag und
    dann gehen sie zusammen zum Auto.*
    The employee fills out a few documents. Liza reads
    the conditions. Luckily, there is no fine print. She
    signs the contract, and then they walk together to
    the car.

12. Liza: **Ja, das Auto sieht stark genug aus und ist in
    einem guten Zustand. Damit kommen wir be-
    stimmt durch den dicksten Schnee. Aber Mo-
    ment mal! Das Auto ist ja mit Kupplung. Ich
    habe bisher nur Automatikwagen gefahren.**
    Yes, that car looks strong enough and is in good con-
    dition. We get through the thickest snow with that.
    But just a moment! The car has manual transmis-
    sion. I've only driven cars with automatic transmis-
    sion so far.

13. Angestellter: **Was, Sie können nicht mit Kupplung
    fahren? Dann gebe ich Ihnen besser eine kleine
    Fahrstunde. Die erste Regel ist Koordination. Sie
    müssen das Kupplungspedal langsam kommen
    lassen nach dem Schalten, und dann Gas geben.**
    What, you can't drive stick? Then I'd better give you
    a little driving lesson. The first rule is coordination.
    You have to let go of the clutch slowly after shifting,
    and then push the gas pedal.

14. *Nur wenige Minuten später auf dem Parkplatz
    bekommt Liza es schon beim dritten Versuch in den
    Griff.*
    A few minutes later, in the parking lot, Liza has got-
    ten the hang of it on only the third try.

15. Liza: **Oh, ich verstehe! Es ist fast so wie mit zwei
    Stöcken in der Luft zu jonglieren. Zum Beispiel,**

man wirft einen Stock und wartet gelassen darauf, den anderen zu fangen.

Oh, I understand. It's almost like juggling two sticks in the air. For instance, you throw one stick, and you calmly wait to catch the other.

16. Angestellter: **Das ist genau der Punkt. Ein guter Vergleich!**

That's exactly the point. A good comparison!

17. Liza: **Es ist interessanter als ich dachte. Aber auf jeden Fall sind noch zwei andere gute Autofahrer mit mir unterwegs.**

It's more interesting than I thought. But just in case, there are two other good drivers with me on the road.

18. Angestellter: **Na, dann kann ja nichts schief gehen. Gute Fahrt!**

Well, then nothing can go wrong. Have a nice trip!

B. NOTES

1. *etwas erledigen* (to take care of) is also used for running errands: *Ich muss etwas in der Stadt erledigen.* (I have to run some errands in the city.) Don't use the expression with *jemand* (somebody), because that sounds more like an organized-crime "hit"! Another use of the word is: *Ich bin total erledigt.* (I'm totally exhausted.)

2. There are several verbs for "to change" in German: *ändern* (to alter something that already exists, e.g., clothes), *wechseln* (to exchange something like money or replace one piece of clothing with another), *tauschen* (to trade one item for another), and

umtauschen (to exchange something at the store): *Ich habe meine Meinung geändert.* (I changed my mind.)

6./11./12. There are at least six words for different types of conditions in German: *das Verhältnis* (a relative condition, e.g., road conditions in the winter, plural use), *der Zustand* (the physical condition of something, as in a car or a person), *die Bedingung* (a condition that has to be met, as in a contract), *die Kondition* (the condition of a business deal, but also athletic endurance), *die Voraussetzung* (a condition that has to exist, like a prerequisite), and finally *die Verfassung* (usually the mental condition of a person, the constitution).

14. *etwas in den Griff bekommen* (to get the hang of something)

18. The idiom *Dann kann nichts schief gehen* (lit.: Then nothing can go crooked) is used as an assurance that nothing can go wrong.

Culture Notes

While cars with automatic transmissions are widely available, manual transmissions are still the norm. This is mostly due to the fact that many drivers prefer a manual transmission because it makes driving seem sportier, not necessarily on the *Autobahn*, but when driving up and down winding country roads. Car rental companies usually have both types available, but if you prefer an automatic, you need to specify it. Cars that are most suited for mountain driving are almost exclusively manual. You have much better maneuvering possibilities with a stick shift in heavy winter conditions up and down alpine roads.

C. GRAMMAR AND USAGE

1. Comparative and Superlative

All comparatives are formed in German by adding *-er* to the stem of the adjective (or adverb) plus the appropriate adjective ending. As in English, some are irregular. Note that *mehr* (more) is only the comparative of *viel* (much); it isn't used as in the English "more interesting" or "more maneuverable." In German, even longer adjectives build their comperatives with *-er* endings:

Es ist billiger als ich dachte.
   It's cheaper than I thought.

Im Sommer ist es schöner hier als im Winter.
   It's more beautiful here in the summer than in winter.

Ich nehme das bessere Auto.
   I'll take the better car.

The superlative is formed by adding *-(e)st* and the proper adjective ending. There are two ways to use the superlative in German. One precedes a noun:

Die interessantesten Erfahrungen macht man auf der Reise.
   One has the most interesting experiences while traveling.

When the superlative is used as a predicative adjective (after a form of *sein,* for example) or an adverb, it is formed with *am* and the ending *-(e)sten*:

Der Flug war am teuersten.
   The flight was the most expensive.

Mit dem Zug geht es am schnellsten.
   It's fastest by train.

The most common irregular comparatives and superlatives are: *gut* (good, well), *besser* (better), *best-* (best);

viel (much), *mehr* (more), *meist-* (most); *gern* (gladly), *lieber* (preferably), *liebst-* (favorite); *hoch* (high), *höher* (higher), *höchst-* (highest). Short adjectives sometimes change their stem vowel to an umlaut: *kalt* (cold), *kälter* (colder); *groß* (big), *größer* (bigger). Adjectives that end in *-el* usually drop the *-e-* in the comparative: *dunkel* (dark), *dunkler* (darker).

Das Auto ist gut in der Stadt, besser auf dem Land und am besten in den Bergen.
That car is good in the city, better in the country, and best in the mountains.

Note that adjectives that already describe the highest degree do not have a comparative or superlative form:

Das ist die optimale Lösung.
That's the optimal solution.

2. *als* vs. *wie*

The two conjunctions *als* (than) and *wie* (as), used in comparisons, are easily confused with each other. They are never interchangeable. *Als* is used strictly with comparatives, e.g., *größer als* (larger than), whereas *so . . . wie* (as . . . as) compares adjectives or adverbs in the positive form, e.g., *so schön wie* (as beautiful as). Look at the following examples:

Das Auto ist schneller als ich dachte.
The car is faster than I thought.

Es ist doppelt so groß wie das alte Auto.
It's twice as big as the old car.

3. Quantifiers

Most quantifiers follow the endings of the indefinite articles (definite article for plurals). The common ones are: *viel* (much), *viele* (many), *wenig* (a little), *wenige* (not many), *mehr* (more), *mehrere* (several), *einige* (a few), and *manche* (some):

Wie viele Stunden wartest du schon?
How many hours have you been waiting?

Sie hat nur wenig Zeit.
She only has a little time.

In mehreren Hotels ist das Frühstück im Zimmerpreis mit einbegriffen.
In several hotels, breakfast is included.

Note that some quantifiers are mostly used with articles in German. They take on the endings of adjectives in this case:

Wir nutzen die wenige Zeit.
We make use of the little time.

Woher kommen die vielen Leute auf der Straße?
Where do the many people in the street come from?

4. Ordinal Numbers

Ordinal numbers have the same endings as adjectives in German. They are formed as follows: Just as in English, *der erste* (the first), *der zweite* (the second), and *der dritte* (the third) are irregular. Numbers four to nineteen add *-te* to their names: *der vierte* (the fourth), *der fünfte* (the fifth), etc. The number seven drops the *-en*: *der siebte* (the seventh). Numbers twenty through one hundred add *-ste*: *der dreiundzwanzigste* (the twenty-third), *der siebenunddreißigste* (the thirty-seventh):

Es ist bereits das dritte Mal.
It's already the third time.

Ich muß am einundzwanzigsten August in München sein.
I have to be in Munich on the twenty-first of August.

Nach dem siebten Versuch hat es geklappt.
After the seventh try it worked out.

EXERCISES

A. Change the adjectives or adverbs into their comparative forms.

1. *Ich nehme das große Auto.*

2. *Es ist gut so!*

3. *Dieses Haus ist hoch.*

4. *Sie isst gern Spaghetti.*

5. *Das gute Auto hat Vierradantrieb.*

6. *Das Hotel ist bequem.*

7. *Die schöne Landschaft haben wir gesehen.*

8. *Der Plan ist intelligent.*

9. *Was ist preiswert?*

10. *Das billige Auto ist schlecht für die Berge.*

B. Change the adjectives or adverbs in exercise A to the superlative.

C. Choose *als* or *wie*:

1. *Das Hotel ist besser _____ das andere.*

2. *Wir haben heute mehr Zeit _____ gestern.*

3. *Der Weg ist halb so weit _____ der andere.*

4. *Der Berg ist nicht höher _____ 2000 Meter.*

5. *Das Hotel ist so gut _____ das in München.*

6. *Nichts ist wichtiger _____ Zeit.*

7. *Kostet es wesentlich mehr _____ geplant?*

8. *Wir lösen das Problem schneller _____ erwartet.*

9. *Das Auto ist doppelt so stark* _____ *das andere.*

10. *Ich habe weniger Zeit* _____ *du.*

D. Choose the correct translation:

1. She is more tired than he.
   a) *Sie ist mehr müde als er.*
   b) *Sie ist müder als er.*
   c) *Sie ist müde wie er.*
   d) *Ihm ist müder als ihr.*

2. That's the highest mountain.
   a) *Das ist der höhere Berg.*
   b) *Das ist der höchste Berg.*
   c) *Das ist höher als Berg.*
   d) *Das ist der Berg am höchsten.*

3. Just a few people come here.
   a) *Manche Leute kommen hierher.*
   b) *Wenige Leute kommen hierher.*
   c) *Die wenigen Leute kommen hierher.*
   d) *Einige Leute kommen hierher.*

E. Add the correct ending to the ordinal numbers:

1. *Die erst*_____ *Regel ist Konzentration.*

2. *Sie hat am siebzehn*_____ *April Geburtstag.*

3. *Heute ist der dreißig*_____ *August.*

4. *Es klappte beim dritt*_____ *Versuch.*

5. *Ist morgen der sieb*_____ *oder der acht*_____ *September?*

Answer Key

A. 1. *größere*; 2. *besser*; 3. *höher*; 4. *lieber*; 5. *bessere*;
   6. *bequemer*; 7. *schönere*; 8. *intelligenter*; 9. *preis-
   werter*; 10. *billigere, schlechter*.

B. 1. *größte*; 2. *am besten*; 3. *am höchsten*; 4. *am liebsten*;
   5. *beste*; 6. *am bequemsten*; 7. *schönste*; 8. *am intelli-
   gentesten*; 9. *am preiswertesten*; 10. *billigste, am
   schlechtesten*.

C. 1. *als*; 2. *als*; 3. *wie*; 4. *als*; 5. *wie*; 6. *als*; 7. *als*; 8. *als*;
   9. *wie*; 10. *als*.

D. 1. b; 2. b; 3. b.

E. 1. *erste*; 2. *siebzehnten*; 3. *dreißigste*; 4. *dritten*;
   5. *siebte, achte*

LESSON 14

IN DER WERKSTATT: WERTVERDOPPELUNG?
AT THE REPAIR SHOP: TWICE THE VALUE?

A. DIALOGUE

1. *Auch Michael hat heute Morgen mit Autos zu tun. Aber dies ist eine ganz andere Erfahrung. Die tägliche Autofahrt den steilen Berg hinauf hat an seinem Auto Spuren hinterlassen, und jetzt scheint der Auspuff zu fehlen. Er ist jetzt in der Werkstatt und spricht mit einem Mechaniker:*
   Michael is also dealing with cars this morning. But this is quite a different experience. The daily trip up the mountain has taken its toll on his car, and now he seems to be missing an exhaust pipe. He's now at the repair shop speaking to a mechanic:

2. Michael: **Guten Morgen. Kann ich für dieses Auto einen neuen Auspuff bekommen?**
   Good morning. Can I get a new exhaust pipe for this car?

3. *Der Mechaniker wirft einen kurzen Blick auf das Auto:* **Scheint mir ein fairer Tausch zu sein.**
   The mechanic takes a quick look at the car: Seems like a fair exchange to me.

4. *Michael lächelt:* **Ich weiß, ich habe es zehn lange Jahre benutzt, und es hat mich nie enttäuscht. Es ist recht verbeult, aber es fährt immer noch ganz gut.**
   Michael smiles: I know, I've used it for ten long years, and it's never let me down. It's pretty banged up, but it still drives quite well.

5. Mechaniker: **Sollen wir auch eine Inspektion machen?**
Should we do an inspection, too?

6. Michael: **Ja, die ist sowieso bald fällig! Aber bevor Sie etwas reparieren, möchte ich es wissen.**
Yes, that's due soon anyway! But before you repair anything, I'd like to know what it is.

7. Mechaniker: **Kommen Sie doch heute am späten Nachmittag zurück. Dann wissen wir sicher mehr.**
Why don't you come back late this afternoon? We'll definitely know more by then.

8. *Es ist vier Uhr nachmittags, und Michael ist wieder in der Werkstatt.*
It's four o'clock in the afternoon, and Michael is back at the garage.

9. Mechaniker: **Ich denke, Sie werden angenehm überrascht sein.**
I think you'll be pleasantly surprised.

10. *Michael denkt:* **Bedeutet dieser Satz nicht immer etwas Schlechtes?**
Michael thinks: Doesn't this sentence always mean something bad?

11. Mechaniker: **Ich habe gute und ein paar schlechte Nachrichten. Der Motor ist in hervorragendem Zustand für einen Kilometerstand von 150.000 aber das Getriebe liegt in den letzten Zügen. Und dann brauchen Sie natürlich einen neuen Auspuff. Nun, ich meine, überhaupt einen.**
I have good news and some bad news. The motor is in excellent condition for 93,000 miles, but the transmission is about to give out. And then you'll

need a new exhaust pipe, of course. Well, I mean, an
exhaust pipe, period.

12. Michael: **Ja, den muss ich letzte Woche verloren
    haben. Wie viel wird das alles kosten?**
    Yes, I must have lost the old one last week alto-
    gether. How much will all that cost?

13. Mechaniker: **Einen Moment! Ich muss es am
    Computer berechnen.**
    One moment! I have to total it on the computer.

14. *Schlechte Nachrichten sind zu erwarten, denkt
    Michael. In diesem Moment läuft ein kleiner Junge
    auf ihn und sein Auto zu.*
    Bad news is ahead, Michael thinks. At that moment,
    a little boy runs towards him and his car.

15. Junge: **Wollen Sie den Wert von diesem Auto ver-
    doppeln? Mit wenig Geld?**
    Do you want to double the value of this car with lit-
    tle money?

16. Michael: **Ja natürlich, nichts lieber als das!**
    Yes, of course, nothing would please me more!

17. Junge: **Volltanken!**
    Fill it up with gas!

B. NOTES

1. *zu tun haben mit* (to have something to do with, to
   deal with). *Es hat nichts damit zu tun.* (It has nothing
   to do with that.)

Es hat Spuren hinterlassen. (It has taken its toll. [lit.: left traces])

4. *recht* (right) is often used as "quite." *Das ist recht schön!* (That's quite nice!) *Das ist mir nicht recht.* (That doesn't suit me right.) *Das Recht* (the law/the right).

6. *fällig* (due). *Die Telefonrechnung ist am 25. d.M. fällig.* (The telephone bill is due on the 25th of the month.) *d.M.* means *des Monats.*

11. *die Nachricht* (message), *die Nachrichten* (news).
    Note that the period and the comma are reversed in German: *15.000,00* = 15,000.00.
    Es liegt in den letzten Zügen. (It's on its last breath.)

16. *Nichts lieber als das!* ([lit.: Nothing more gladly than that!] Nothing would please me more!)

Culture Notes

On top of the inspection by the dealership, cars have to go through meticulous testing by the *TÜV*, the *Technischer Überwachungsverein* (Technical Inspection Agency). Repair shops and dealerships can only make sure that the requirements of the *TÜV* are met, but can't issue the sticker themselves. The German term *die Garage* only refers to private parking garages; a large parking garage is called *das Parkhaus*. If you need to go to a repair shop *(die Autowerkstatt)*, ask for an estimate *(der Kostenvoranschlag)*. You don't have to be concerned about "false" repairs, but car repair shops are not cheap, either.

C. GRAMMAR AND USAGE

1. Inseparable Verb Prefixes

You've seen with the separable prefix verbs that a prefix can change the meaning of a verb completely. This is also the case for inseparable prefixes. They are easier to use in all tenses, partly because they are inseparable from the verb, partly because they usually don't add the *ge-* in the past participle. The most common ones are: *ver-, zer-, ent-, be-, ge-, emp-, ent-, wider-, miss-, er-, de-, re-,* and almost all verb combinations with the prepositions *hinter, unter, durch, um, gegen,* and *über.*

kommen	to come	*bekommen*	to receive/to get
fangen	to catch	*empfangen*	to receive/to welcome
zählen	to count	*erzählen*	to tell, to recount
sehen	to see	*übersehen*	to miss seeing
stören	to disturb	*zerstören*	to destroy
suchen	to search	*versuchen*	to try
hören	to hear	*gehören*	to belong

Es hinterläßt Spuren am Auto.
It's taking a toll on the car.

Er unterschreibt den Brief.
He's signing the letter.

Er hat einen neuen Auspuff für sein Auto bekommen.
He got a new exhaust pipe for his car.

Er hat den Wert verdoppelt.
He doubled the value.

2. Demonstratives

There are three ways of using demonstratives in German. The easiest to use are *dies* (this) and *das* (that/this) as pronouns that don't relate to a specific gender. Note that here they are not used as replacement for articles (*das*

just happens to be the neuter article "the" as well as
"that").

Dies ist Frau Martin und das ist Herr Schulz.
   This is Mr. Martin and that is Mr. Schulz.

If the demonstrative replaces the definite article, its endings are the same as the article. Note that the demonstratives for "that" are the same as the articles. It's common to
use an additional adverb to make the location more clear:

Ich brauche für dieses Auto einen neuen Auspuff.
   I need a new exhaust pipe for this car.

In diesem Sommer fahren wir nach Wien.
   This summer, we'll go to Vienna.

Die Jacke liegt auf dem Regal dort.
   The (that) jacket is lying on that shelf there.

The third and last possibility is to use demonstratives as
pronouns that replace and clearly relate to a specific
noun. This is rarely used in writing.

Den habe ich letzte Woche verloren.
   I lost that / the old one last week. (an item of masculine gender)

Dieses habe ich schon gelesen.
   I've read this one already.

3. Common Noun Suffixes

   In previous lessons you've seen that certain suffixes may
   very likely indicate a certain gender. There are a number
   of very common suffixes that always make the noun feminine in gender: *-heit, -keit, schaft, -ung, -ion, -enz,* and *–ei.*

die Erfahrung	experience
die Inspektion	inspection
die Gesundheit	health
die Wirtschaft	economy

| *die Konditorei* | café, cake shop |
| *die Konkurrenz* | competition |

Common nouns with the endings *-ling, -iker, -ist, -eur,* and *-ismus* are always masculine:

der Optimist	optimist
der Mechaniker	mechanic
der Ingenieur	engineer
der Schmetterling	butterfly
der Idealismus	idealism

4. *meinen* vs. *bedeuten*

These two verbs are commonly mixed up. The meaning becomes clearer when the nouns are used: *die Meinung* (opinion), *die Bedeutung* (the meaning). When used as verbs, a person can *meinen* (mean) something, as in having an opinion, but only things can *bedeuten* (mean) something, as in having a definition.

Ich meine die Jacke dort.
   I mean that jacket there.

Was meinst du?
   What do you think? What's your opinion?

Was bedeutet das?
   What does that mean?

EXERCISES

A. Choose the correct inseparable prefix:

1. *Was _____ deutet denn das?*

2. *Ich habe jedes Wort _____ standen.*

3. *Er weiß nicht, ob er das kann, aber er wird es _____ suchen.*

4. *Bitte _____ schreiben Sie den Brief.*

5. *Sie _____ sucht ihre Freunde in Hannover.*

6. *Ich kann mich nicht _____ scheiden.*

7. *Dieses Restaurant können wir sehr _____ fehlen.*

8. *Das Kaufhaus ist total _____ laufen.*

9. *Ich möchte mir das erst _____ legen.*

10. *Bitte _____ brechen Sie das Glas nicht.*

B. Choose the correct translation. Several answers might apply:

1. They drive this car.
   a) *Sie fahren mit diesem Auto.*
   b) *Sie fahren mit dies Auto.*
   c) *Sie fährt mit diesem Auto.*
   d) *Sie fahren mit diesen Auto.*

2. This I don't want!
   a) *Dieses möchte ich nicht!*
   b) *Diesen möchte ich nicht!*
   c) *Diese möchte ich nicht!*
   d) *Dies möchte nicht!*

3. I'll take this car and you take that one.
   a) *Ich nehme dieses Auto und du nimmst dort.*
   b) *Ich nehme diesen Auto und du nimmst das.*
   c) *Ich nehme dieses Auto und du nimmst das.*
   d) *Ich nehme dies Auto und du nimmst den.*

C. Choose the correct article and noun suffix:

1. *Das ist _____ beste Gelegen _____ .*

2. *_____ Wirt _____ wird wieder besser.*

3. *_____ Konkurr _____ ist groß.*

   4. *Wo ist _____ Mechan_____?*

   5. *Wie ist ___ Gesund_____?*

D. Choose the conjugated form of *meinen* or *bedeuten:*

   1. *Was _____ du zu diesem Thema?*

   2. *Der Mechaniker _____, das Auto ist nicht in Ordnung.*

   3. *_____ das, ich muß mein Auto reparieren?*

   4. *Das hat nichts zu _____!*

   5. *Was _____ Michael dazu?*

E. Change the following sentences into the present tense:

   1. *Das habe ich nicht verstanden.*

   2. *Er hat den Vertrag unterschrieben.*

   3. *Das habe ich mir lange überlegt.*

   4. *Das Buch hat mir gut gefallen.*

   5. *Sie haben ihn in München besucht.*

   6. *Er hat seine Brieftasche irgendwo verloren.*

   7. *Sie haben mir von ihrer Reise erzählt.*

   8. *Wir haben uns über die Wirtschaft unterhalten.*

   9. *Ich habe den Scheck bekommen.*

   10. *Er hat die Krankheit gut überstanden.*

Answer Key

A. 1. *be-*; 2. *ver-*; 3. *ver-*; 4. *unter-*; 5. *be-*; 6. *ent-*; 7. *emp-*; 8. *über-*; 9. *über-*; 10. *zer-*

B. 1. a; 2. a, b, c; 3. c

C. 1. *die -heit*; 2. *Die -schaft*; 3. *Die -enz*; 4. *der -iker*; 5. *die -heit*

D. 1. *meinst*; 2. *meint*; 3. *Bedeutet*; 4. *bedeuten*; 5. *meint*

E. 1. *Das verstehe ich nicht.* 2. *Er unterschreibt den Vertrag.* 3. *Das überlege ich mir lange.* 4. *Das Buch gefällt mir gut.* 5. *Sie besuchen ihn in München.* 6. *Er verliert seine Brieftasche irgendwo.* 7. *Sie erzählen mir von ihrer Reise.* 8. *Wir unterhalten uns über die Wirtschaft.* 9. *Ich bekomme den Scheck.* 10. *Er übersteht die Krankheit gut.*

LESSON 15

AUF DEM ALPENPASS: WER HERAUFKOMMT, MUSS HINUNTER?
ON THE ALPINE PASS: WHO GOES UP, MUST GO DOWN?

A. DIALOGUE

1. *Nach einer Übernachtung in einem Hotel am See, sind Liza, Shawn und Klaus jetzt in der Schweiz. Sie fahren gerade eine schmale Pass-Straße hoch. Sie sind bereits so hoch auf dem Berg, dass die Straße zunehmend enger wird und Schnee teilweise die Straße blockiert.*

   After an overnight stay at a hotel on a lake, Liza, Shawn, and Klaus are now in Switzerland. They are driving up a narrow alpine road. They're already so high up the mountain that the street is becoming increasingly narrow, and snow is partially blocking the road.

2. **Shawn: Ich bin eigentlich überrascht, dass hier nicht mehr Verkehr ist. Bisher sind uns erst wenige Autos begegnet.**

   I'm actually surprised that there isn't more traffic here. So far we've come across very few cars.

3. **Klaus: Nur Einwohner und Touristen nehmen diese Pass-Straße, weil sie doch recht schmal ist. Leute, die kommerziell unterwegs sind, nehmen den Tunnel. Es geht schließlich viel schneller. Wir haben Glück, dass der Pass nicht geschlossen ist, da oft die Schneemassen Teile der Straße blockieren.**

   Only locals and tourists take this alpine road, because it's so narrow. People who use the road commercially take the tunnel. It's a lot faster, after all. We're lucky that the pass isn't closed, because large amounts of snow often block parts of the road.

4. *Plötzlich sehen sie ein Auto aus der anderen Richtung näher kommen, dessen Fahrer auf die Hupe drückt.*
Suddenly, they see a car approaching from the other direction, and its driver honks the horn.

5. Liza: **Wenn man vom Teufel spricht! Was machen wir denn da? Die Straße ist doch viel zu eng hier für zwei Autos nebeneinander.**
Speak of the devil! What are we going to do? The road is much too narrow here for two cars next to each other.

6. *Das Auto, das ihnen entgegenkommt, hält direkt vor ihnen, und der Fahrer steigt aus. Klaus öffnet das Seitenfenster.*
The car that's approaching stops right in front of them, and the driver gets out. Klaus opens the side window.

7. Fahrer: **Grüezi! Sie müssen zurück bis zur nächsten Ausweichstelle. Es ist ein ungeschriebenes Gesetz hier! Wer den Berg heraufkommt, muss hinunter.**
Greetings! You have to go back to the last passing spot. It's an unwritten law here. Whoever comes up the mountain, has to go down.

8. Klaus: **Grüezi! Ja natürlich.**
Greetings! Yes, of course!

9. *Klaus fährt den Wagen langsam rückwärts bis zur nächsten Ausweichstelle, die ungefähr fünfzig Meter weiter unten liegt. Die drei Freunde steigen*

aus. Der Fahrer des anderen Autos winkt ein Dankeschön.

Klaus drives the car slowly backwards to the nearest passing spot, which is located about fifty meters down. The three friends get out of the car. The driver of the other car waves a thank-you.

10. Shawn: **Großartig, dass wir hier ausgestiegen sind. Seht doch mal den atemberaubenden Bergsee dort unten.**

    It's great that we got out here! Just take a look at that breathtaking mountain lake down there.

11. Liza: **Ich habe noch nie in meinem Leben einen so blauen See gesehen. Ist ja wirklich so klar wie Kristall.**

    I've never seen such a blue lake in my life. It's really as clear as crystal.

12. Klaus: **Das Hotel auf dem Gipfel, in dem wir heute übernachten, soll auch einen Blick auf einen Bergsee haben.**

    The hotel at the mountain peak where we're staying tonight is said to have a view of a mountain lake too.

13. Shawn: **Fantastisch! Ich kann es kaum erwarten. Lass uns fahren, bevor du anfängst zu jodeln.**

    Fantastic! I can hardly wait. Let's go before you start yodeling.

14. Liza: **Shawn, jetzt hast du ihn auf die Idee gebracht! Es gibt keine Wölfe hier, oder?**

    Shawn, now you gave him the idea! There are no wolves around here, are there?

15. Klaus: **Keine Wölfe hier! Außerdem weißt du, Liza, dass ich nicht mit den Wölfen heule.**

No wolves around here! Besides, you know, Liza, that I don't howl with the wolves.

16. *Nach einer weiteren Stunde Fahrt durch dicken Schnee erreichen sie endlich das Hotel am Gipfel. Nachdem sie im Hotel einchecken, gehen sie in ihre Zimmer und dann in den heißen Whirlpool auf der Terrasse. Vor ihnen prasselt ein Feuer im offenen Kamin, und nicht weit von ihnen sehen sie einen tiefblauen Bergsee, der von Schnee bedeckten Bergen umgeben ist. Liza nimmt ein Schlückchen von ihrem heißen Glühwein und sagt:*
After another hour's drive through the thick snow, they finally reach the hotel at the peak. After they check in at the hotel, they go to their rooms, and then they're in the hot whirlpool on the terrace. In front of them a crackling fire burns in the open fireplace, and not far away they can see a deep blue mountain lake that is surrounded by snow-covered mountains. Liza takes a sip from her hot mulled wine, and says:

17. Liza: **Michael weiß wirklich, welche Reiseziele am besten sind. Das ist so viel schöner, als ich es mir jemals vorgestellt habe. Das nächste Mal müssen wir mindestens eine Woche hier bleiben.**
Michael really knows which travel destinations are the best. This is so much more beautiful than I ever imagined. Next time, we have to spend at least a week here.

18. Klaus: **Ja, und ich habe bisher immer gedacht, dass mein Urlaub an einem sonnigen Strand sein muß. Leider können wir jetzt unsere Pläne nicht ändern, da ich unbedingt am Einundzwanzigsten in München sein muss.**

Yes, and I've always thought up to now, that my
vacation has to be on a sunny beach. Unfortunately,
we can't change our plans now, because I have to be
in Munich on the twenty-first.

19. *Shawn grinst:* **Das hat nicht etwa etwas mit einer
    gewissen Dame zu tun, die du in Hannover in der
    U-Bahn getroffen hast, oder?**
    Shawn grins: That wouldn't by any chance have
    anything to do with a certain lady you met on the
    Hannover subway, would it?

20. Klaus: **Nun, ich kann's nicht bestreiten.**
    Well, I can't deny it.

21. Liza: **Aber jetzt lasst uns erst einmal zum Abend-
    essen gehen, denn die Schweizer Küche soll hier
    auch ausgezeichnet sein.**
    But for now, let's go to dinner, because the Swiss
    cuisine is said to be excellent here as well.

22. Klaus: **Das brauchst du uns nicht zweimal zu
    sagen, nicht wahr Shawn?**
    You don't have to tell us twice, right Shawn?

23. Shawn: **Absolut nicht! Ich hatte keine Ahnung,
    wie hungrig Bergluft macht.**
    Absolutely not! I had no idea how hungry mountain
    air can make you.

B. NOTES

1. Both *schmal* and *eng* are adjectives that mean "narrow," but *schmal* has more the meaning of very lim-
   ited width, and *eng* means something that is hard to
   get through. It can also refer to tight clothing: *Die
   Jacke ist zu eng.* (The jacket is too tight.)

2. *bisher* (up to now).

3. *Pass-Straße* (alpine road) can also be written as one word: *die Passstraße*. For style purposes, most people prefer to hyphenate compound nouns that have three of the same consonants in a row: *die Schiff-Fahrt* or *die Schifffahrt* (boat ride).

   Teil (part) can mean two different things, but they are different in gender: *der Teil* (part of something), *das Teil* (part as in 'car part'), *das Teilchen* (particle).

4. and 6. *näherkommen* (to approach, to come closer), *entgegenkommen* (to approach from the other direction).

5. *Wenn man vom Teufel spricht, dann kommt er* (If one speaks of the devil, he appears) is mostly shortened, as in English: *Wenn man vom Teufel spricht!* (Speaking of the devil!)

7. *Grüezi* (lit.: Greetings to you) is only used in Switzerland and sometimes in Liechtenstein.

9. The verb *winken* (to wave) is commonly mixed up with *zwinkern* (to wink at somebody) and *blinzeln* (to wink, to blink). But: *der Wink* (the hint, the cue).

14. The idiom *jmdn. auf eine Idee bringen* (lit: to bring someone to an idea) means to give someone an idea: *Das bringt mich auf eine Idee!* (That gives me an idea!)

15. The saying *mit den Wölfen heulen* (lit.: to howl with the wolves) is used to describe an opportunist, or one who always agrees with the masses (to run with the pack). In the dialogue, it's just a play on words, of course.

16. The verb *prasseln* (to burn with a crackling sound) can also describe the sound of heavy raindrops or

quick, relentless words: *Der Regen prasselt an die Fensterscheibe.* (The rain is drumming on the windowpane). *Die Worte der Kritik prasselten auf ihn nieder.* (The words of criticism rained down on him.) *Im Kamin prasselte ein Feuer.* (A fire crackled in the fireplace.)

18. *unbedingt* (absolutely, under any circumstance).

19. It's easy to mix up *etwas* (something, some, a little) and *etwa* (about, perhaps, really, in a way). *Es ist etwas kalt hier.* (It's a little cold here.) *Ist das etwa wahr?* (Is that really true?) *Der Berg ist etwa 3000 Meter hoch.* (The mountain has an altitude of about 3,000 meters.)

Culture Notes

Alpine roads *(der Alpenpass, die Pass-Straße)* are indeed mostly used by tourists and locals in all four German-speaking countries. There are more efficient tunnels through the Alps almost everywhere, often stretching for many miles on end. Some passes over the mountains are very narrow, and often closed because of large amounts of snow blocking parts of the road. There is also the chance of avalanches *(die Lawine)*, but the largest parts of the roads are built away from where heavy avalanches usually occur. The chances of being caught in one are very low, but having some driving experience in thick snow conditions is highly recommended. But the breathtaking views and many of the hotels and cozy alpine huts certainly make a visit worth your while.

It's customary for the car going up the mountain to back down to the last passing place if another car coming down the mountain is unable to pass. This is not the law but comparable to letting people come out of a door first, before you go in, as a courtesy. And no, there are hardly any animals in the Alps that are harmful to humans. There are only about ten to fifteen bears estimated to live in remote regions of the Alps. Wolves have been reported just once or twice in the last decade, but they avoid humans. If you ever find a brilliant white flower called an *Edelweiß*, don't pick it. They are under enviromental protection and extremely rare. They only exist in the Alps, the Pyrenees and the Carpathian Mountains, and any attempt to grow them anywhere else has failed. A variation of the plant exists in the mountains of Japan.

C. GRAMMAR AND USAGE

1. Clauses with Relative Pronouns (Relative Clauses)

The word order of a relative clause is slightly different from English, since the verb stands at the end of the clause. The relative clause starts with a relative pronoun, which in German is the same as the definite article, except in the genitive case (*des* becomes *dessen*, *der* becomes *deren*) and in the dative plural (*den* becomes *denen*):

Das ist der Mann, der das rote Auto fährt.
That's the man who drives the red car.

Das Buch, das ich gekauft habe, ist sehr gut.
The book that I bought is very good.

Er fährt zur Ausweichstelle, die zwanzig Meter zurück liegt.
He is driving to the passing spot, which is located twenty meters back.

Note that the relative pronoun must reflect the case that shows its function in the relative clause and the gender of the noun it refers to.

Der Wagen, den ich gekauft habe, ist sehr gut.
The car that I bought is very good.

Der Fahrer, dessen Auto den Berg herunter kam, steigt aus.
> The driver, whose car came down the mountain, is getting out.

Das Hotel, in dem wir übernachten, ist fantastisch.
> The hotel, in which we're staying overnight, is fantastic.

Alle Hotels, in denen wir wohnten, waren ausgezeichnet.
> All hotels in which we stayed were excellent.

2. Clauses with Subordinating Conjunctions

In previous lessons, you came across many conjunctions that don't change the word order of the clause they introduce. They were coordinating conjunctions, introducing another main (independent) clause. But with the large number of subordinating conjunctions that introduce a dependent (or subordinate) clause, the verb is placed at the end of the clause, just as in the relative clause. The most common subordinating conjunctions are: *als* (when [past], as), *nachdem* (after), *bevor* (before), *seitdem* (since the time), *bis* (until), *während* (while, whereas), *wie* (as), *weil, da* (because, since), *obwohl/obgleich* (even though), *wenn* (when, if), *dass* ([so] that), *damit* (so that), and *ob* (whether).

Nachdem sie eingecheckt haben, gehen sie in (auf) ihre Zimmer.
> After they've checked in, they go to their rooms.

Bevor sie zum Abendessen gehen, nehmen sie ein heißes Bad.
> Before they go to dinner, they take a hot bath.

Während sie im Whirlpool sind, können sie die Berge sehen.
> While they're in the whirpool, they can see the mountains.

Da es hier so schön ist, möchte Liza wiederkommen.
Because it's so beautiful here, Liza wants to come back.

Wenn ich in den Bergen bin, werde ich immer hungrig.
Whenever I'm in the mountains, I get hungry.

Ich weiß nicht, ob das Wetter so bleibt.
I don't know whether the weather will stay like that.

Note that *als* (when) almost always refers to a past event:

Als Shawn den Bergsee sah, war er beeindruckt.
When Shawn saw the mountain lake, he was impressed.

3. *das* vs. *dass*

When *das* is used as a relative pronoun, it's easy to mix it up with the conjunction *dass* (that). Compare the following sentences:

Sie hoffen, dass das andere Auto vorbeifahren kann.
They hope that the other car can pass.

Das Hotel, das sie gewählt haben, ist großartig.
The hotel that they've chosen is great.

Schade, dass wir nicht länger bleiben können.
It's too bad that we can't stay longer.

Ich wusste nicht, dass das das Hotel ist.
I didn't know that that is the hotel.

As in English, *dass* (that) is often left out. The word order changes back to regular in this instance:

Er hatte immer geglaubt, er wollte im Urlaub lieber an den Strand.
but: *Er hatte immer geglaubt, dass er im Urlaub lieber an den Strand wollte.*
He'd always believed (that) he'd prefer the beach on vacation.

4. Clauses with Interrogatives

Subordinate clauses can also be introduced by interrogatives. They follow the same word order rules. The verb is placed at the end of the clause:

Wir wissen nicht, wann wir das nächste Mal herkommen.
  We don't know when we'll come here next.

Er weiß wirklich, welche Reiseziele am besten sind.
  He really knows which travel destinations are the best.

Wir haben uns entschieden, wohin wir in unserem nächsten Urlaub fahren.
  We've decided where we'll go on our next vacation.

Es ist klar, wer nächstes Jahr wieder herkommt.
  It's clear who will come back next year.

EXERCISES

A. Choose *dass* or *das*:

1. *Das ist das Buch, _____ ich gelesen habe.*

2. *Wussten Sie, _____ es in den Alpen Bären gibt?*

3. *Er hat mir gesagt, _____ er morgen hier sein wird.*

4. *Das Hotel, _____ in den Alpen liegt, ist sehr schön.*

5. *Es gefällt ihnen so gut, _____ sie bald wiederkommen wollen.*

6. *Ich bin überrascht, _____ hier so wenig Verkehr ist.*

7. *Das Auto, _____ ich gekauft habe, steht in der Garage.*

8. *Glauben Sie, _____ _____ Wetter so bleibt?*

9. *Ich glaube nicht, _____ ich jemals einen tiefer blauen See gesehen habe.*

10. *Ist _____ _____ Hotel, _____ in den Alpen liegt?*

B. Choose the correct translation:

1. They like the Alps, even though it is cold.
   a) *Sie mögen die Alpen, obwohl es kalt ist.*
   b) *Sie mögen die Alpen, obwohl es ist kalt.*
   c) *Sie mögen die Alpen, obwohl kalt es ist.*
   d) *Sie mögen die Alpen, obwohl ist es kalt.*

2. After they've gotten out of the car, they see a lake.
   a) *Nachdem sie aus dem Auto ausgestiegen sind, sehen sie einen See.*
   b) *Nachdem sie aus dem Auto ausgestiegen sind, einen See sie sehen.*
   c) *Nachdem sie ausgestiegen aus dem Auto sind, sehen sie einen See.*
   d) *Nachdem aus dem Auto ausgestiegen sie sind, sehen sie einen See.*

3. It looks as if the weather is staying nice.
   a) *Es sieht so aus, als ob das Wetter bleibt schön.*
   b) *Es sieht so aus, als ob das Wetter schön bleibt.*
   c) *Es sieht so aus, als ob schön das Wetter bleibt.*
   d) *Es sieht so aus, als ob bleibt das Wetter schön.*

C. Choose *als* or *wenn*:

1. *Wir hatten viel Vergnügen, _____ wir in den Alpen waren.*

2. *_____ ich nach München gefahren bin, war das Wetter gut.*

   3. *Was machen Sie, _____ Sie in den Alpen sind?*

   4. *Er war sehr überrascht, _____ er den See sah.*

   5. *_____ das Wetter gut ist, gehe ich immer schwimmen.*

D. Answer the following questions, starting with *Ich weiß nicht, . . .*

   1. *Was machst du heute Abend?*

   2. *Wo ist meine Brieftasche?*

   3. *Wessen Buch ist das?*

   4. *Wann kommt er wieder?*

   5. *Welches Auto muß warten?*

E. Add the correct relative pronoun:

   1. *Das Buch, in _____ ich lese, ist auf Deutsch.*

   2. *Die Berge, auf _____ Schnee liegt, liegen am Hotel.*

   3. *Dort ist das Hotel, in _____ wir wohnen.*

   4. *Der See, _____ wir gesehen haben, war klar wie Kristall.*

   5. *Wo ist die Karte, _____ ich dir gegeben habe?*

Answer Key

A. 1. *das*; 2. *dass*; 3. *dass*; 4. *das*; 5. *dass*; 6. *dass*; 7. *das*;
   8. *dass, das*; 9. *dass*; 10. *das, das, das*.

B. 1. a; 2. a; 3. b

C. 1. *als*; 2. *Als*; 3. *wenn*; 4. *als*; 5. *Wenn*

D. 1. . . . *was ich heute Abend mache.* 2. . . . *wo deine
   Brieftasche ist.* 3. . . . *wessen Buch das ist.* 4. . . . *wann
   er wiederkommt.* 5. . . . *welches Auto warten muß.*

E. 1. *dem*; 2. *denen*; 3. *dem*; 4. *den*; 5. *die*

LESSON 16

IN DER BANK: ICH FREUE MICH, IHNEN MITTEILEN ZU DÜRFEN . . .
AT THE BANK: I'M HAPPY TO INFORM YOU . . .

A. DIALOGUE

1. *Wir haben lange nichts von Shannon und ihren Gastgebern in Hannover gehört. Shannon ist gerade am Geldautomaten ihrer internationalen Bank. Bevor sie Geld abhebt, checkt sie ihren Kontostand. Sie wirft einen Blick auf die Quittung und ist schockiert. Es scheint fast kein Geld mehr auf ihrem Konto zu sein, obwohl sie vor ihrer Reise eine sehr große Summe eingezahlt hatte. Sie geht in die Bank, um mit einem Bankangestellten zu sprechen. Sie weiß nicht, dass ihr eine weitere Überraschung bevorsteht:*
   We haven't heard from Shannon and her hosts in Hannover for a long time. Shannon is just at the ATM of her international bank. Before she withdraws money, she checks her account balance. She looks at the receipt, and is shocked. It seems there is almost no money in her account, even though she deposited a large sum before her trip. She walks into the bank to speak with a representative, not knowing that another surprise is ahead:

2. Shannon: **Ich habe gerade versucht, Geld am Automaten abzuheben, und es fehlt eine sehr große Summe auf meinem Konto.**
   I just tried to withdraw money at the machine, and a large amount of money is missing from my account.

3. Bankangestellter: **Hatte irgendjemand außer Ihnen Zugang zu ihrer Karte und der Geheimnummer?**
Did anyone besides you have access to your card and PIN-Number?

4. Shannon: **Nein, ganz bestimmt nicht! Ich habe die Karte immer bei mir. Und die Nummer habe ich nirgendwo aufgeschrieben.**
No, definitely not. I always have the card with me. And I haven't written down the number anywhere.

5. Bankangestellter: **Irgendwelche laufenden Kosten, automatische Überweisungen oder Abbuchungen vielleicht?**
Any ongoing costs, automatic transfers or deductions perhaps?

6. Shannon: **Nein, überhaupt keine bis auf die monatlichen Kontogebühren.**
No, none at all, other than the monthly account fees.

7. Bankangestellter: **Dann ist es sicher nur ein Buchungsfehler der Bank. Innnerhalb weniger Tage werden wir diesen Fehler sicher korrigiert haben.**
Then it has to be just an accounting error on the part of the bank. We'll surely have the mistake corrected in a matter of days.

8. Shannon: **Aber ich bin im Urlaub. Ich hebe laufend Geld von meinem Konto ab. Ich kann doch nicht die verbleibenden zwei Wochen mit meiner Kreditkarte leben.**
But I'm on vacation. I constantly withdraw money from my account. I can't live on my credit card for the remaining two weeks.

9. Bankangestellter: **Ich kann natürlich im Computer nachsehen. Erinnern Sie sich an alle geführten Transaktionen während der letzten Tage?**
   I can look it up in the computer, of course. Do you remember all the transactions you made during the past few days?

10. Shannon: **Ja, ich denke schon.**
    Yes, I think so.

11. *Der Angestellte gibt Shannons Informationen in den Computer ein und fragt:* **Also vor einer Woche haben Sie die letzte Einzahlung gemacht, nicht wahr?**
    The employee enters Shannon's information into the computer, and asks: So, a week ago you made the last deposit, right?

12. Shannon: **Nein, vor drei Wochen. Und ich habe seitdem fünf Abhebungen gemacht.**
    No, three weeks ago, and I've made five withdrawals since then.

13. Bankangestellter: **Das sehe ich auch hier auf meinem Bildschirm, und eine weitere Einzahlung von 4.000 Euro letzte Woche.**
    I see that also on my screen here, and an additional deposit of 4,000 euros last week.

14. Shannon: **Das ist sicher eine Einzahlung von meiner Firma. Aber dann ist die fehlende Summe ja noch größer!**
    That must be a deposit from my company. But then the missing sum is even larger!

15. Bankangestellter: **Ich weiß leider wirklich nicht, wo der Fehler liegen kann. Aber darf ich Sie**

**vielleicht bitten, bis morgen zu warten?
Schließlich haben Sie ja noch eine recht große
Summe auf dem Konto.**

Unfortunately, I really don't know where the mistake could be. But may I ask you perhaps, to wait
until tomorrow? After all, you do still have a rather
large amount in your account.

16. Shannon: **Sie nennen zwölf Euro eine große
    Summe?**

    You're calling twelve euros a large amount?

17. *Der Bankangestellte lächelt:* **Nein, ich freue mich
    Ihnen mitteilen zu dürfen, dass Sie 12.000 Euro
    auf Ihrem Konto haben.**

    The bank employee smiles: No, I'm happy to inform
    you that you have 12,000 euros in your account.

18. *Shannon sieht auf ihre Quittung vom Geldauto-
    maten und lacht:* **Verzeihung! Ich hatte ganz
    vergessen, dass man Zahlen in Europa anders
    schreibt. Der Punkt ist ja gar nicht der Dezi-
    malpunkt wie in Amerika. Vielen herzlichen
    Dank für Ihre Hilfe.**

    Shannon looks at her receipt from the ATM and
    laughs: Excuse me! I completely forgot that you
    write numbers differently in Europe. The period
    isn't the decimal point at all, as in America. Thank
    you so much for your help.

19. Bankangestellter: **Keine Ursache! Ich bin nur
    froh, dass wir dieses besorgniserregende Prob-
    lem so einfach lösen konnten.**

    Don't mention it! I'm just glad that we were able to
    solve this worrisome problem so easily.

B. NOTES

1. *der Geldautomat* (ATM-machine). Also known as
   der Bankomat. The word *ATM-Maschine* (pron.: Ah-
   teh-em) is also commonly used in Germany.

2. *Geld abheben* (to withdraw money), *Geld einzahlen*
   (to deposit money).

3. *die Geheimnummer* (lit.: secret number). The word
   PIN-Nummer is also used.

4. *etwas bei sich haben* (to have sth. with you). *Ich
   habe meine Karte nicht bei mir.* (I don't have my
   card with me). Same meaning: *Ich habe meine Karte
   nicht dabei.*

6. *bis auf* (except, all but). *Bis auf einen Tag schien die
   Sonne.* (All but one day, the sun was shining.)

7. *innerhalb weniger Tage* (in a matter of days).

13. *der Bildschirm* (computer or TV screen), *der Schirm*
    (umbrella).

16. The two verbs *nennen* (to call, to give a name to) and
    heißen (to be called) are often confused with each
    other: *Das nenne ich Glück!* (I call that being
    lucky!). *Wie heißt das?* (What is it called?) Remem-
    ber that *heißen* is never an action of a person, since
    the object or person in question is already named;
    nennen, on the other hand, can be used as an action.
    Wie nennt ihr euer Baby? (What will you name your
    baby?)

17. *Wir freuen uns, Ihnen mitteilen zu dürfen, . . .* (We
    are happy to inform you . . .) is also a very common
    phrase in business letters.

19. *Keine Ursache!* (lit.: No cause!) is often used as a reply to an expression of thanks, and means "Don't mention it!" or "You're welcome!"

The adjective *besorgniserregend* (worrisome, alarming) is written as two words when used as a verb and noun: *Das Gewitter erregt Besorgnis.* (The thunderstorm causes alarm.)

Culture Note

In many larger cities in Germany, you can also find branches of some American banks. ATMs are as numerous as in America. Even though hotels, restaurants, and most stores accept at least one major credit card (the same ones as in America), the much more common German credit card is similar to a debit card, where the full amount is deducted once a month from a bank account. Note that the decimal point and the comma in numbers are reversed in Europe (*3.000* = 3,000).

C. GRAMMAR AND USAGE

1. The Present Participle

In English, the present participle is the verb form ending in -ing. In German, it ends in *-end*: *schreibend, gehend,* etc. Present participles are not used in German with the present continuous tense (e.g., I'm <u>writing</u> a letter), but frequently as an adjective (the <u>falling</u> rain) or as part of a descriptive clause (Still <u>thinking</u> about her vacation, Liza . . .). If used as an adjective preceding a noun, the present participle will take adjective endings.

Die laufenden Gebühren buchen wir von Ihrem Konto ab.
We'll deduct the recurring (lit.: running) fees from your account.

Sie verbringt die verbleibende Zeit im Süden.
> She's spending the remaining time in the South.

Immer noch an die schöne Reise denkend, fliegen sie zurück nach Hause.
> Still thinking of the beautiful trip, they are flying back home.

2. Past Participles vs. Present Participles as Adjectives

The past participle, like the present participle, can be used as an adjective. Note that the present participle always describes an ongoing event, while the past participle as an adjective can only describe an already finished action. Compare the following examples:

Der schreibende Student sitzt am Computer.
> The writing student (student who is writing) is sitting at the computer.

Der geschriebene Brief liegt auf dem Schreibtisch.
> The written letter (letter that has been written) is lying on the desk.

Die schockierende Quittung zeigt einen Kontostand von zwölf Euro.
> The shocking receipt shows an account balance of twelve euros.

Die schockierte Shannon spricht mit einem Bankangestellten.
> The shocked Shannon is speaking to a bank employee. (In German you often use definite articles with names, even without adjectives.)

3. Infinitives with *zu*

As in English, infinitives in clauses are mostly used with the preposition *zu* (to). In German, the infinitive is usually placed at the end of the sentence:

Es scheint kein Geld auf ihrem Konto zu sein.
There seems to be no money in her account.

Darf ich Sie bitten, bis morgen zu warten?
May I ask you to wait until tomorrow?

Sie erinnert sich, Geld eingezahlt zu haben.
She remembers having deposited money.

With separable verbs, the *zu* is placed between the prefix and the verb:

Ich habe vergessen, die Zahl aufzuschreiben.
I forgot to write down the number.

4. Clauses with *um zu*

When the infinitive describes a purpose, *um zu* (in order to) is used in German:

Er braucht seinen Pass, um in die Schweiz zu reisen.
He needs his passport (in order) to travel to Switzerland.

Sie mietet ein Auto, um in den Urlaub zu fahren.
She is renting a car in order to go on vacation.

Sie geht an den Bankomat um Geld abzuheben.
She is going to the ATM (in order) to withdraw money.

EXERCISES

A. Choose the present or past participle as an attribute (verbal adjective):

1. *Die _____ Kosten bezahlt sie mit Scheck. (laufen)*

2. *Der _____ Mann wartet auf den Zug. (lesen)*

3. *Sie bringt den _____ Brief zur Post. (schreiben)*

4. *Die _____ Lehrerin sitzt am Schreibtisch. (schreiben)*

5. *Die _____ Summe ist hoch. (fehlen)*

6. *Das _____ Problem ist gelöst. (Besorgnis erregen)*

7. *Dort ist die _____ Brieftasche. (verlieren)*

8. *Der _____ Urlauber macht ein Foto. (überraschen)*

9. *Das ist ein _____ Blick auf die Berge. (überraschen)*

10. *Sie legt das _____ Buch auf den Tisch. (lesen)*

B. Choose the correct translation(s):

   1. We'll spend the remaining week in the South.
     a) *Wir verbringen die verbleibene Woche im Süden.*
     b) *Wir verbringen die vergebliebene Woche im Süden.*
     c) *Wir verbringen die verbleibende Woche im Süden.*
     d) *Wir verbringen die verbleiben Woche im Süden.*

   2. I'm glad about the corrected error.
     a) *Ich freue mich über den korrigierten Fehler.*
     b) *Ich freue mich über den korrigierenden Fehler.*
     c) *Ich freue mich über den Fehler korrigiert.*
     d) *Ich freue mich über den Fehler korrigierend.*

   3. The view is breathtaking.
     a) *Der Ausblick ist atemberaubt.*
     b) *Der Ausblick ist atemgeraubt.*
     c) *Der Ausblick ist atemberaubender.*
     d) *Der Ausblick ist atemberaubend.*

C. Change the sentences to an infinitive with *zu* using the verbs in parentheses:

1. *Er freut sich über das Photo. (scheinen)*

2. *Wir bleiben bis morgen. (hoffen)*

3. *Er konzentriert sich auf das Buch. (versuchen)*

4. *Wir erinnern uns an die Zeit. (glauben)*

D. Combine the sentences using *um zu* (in order to):

1. *Sie geht in die Bank. Sie spricht mit einem Ange-stellten.*

2. *Wir besuchen die Schweiz. Wir sehen die Alpen.*

3. *Ich gehe ins Kaufhaus. Ich kaufe eine Jacke.*

4. *Er fährt zur Werkstatt. Er lässt sein Auto reparieren.*

5. *Ich miete ein Auto. Ich fahre in den Urlaub.*

Answer Key

A. 1. *laufenden*; 2. *lesende*; 3. *geschriebenen*;
    4. *schreibende*; 5. *fehlende* 6. *besorgniserregende*;
    7. *verlorene*; 8. *überraschte*; 9. *überraschender*;
    10. *gelesene*

B. 1. c; 2. a; 3. d

C. 1. *Er scheint sich über das Photo zu freuen.* 2. *Wir hof-
    fen bis morgen zu bleiben.* 3. *Er versucht sich auf das
    Buch zu konzentrieren.* 4. *Wir glauben, uns an die Zeit
    zu erinnern.*

D. 1. *Sie geht in die Bank, um mit einem Angestellten zu
    sprechen.* 2. *Wir besuchen die Schweiz, um die Alpen
    zu sehen.* 3. *Ich gehe ins Kaufhaus, um eine Jacke zu
    kaufen.* 4. *Er fährt zur Werkstatt, um sein Auto re-
    parieren zu lassen.* 5. *Ich miete ein Auto, um in den
    Urlaub zu fahren.*

LESSON 17

AUF DEM POSTAMT: AUSSERHALB DER BOX?
AT THE POST OFFICE: OUTSIDE THE BOX?

A. DIALOGUE

1. *Shannon und Dorothee sind zusammen auf der Post. Shannon möchte ein paar CDs nach Amerika schicken und Dorothee hat einen Einschreibebrief aufzugeben. Sie warten in der Schlange.*
   Shannon and Dorothee are together at the post office. Shannon wants to send a few CDs to America, and Dorothee has a registered letter to send. They're waiting in line.

2. Shannon: **Werden die Päckchen einfach am Schalter abgegeben oder muss ich noch ein Formular ausfüllen?**
   Are the packages simply handed in at the counter, or do I have to fill out a form?

3. Dorothee: **Ich habe wirklich keine Ahnung. Postangelegenheiten werden in unserer Familie möglichst vermieden. Man muss immer so lange warten.**
   I really have no idea! If possible, postal matters are avoided in our family. You always have to wait so long.

4. Shannon: **Das macht wohl niemand gern. Es scheint in Amerika nicht viel anders zu sein.**
   Nobody likes to do that. It doesn't seem to be much different in America.

5. Postbeamter: **Was kann ich für Sie tun, meine Damen?**
What can I do for you, ladies?

6. Shannon: **Ich möchte diese beiden CD-Päckchen mit Luftpost nach Amerika schicken.**
I want to send these two CD packages by airmail to America.

7. Postbeamter: **Fast alles wird heute mit Luftpost geschickt. Dafür muss allerdings eine Zoller-klärung ausgefüllt werden. Aber ich sehe gerade, dass beide an die gleiche Adresse gehen.**
Almost everything is sent by airmail today. A customs delaration has to be filled out for that, though. But I see now that both packages are going to the same address.

8. Shannon: **Ja!**
Yes!

9. Postbeamter: **Das kostet fast doppelt so viel. Warum schicken Sie nicht beide Päckchen zusammen?**
That's almost twice as expensive. Why don't you send both packages together?

10. Shannon: **Großartig! Und wie mache ich das?**
Great! And how do I do that?

11. *Der Beamte gibt Shannon die Zollerklärung und etwas Klebeband.*
The clerk hands Shannon the customs declaration and some adhesive tape.

12. Postbeamter: **Kleben Sie sie einfach mit diesem Band zusammen. Das kann hier gleich an der Seite des Schalters gemacht werden.**

Just stick them together with this tape. That can be
done right here on the side of the counter.

13. *Der Postbeamte wendet sich an Dorothee:* **Sind Sie
zusammen hier, oder haben Sie auch einen
Wunsch?**
The postal clerk turns to Dorothee: Are you here
together, or do you also need something?

14. Dorothee: **Beides! Ich möchte dieses Einschreiben
aufgeben.**
Both! I'd like to send this registered letter.

15. Postbeamter: **Dafür muss leider auch ein Zettel
ausgefüllt werden.**
For that you'll have to fill out a slip as well.

16. *Während Dorothee und Shannon auf die Seite treten,
kommt ein Mann mit einem Stuhl an den Schalter:*
**Ich möchte diesen Stuhl an meine Tochter nach
Frankfurt schicken.**
While Dorothee and Shannon step to the side, a man
with a chair approaches the counter: I want to send
this chair to my daughter in Frankfurt.

17. Postbeamter: **Tut mir Leid, aber derartige
Sendungen werden von der Post nicht akzeptiert.
Aber ich sehe gerade, die Beine und die Lehne
sind ja angeschraubt. Warum machen Sie sie
nicht ab, kaufen einen unserer Postkartons mit
etwas Luftpolsterfolie, und ab geht die Post?**
I'm sorry, but those kinds of shipments are not
accepted by the post office. But I see that the legs
and the back are screwed on. Why don't you take
them off, buy one of our postal cartons with some
bubble wrap, and off it goes?

18. *Shannon and Dorothee kommen zurück an den
Schalter mit den ausgefüllten Zetteln.*

Shannon and Dorothee come back to the counter with their slips filled out.

19. Dorothee: **Ich bin wirklich überrascht, was für einfache Lösungen hier für den Postkunden gefunden werden. Hier wird ja wirklich außerhalb der Box gedacht.**
I'm really surprised at what simple solutions are found for the postal customer here. You really think outside the box here.

20. *Der Postbeamte lächelt:* **Nun, es ist wirklich ganz das Gegenteil! Das Prinzip ist, alles in die Box zu bekommen.**
The post office clerk smiles: Well, it's really quite the opposite! The principle is to get it all inside the box.

B. NOTES

1. There are three verbs for "to send" in German: *schicken* (to send), *senden* (to send, to broadcast), and *aufgeben* (to send at the post office).

2. The noun *der Schalter* means "counter" as well as "switch": *der Bankschalter* (counter at the bank), *der Lichtschalter* (light switch).

6. *das Päckchen* (small package, parcel), *das Paket* (package).

11./12. *das Klebeband* (adhesive tape), *kleben* (to stick, to glue).

15. *Der Zettel* (slip) can stand for any loose piece of paper, *das Blatt Papier* (sheet of paper), *das Formular* (the pre-printed form).

17. The English word *das Bubble-Wrap* is just as commonly used for *die Luftpolsterfolie* in German.

20. *Das Gegenteil* (the opposite) is often used idiomatically: *Ganz im Gegenteil!* (Quite the opposite!)

Culture Notes

The German Post *(Deutsche Bundespost)* used to be a monopoly and it included the only telephone company and the postal bank *(die Postbank)* as well. But now several competitors have emerged, especially for overnight and parcel delivery. The quality of service has dramatically increased and waiting times at the post office are now about half of what they were ten years ago, on average about seven minutes. Even though the post office doesn't operate as a telephone service provider anymore, it is possible to make long distance calls at many post offices. This is also the case in Austria, Switzerland, and Liechtenstein.

C. GRAMMAR AND USAGE

1. The Passive Voice

As shown in Lesson 8, the verb *werden*, on its own, means "to become," and it is also used as an auxiliary to form the future tense. *Werden* has a third use, to form the passive voice, which in English is shown as a form of "to be" with the past participle of a verb: The active sentence *Ich öffne die Tür* (I'm opening the door) in the passive voice becomes *Die Tür wird geöffnet* (The door is being opened). As in English, the former object of the sentence becomes the subject, and the former subject is demoted, so that it may not appear at all.

Päckchen werden am Schalter abgegeben.
   Small packages are handed in at the counter.

Der Brief wird geschrieben.
    The letter is being written.

The former subject can be added with the prepositions *von* or *durch*, meaning "by" or "with," just as in English.

Derartige Sendungen werden von uns nicht akzeptiert.
    Such mailings are not accepted by us.

Alle Klienten werden durch die Post benachrichtigt.
    All clients are informed by/through the mail.

Der Zettel wurde von ihnen ausgefüllt.
    The piece of paper was filled out by them.

The passive voice uses *worden* instead of *geworden* in the perfect tenses:

Das Buch ist mir gegeben worden.
    The book has been given to me.

Das Auto war kürzlich repariert worden.
    The car had recently been repaired.

Note that two forms of *werden* are required in the future tense of the passive voice. In conversations, the second *werden* is often left out if the future is clearly indicated:

Die Rechnung wird heute bezahlt (werden).
    The bill will be paid today.

2. Modal Verbs with the Passive Voice

In German, modal verbs are commonly used with the passive voice. *Werden* is placed at the end of the sentence, just like any other verb when a modal verb is used in the active voice. The past participle of a verb, together with the infinitive of *werden,* is called the passive infinitive.

Der Brief muss heute geschrieben werden.
    The letter has to be written today.

Das kann auch morgen gemacht werden.
That can also be done tomorrow.

Der Termin darf nicht vergessen werden.
The appointment must not be forgotten.

3. The Stative Passive

The stative passive simply involves a form of "to be" and a past participle, both in English and in German. It describes a state or action that has been completed. It is easy to form; it is identical with sentences that use the past participle as predicative adjective with "to be." Compare the passive voice with the stative passive in the first example below:

Die Post wird geschlossen. Die Post ist geschlossen.
The post office is (being) closed. The post office is closed.

Das Formular ist ausgefüllt.
The form is filled out.

Leider war die Bank noch nicht geöffnet.
Unfortunately, the bank wasn't open(ed) yet.

4. *Tun* vs. *Machen*

A common mix-up involves the verbs *tun* (to do) and *machen* (to make). But in fact, with the exception of some idiomatic expressions, *tun* is rarely used. As a general rule, use *machen* when in doubt. And don't forget that in German, unlike English, neither *tun* nor *machen* is used to form questions (does it . . . ?) or negatives (it doesn't . . .).

Er macht seine Hausaufgaben.
He's doing his homework.

Wie macht man das?
How does one do (go about doing) that?

Das tut nichts zur Sache!
  That doesn't matter!

Sie macht sich keine Sorgen.
  She doesn't worry about it.

Das tut mir Leid!
  I'm sorry about that!

Können Sie das bis Montag machen?
  Can you do that by Monday?

Er macht sich auf den Weg.
  He's (getting) on his way.

EXERCISES

A. Make the following sentences passive:

  1. *Er schreibt einen Brief.*

  2. *Sie findet eine Lösung für das Problem.*

  3. *Man schickt einen Brief auf der Post ab.*

  4. *Wo telefoniert man hier?*

  5. *Die Post akzeptiert keine unverpackten Artikel.*

  6. *Ich mache meine Hausaufgaben.*

  7. *Wir vermeiden lange Wartezeiten.*

  8. *Die junge Frau las ein Buch.*

  9. *Das macht niemand gern.*

  10. *Sie schickte die Päckchen zusammen.*

B. Add the modal verb in parentheses:

  1. *Ihr Auto wird repariert. (müssen)*

  2. *Das Buch wird umgetauscht. (können)*

3. *Der Brief wurde von mir gelesen. (sollen)*

4. *Das wird bis morgen erledigt. (müssen)*

5. *Das Päckchen wird nach Amerika geschickt. (sollen)*

C. Choose the correct translation:

1. The customs declaration has been filled out.
   a) *Die Zollerklärung ist ausfüllen worden.*
   b) *Die Zollerklärung wurde ausgefüllt.*
   c) *Die Zollerklärung ist ausgefüllt worden.*
   d) *Die Zollerklärung wird ausgefüllt werden.*

2. The photo will be sent this week.
   a) *Das Photo wird diese Woche schicken werden.*
   b) *Das Photo wird diese Woche geschickt werden.*
   c) *Das Photo wird diese Woche geschickt worden sein.*
   d) *Das Photo will diese Woche geschickt werden.*

3. The bank is opened at 9 o'clock.
   a) *Die Bank wird um 9 Uhr geöffnet werden.*
   b) *Die Bank wird um 9 Uhr geöffnet.*
   c) *Die Bank wird 9 Uhr öffnen.*
   d) *Die Bank wird um 9 Uhr öffnen werden.*

D. Translate the following sentences.

1. This counter is closed.

2. It is being opened at 9 o'clock.

3. Now, the form is filled out.

4. How is that being done?

5. Everything is (being) sent by airmail.

E. Use *machen* or *tun*:

1. *Das _____ nichts!* (Don't mention it.)

2. *Was _____ Sie in Ihrem nächsten Urlaub?*

3. *Ich hoffe, Sie _____ sich keine Sorgen.*

4. *Es _____ mir wirklich sehr Leid!*

5. *Ist es nicht Zeit, sich auf den Weg zu _____?*

Answer Key

A. 1. *Ein Brief wird (von ihm) geschrieben.* 2. *Eine Lösung für das Problem wird (von ihr) gefunden.* 3. *Ein Brief wird auf der Post abgeschickt.* 4. *Wo wird hier telefoniert?* 5. *Unverpackte Artikel werden von der Post nicht akzeptiert.* 6. *Die Hausaufgaben werden von mir gemacht.* 7. *Lange Wartezeiten werden von uns vermieden.* 8. *Ein Buch wurde von der jungen Frau gelesen.* 9. *Das wird von niemand gern gemacht.* 10. *Die Päckchen wurden von ihr zusammen geschickt.*

B. 1. *Ihr Auto muss repariert werden.* 2. *Das Buch kann umgetauscht werden.* 3. *Der Brief sollte von mir gelesen werden.* 4. *Das muss bis morgen erledigt werden.* 5. *Das Päckchen soll nach Amerika geschickt werden.*

C. 1. c; 2. b; 3. b

D. 1. *Dieser Schalter ist geschlossen.* 2. *Er wird um 9 Uhr geöffnet.* 3. *Jetzt ist das Formular ausgefüllt.* 4. *Wie wird das gemacht?* 5. *Alles wird mit **Luftpost** geschickt.*

E. 1. *macht*; 2. *machen*; 3. *machen*; 4. ***tut***; 5. *machen*

LESSON 18

IM HOTEL: DER HEURIGE GEHT AUF KOSTEN DER MAUS?
AT THE HOTEL: DINNER IS ON THE MOUSE?

A. DIALOGUE

1. *Liza, Shawn und Klaus sind nach ihrer Autofahrt durch die Alpen in Wien angekommen. Ihr Hotel in der Wiener Altstadt war nicht schwer zu finden. Es ist erst halb drei am Nachmittag, und sie befinden sie sich an der Rezeption.*

   After their trip through the Alps, Liza, Shawn, and Klaus have arrived in Vienna. Their hotel in the old part of Vienna wasn't difficult to find. It's only two thirty in the afternoon, and they're at the reception desk.

2. Rezeptionist: **Grüß Gott. Herzlich willkommen im Hotel Sternschnupperl, meine Herrschaften.**

   Greetings. Welcome at the Hotel *Sternschnupperl*, Ma'am, Gentlemen.

3. Shawn: **Grüß Gott. Wir haben eine Reservierung für ein Einzelzimmer und ein Doppelzimmer.**

   Greetings. We have a reservation for a single and a double room.

4. Rezeptionist: **Ach ja, hier habe ich Ihre Reservierung. Wenn Sie sich hier bitte eintragen möchten, kann ich unterdessen schon ihr Gepäck auf die Zimmer bringen lassen.**

   Ah, yes, I have your reservation right here. If you want to sign in right here, I'll have your luggage brought to your rooms in the meantime.

5. Liza: **Ist es möglich, ein paar Kleidungsstücke bis morgen früh reinigen zu lassen?**
Would it be possible to have some items of clothing cleaned by tomorrow morning?

6. Rezeptionist: **Selbstverständlich, gnädige Frau! Wenn Sie sie vor drei Uhr abholen lassen, werden sie schon heut' Abend um Viertel nach sechs gereinigt sein.**
Of course, Ma'am! If you have them picked up before three o'clock, they'll be cleaned by a quarter after six this evening.

7. Liza: **Wunderbar! Wie viel Uhr ist es jetzt?**
Wonderful! What time is it now?

8. Rezeptionist: **Es ist jetzt genau zwei Uhr zweiundvierzig.**
It's now exactly two forty-two.

9. *Kurze Zeit später sind die drei Freunde in ihren gemütlichen Hotelzimmern. Es klopft an der Tür.*
A short time later, our three friends are in their cozy rooms. There's a knock on the door.

10. Liza: **Sind Sie hier, um die Wäsche abzuholen?**
Are you here to pick up the laundry?

11. Page: **Ja, deswegen bin ich hier. Aber ich kann später z'rückkommen, wenn Sie noch nicht soweit sind.**
Yes, that's what I'm here for. But I can come back later, if you're not ready.

12. Liza: **Nein, das ist nicht notwendig. Es dauert nur eine Minute. Shawn, gib mir doch bitte meinen Koffer. Danke! Das ist wirklich ein fantas . . . aaaah! Dort in der Ecke sitzt ja eine Maus!**

No, that won't be necessary. It'll just take a minute.
Shawn, would you please hand me my suitcase?
Thanks. That's really a fantas . . . aaaah! There's a
mouse in that corner!

13. Page: **Oh Graislicher . . . ! Ich ruf' gleich die
    Hausinspektion.**
    Terrible . . . ! I'll call hotel maintenance right away.

14. *Wenige Minuten später kommt die Direktorin des
    Hotels:* **Um Himmels Willen! Die Maus sitzt ja
    immer noch dort in der Ecke!**
    Several minutes later the director of the hotel
    appears: For heaven's sake! The mouse is still sitting
    in the corner there!

15. Shawn: **Meiner Meinung nach scheint sie sich
    dort auch ganz wohl zu fühlen.**
    In my opinion it seems to be quite comfortable over
    there.

16. *Unterdessen hat sich eine kleine Gesellschaft ange-
    sammelt. Niemand hat das Mädchen bemerkt, das ins
    Zimmer gekommen ist.*
    Meanwhile a small group gathers. Nobody has
    noticed the little girl who has come into the room.

17. Mädchen: **Oh, da ist er ja, mein kleiner Felix!**
    Oh, there he is, my little Felix!

18. Hoteldirektorin: **Na, da fällt mir ja ein Stein vom
    Herzen! Zumindest haben wir kein Mäusepro-
    blem im Hotel.**
    Well, that takes a load off my mind! At least we
    don't have a problem with mice in the hotel.

19. Mädchen: **Oh, Entschuldigung! Das ist ja gar nicht mein Felix!**
Oh, I'm sorry! That isn't my Felix after all!

20. Hoteldirektorin: **Wie bitte?**
What?

21. Mädchen: **Kleiner Scherz meinerseits! Natürlich ist das meine Maus.**
Just kidding! Of course it's my mouse.

22. Hoteldirektorin: **Versprich mir, dass du in Zukunft besser auf sie aufpasst!**
Promise me that you'll watch it better in the future!

23. *Die Direktorin des Hotels wendet sich Liza, Shawn und Klaus zu:* **Und heute Abend geht der *Heurige* mit *Brettjause* in uns'rer *Schmankerlstuben* für Sie auf Kosten des Hotels.**
The director of the hotel turns to Liza, Shawn, and Klaus: And tonight, the *Heurige* with *Brettjause* in our Schmankerl Restaurant is on the hotel for you.

24. Shawn: **Aber es war doch nur eine winzige Maus!**
But it was just a tiny mouse after all!

25. Hoteldirektorin: **Aber ich schlafe heute Nacht sehr viel besser, wenn Sie die winzige Maus nicht an die große Glocke hängen!**
But I'll sleep a lot better tonight, if you keep the tiny mouse a big secret.

26. Klaus: **Wir werden mucksmäuschenstill sein!**
We'll be silent as a mouse!

27. Liza: **Natürlich behalten wir das für uns. Meiner Meinung nach ist Ihr Hotel ganz hervorragend. Aber wir beeilen uns besser, damit wir vor dem**

***Heurigen* noch genug Zeit haben für den Wiener *Prater*.**

Of course we'll keep it to ourselves. In my opinion, your hotel is outstanding. But we'd better hurry up, so we have enough time to visit the Vienna *Prater* before the *Heurigen*.

B. NOTES

1. *Die Altstadt* (lit.: old part of the city) is usually identical with "downtown" in most cities.

2. *Grüß Gott* (lit.: God greets you) is the common greeting in Austria and southern Germany, even for non-religious people.

   Die Sternschnuppe (shooting star) is used here as a diminutive in the name of the hotel. In Southern Germany and Austria, the endings *-erl* (Bavaria and Austria) and *-le* (Swabia) are more common as a term of endearment than *-chen* or *-lein*: *das Häuserl, das Häusle* (little house).

6./11./23. In the Austrian and Southern German dialects, the final *-e* of many words and some vowels within words (especially before *-r*) are often not pronounced in the spoken language: *heut'* instead of *heute* (today), *z'rückkommen* instead of *zurückkommen* (to come back), *uns'rem* instead of *unserem* (our).

13. *graislich* (terrible) is Bavarian and Austrian: *Oh Graislicher!* (Oh, terrible!)

21. *der Scherz* (practical joke).

23. *Die Brettjause* (lit.: feast on the wooden board) is a wooden platter of different types of food that is often served in the *Heurigen* restaurants in and around

Vienna. *Der Heurige* (the one of this season) is the young wine served in these restaurants. *Die Schmankerlstuben* is also an Austrian and Bavarian term referring to a gourmet but cozy country restaurant in the style of the region. *Die Stube* (parlor), *das Schmankerl* (a delicious local specialty).

25. *etwas an die große Glocke hängen* (lit.: to hang something on the large bell) is idiomatic for making a big fuss about something. The saying originates from the ringing of church bells, an old way of notifying everyone for miles around of unusual happenings.

27. The *Prater* is Vienna's permanent amusement park with many "old-fashioned" but fun attractions, and of course the famous ferris wheel, the symbol of Vienna.

Culture Notes

Vienna is known for very friendly customer service. It is known as the *Wiener Charme* (Viennese charm). You might not only be addressed with *Mein Herr* (Sir) and *Gnädige Frau* (Milady), but it is absolutely not uncommon to be addressed with titles you don't even possess, just to give customers an aura of importance.

Vienna is also well-known for its famous *Heurige* restaurants. *Heurig* means "of this year, of this season." The term originally referred to the new young wine of the current year, served from November 11 on (and for the following 300 days), but its meaning has changed over the centuries to include the restaurants on the outskirts of town that serve this wine. A green *Buschen* (fir sprig) on the door is the sign that the wine is available. For hundreds of years, people from all walks of life have been coming together to sit at the wooden tables and enjoy a hearty meal with the young wine after all the work is done. Often, it may be more wine than food, but in any event, *Heurige* is one of the few words that needs several English words to describe it: "Dinner and all."

C. GRAMMAR AND USAGE

1. The Real Conditional

The real conditional is used for events that actually occur if certain conditions are met, just like the English "We'll go to the beach if it stops raining." So, the real conditional expresses more of a contingency than a hypothetical situation, as opposed to the unreal conditional, "we would go to the beach if it weren't raining." German uses mostly the conjunction *wenn* (if, only if) in conditionals.

Wenn es heute regnet, nehmen wir einen Regenschirm mit.
   If it rains today, we'll take an umbrella with us.

Wenn die Kleidungsstücke vor drei Uhr hier sind, sind sie heute Abend gereinigt.
   If the clothing is here before three o'clock, it'll be cleaned by tonight.

Conditional clauses are dependent clauses. Notice that the verb is at the end of the conditional clause. Also, if the conditional clause is first, the verb in the second clause comes before its subject.

Wenn Sie noch nicht soweit sind, kann ich später zurückkommen.
   I can come back later, if you're not ready yet.

2. The Imperative

There are three imperatives in German, two for the familiar forms *du* and *ihr*, and one for the polite form of address. For almost all verbs the *du* form uses the second person singular of the verb without the *-st* ending: *Gib mir das Buch!* (Give me the book!) The umlaut with irregular verbs is omitted: *Lauf!* (Run!) The older form of regular verbs with an *-e* ending is sometimes used in writing but seldom in spoken language: *Bleibe!* (Stay!) Some verbs however require the *e-* ending for pronunciation purposes: *Öffne das Fenster!* (Open the window!) Exceptions to these rules are *haben* and *sein,* and *werden*: *Hab keine Angst!* (Don't be afraid!), *Sei leise!* (Be quiet!), *Werde bald gesund!* (Get well soon!) Notice that commands in German are always punctuated with exclamation points, whether they are emphatic or not.

Versprich mir, dass du besser darauf aufpasst!
    Promise me that you'll watch it better.

Gib mir doch bitte meinen Koffer!
    Please, hand me my suitcase.

Schreib(e) mir bitte eine Mail!
    Write me an e-mail, please.

The plural familiar imperative form of the verb is always identical to its conjugated form: *Redet nicht darüber!* (Don't talk about it!), *Seid jetzt ruhig!* (Be quiet now!) The verb form of the polite imperative is also identical to its conjugated form, but the pronoun *Sie* is included in the request: *Geben Sie mir das Buch, bitte!* (Please, hand me the book!) Separable verbs are written in two words in all the imperatives.

Bitte nimm meine Einladung an!
    Please accept my invitation.

Sehen Sie sich den Film an!
    Watch that movie.

3. Telling Time

There are several ways to ask the time in German. People on the street usually say one of the following: *Wie*

viel Uhr ist es? Welche Uhrzeit ist es? (What time is it?),
Wie viel Uhr haben wir? (What time do we have?), or *Wie
spät ist es?* (How late is it?) To answer, there is a common
form that people use in the street, and there is the twenty-
four hour system, which is always used on TV and radio,
or for official appointments. Note that if the minutes past
the hour are spelled out, as on a digital clock, then the
usual asumption is that the twenty-four hour system is
being used.

Es ist halb drei. (AM or PM)

Es ist zwei Uhr dreißig. (usually AM)

Es ist vierzehn Uhr dreißig. (PM)
  It's two thirty.

Es ist Viertel vor fünf. (AM or PM)

Es ist vier Uhr fünfundvierzig. (usually AM)

Es ist sechzehn Uhr fünfundvierzig. (PM)
  It's a quarter to five. It's four forty-five.

Es ist zehn nach sieben. (AM or PM)

Es ist sieben Uhr zehn. (usually AM)

Es ist neunzehn Uhr zehn. (PM)
  It's ten past seven.

Es ist zwölf Uhr. (AM or PM)

Es ist null/vierundzwanzig Uhr.
  It's twelve o'clock. (midnight)

Official time follows the twenty-four hour system in
large part because of regional differences in telling time.
Several German dialects also use *Viertel* (a quarter), *halb*
(one half), and *Dreiviertel* (three quarters), meaning "one
quarter . . . ," "one half . . . ," and "three quarters of the
way to the next hour," respectively.

(Viertel vier means three fifteen or a quarter after three; *halb vier* means three thirty or half past three, *Dreiviertel vier* means three forty-five or a quarter to four.) To clear up the confusion, just ask: *Viertel vor oder Viertel nach?* (A quarter to or a quarter after?)

4. Common Genitive Constructions

There are several very common genitive constructions, some including the possessive pronouns. *Meinetwegen* (for my sake, it's okay by me), *meinerseits* (as for me), *keinesfalls* (in no way), *unterdessen* (meanwhile), *meines Erachtens* (in my opinion), and *ungeachtet der Tatsache, dass . . .* (regardless of the fact that . . .) are the most common ones.

Ich bin deinetwegen nach München gekommen.
    I came to Munich because of you.

Seinerseits hat er keine Einwände.
    He, for his part, has no objections.

Sie werden keinesfalls etwas darüber sagen.
    They wouldn't talk about it under any circumstances.

Ungeachtet der Tatsache, dass eine Maus im Hotel war, hatten sie viel Spaß.
    Regardless of the fact that there was a mouse in the hotel, they had a lot of fun.

EXERCISES

A. Combine the sentences with *wenn* or *ob:*

   1. *Wir gehen ins Kino. Das Wetter ist schlecht.*

   2. *Du sagst etwas. Ich höre zu.*

   3. *Wir fahren morgen nach München. Alles ist geplant.*

   4. *Du gibst mir das Buch. Ich sage dir meine Meinung.*

5. *Wir sind früh zurück. Wir gehen ins Restaurant.*

6. *Ich freue mich. Du gibst mir ein Geschenk.*

B. Choose the correct translation:

1. In my opinion, it's a good idea.
   a) *Meiner Meinung nach ist das eine gute Idee.*
   b) *Meine Meinung ist eine gute Idee.*
   c) *Meine Bedeutung ist eine gute Idee.*
   d) *Meiner Meinung zu ist die Idee gut.*

2. It's fine with me, you can visit Vienna.
   a) *Meinetwegen kannst du Wien besuchen.*
   b) *Meiner Meinung nach kannst du Wien besuchen.*
   c) *Unterdessen kannst du Wien besuchen.*
   d) *Unter der Voraussetzung kannst du Wien besuchen.*

3. I, on my part, have no objections.
   a) *Ich habe keine Einwände seinerseits.*
   b) *Meinerseits habe ich keine Einwände.*
   c) *Unterdessen habe ich keine Einwände.*
   d) *Ungeachtet habe ich keine Einwände.*

C. Translate the following time expressions:

1. It's a quarter to four.

2. It's five after twelve.

3. It's half past seven.

4. It's eight PM.

5. It's three quarters past eleven.

D. Translate the imperative:

1. Please give me the book! (to a teacher)

2. Please tell me about it! *(erzählen)* (to a sibling)

3. Forget about it! (to a friend)

4. Please write that down! (to a fellow student)

5. Wait! (to your boss)

E. Add the imperative (singular familiar form):

1. _____ *das bitte* _____ *! (aufschreiben)*

2. *Bitte* _____ *das Buch! (lesen)*

3. _____ *mir* _____ *! (zuhören)*

4. *Bitte* _____ *daran! (denken)*

5. _____ *doch noch eine Tasse! (nehmen)*

Answer Key

A. 1. *Wir gehen ins Kino, wenn das Wetter schlecht ist.*
2. *Wenn du etwas sagst, höre ich zu.* 3. *Wenn alles geplant ist, fahren wir morgen nach München.* 4. *Wenn du mir das Buch gibst, sage ich dir meine Meinung.*
5. *Wenn wir früh zurück sind, gehen wir ins Restaurant.*
6. *Ich freue mich, wenn du mir ein Geschenk gibst.*

Note that you can change the condition to the beginning of the sentence or vice versa; either construction would be correct.

B. 1. a; 2. a; 3. b

C. 1. *Es ist Viertel vor vier.* 2. *Es ist fünf (Minuten) nach zwölf.* 3. *Es ist halb acht.* 4. *Es ist zwanzig Uhr.* 5. *Es ist Viertel vor zwölf.*

D. 1. *Bitte geben Sie mir das Buch!* 2. *Bitte erzähl(e) es mir!* 3. *Vergiss es!* 4. *Bitte schreib(e) das auf!* 5. *Warten Sie, bitte!*

E. 1. *Schreib . . . auf*; 2. *lies*; 3. *Hör . . . zu*; 4. *denk(e)*;
5. *Nimm*

LESSON 19

BEIM ARZT: DAS BRINGT MICH AUF DIE PALME!
AT THE DOCTOR'S: IT'S DRIVING ME UP THE WALL!

A. DIALOGUE

1. *Nach dem Riesenspaß in Wien sind Liza, Shawn und Klaus jetzt auf dem Weg nach München. Zwar ist die Autofahrt nicht sehr lang, aber Klaus fühlt sich heute überhaupt nicht gut.*
   After the great fun in Vienna, Liza, Shawn and Klaus are now on their way to Munich. Even though the trip isn't very long, Klaus doesn't feel good today at all.

2. Liza: **Dir scheint es ja heute wirklich nicht gut zu gehen, Klaus. Es ist ja, als ob du wirklich krank wirst.**
   You really don't seem to be well today, Klaus. It's almost as if you're really getting sick.

3. Klaus: **Es ist höchstwahrscheinlich nur eine kleine Erkältung. Keine Superüberraschung! Wir sind ja in der letzten Woche durch mehrere Klimazonen mit starken Temperaturschwankungen gekommen. In München soll übrigens Föhn sein.**
   It's most likely just a small cold. Not a big surprise! We've come through several climate zones with considerable changes in temperature this past week. By the way, there's supposed to be *Föhn* in Munich.

4. Shawn: **Was ist Föhn?**
   What is *Föhn*?

5. Klaus: **Der Föhn ist eine Warmluftfront, die sich in den Alpen staut. Durch den Druck in der Atmosphäre entstehen plötzlich Höchsttemperaturen in München, selbst im Winter. Ich war zwar noch nie bei Föhn dort, aber ich habe gehört, dass es manchmal eine drückende Hitze gäbe.**

   The *Föhn* is a front of warm air that is held up by the Alps. Because of atmospheric pressure, there are suddenly record temperatures in Munich, even in the winter. Even though I've never been there during *Föhn*, I've heard that it can get awfully hot sometimes.

6. Shawn: **Nach der Kälte in den Alpen habe ich nichts gegen Spitzentemperaturen.**

   After the cold in the Alps, I have nothing against peak temperatures.

7. Liza: **Du scheinst auch hohes Fieber zu haben, Klaus! Vielleicht wäre es besser, wenn du in München zum Arzt gehst.**

   You seem to have a high fever as well, Klaus. Perhaps it would be better if you saw a doctor in Munich.

8. Klaus: **Warten wir's ab, wie ich mich später fühle.**

   Let's wait to see how I feel later on.

9. *Eine Stunde später checken sie im Hotel ein. Da Klaus sich noch schlechter fühlt und Riesenkopfschmerzen hat, geht er zum Hotelarzt.*

   An hour later, they check into the hotel. Since Klaus feels even worse and has a terrible headache, he goes to the hotel physician.

10. Arzt: **Das ist gar nicht ungewöhnlich. Viele Leute werden krank bei dieser plötzlichen Affenhitze.**

That's not unusual at all. Many people get sick in
this sudden heatwave.

11. Klaus: **Aber ich bin erst gerade heute Morgen aus
Wien gekommen. Und vorher waren wir in den
Alpen.**
But I just came from Vienna this morning. And
before, we were in the Alps.

12. Arzt: **Wenn ich richtig vermute, müssten die
ersten Symptome kurz vor München aufgetreten
sein?**
If I assume correctly, the first symptoms occurred
when you were approaching Munich?

13. Klaus: **Ja, als wir ungefähr eine halbe Stunde von
München entfernt waren, bekam ich plötzlich
Kopfschmerzen und Fieber, als ob mir jemand
ständig mit dem Hammer auf den Kopf schlagen
würde. Heute Morgen war alles noch in Ordnung. Wäre es möglich, etwas gegen Fieber und
Schmerzen zu bekommen?**
Yes, when we were about half an hour away from
Munich, I suddenly got the headache and fever, as if
someone were constantly hitting my head with a
hammer. This morning everything was still all right.
Would it be possible to get something for the fever
and the headache?

14. Arzt: **Glauben Sie mir, es ist der Föhn! Höchstwahrscheinlich hat der Klimaumschwung es
noch schlimmer gemacht. Aber die ganze Umge-
bung von München ist vom Föhn betroffen. Morgen fühlen Sie sich wieder wie ein Fisch im
Wasser. Ich gebe Ihnen ein Rezept für heute. In
der Zwischenzeit sollten Sie tief durchatmen.
Föhnluft ist die sauberste Luft die sie je atmen
können.**

Believe me, it's the *Föhn*! Most likely, the change of
climate made it even worse. But the entire area
around Munich is affected by the *Föhn*. Tomorrow
you'll feel just fine again. For today, I'll give you a
prescription. In the meantime, you should breathe
deeply. *Föhn* air is the cleanest air you'd ever
breathe.

15. Klaus: **Na, vielen Dank erst einmal. Ich würde
mich freuen, wenn Sie wirklich Recht hätten,
denn diese Kopfschmerzen bringen mich auf die
Palme.**
Well, thanks a lot for now. I really would be happy,
if you were right, because this headache is driving
me up the wall.

16. Arzt: **Fast jeder Patient, den ich heute hatte, hat
sich über ähnliche Symptome beklagt. Aber ich
wäre wirklich überrascht, wenn Ihnen der Föhn
morgen nicht gefallen würde.**
Almost every patient I've had today has complained
about the same symptoms. But I would be really surprised if you didn't like the *Föhn* by tomorrow.

B. NOTES

1. *auf dem Weg sein* (to be on one's way)

3. *die Temperaturschwankung* (temperature fluctuation). *Schwankung* can be used with other changes
or fluctuations as well, referring to instability: *die
Preisschwankung* (fluctuation in prices).

5. *stauen* (to get stuck), *der Stau* (traffic jam)
    entstehen (to develop, to come into existence)
    zwar (even though) is usually followed by *aber*
(but) in the next clause.

8. *abwarten* (to wait for). *Warten wir ab, wie das Wetter wird.* (Let's wait [to see] how the weather turns out.)

10. The prefix *un-* is similar to English, creating the opposite of many adjectives: *gewöhnlich* (common), *ungewöhnlich* (uncommon).

12. *auftreten* (lit.: to step up) means to occur suddenly.

14. *der Umschwung* (sudden change)
    sich wie ein Fisch im Wasser fühlen (lit.: to feel like a fish in the water) is predictably the opposite of the English saying "like a fish out of water," and means "to feel perfectly all right."
    je can also mean "ever": *Das ist das beste Erlebnis, die ich je gehabt habe!* (That's the best experience I've ever had.)

15. *Das bringt mich auf die Palme* (lit.: It drives me up the palm tree). This means idiomatically, "It drives me up the wall."

Culture Notes

The *Föhn* is a weather condition that happens unpredictably in and around Munich, similar to the *Scirocco*, the *Chinook*, or the *Santa Ana Winds*, but usually without the strong winds. It is caused by a warm front of atmospheric pressure caught by the Alps. While it often rains south of the Alps during *Föhn*, Munich, lying north of them, is immersed in a dry desert-like wind. A sudden temperature increase of up to 40 degrees—even in the middle of winter—can occur during the *Föhn*. When you are in Munich during that rare occasion, you'll have an amazingly clear view of the Alps. The mountains seem to be tangible, rising up right in front of the city and often glowing in an almost mystical purple or orange light. While this causes terrible headaches for some people, others enjoy this unique natural phenomenon so much that there are even *Föhnpartys* in Munich. Rarely lasting more than two or three days, the *Föhn* vanishes as quickly as it appears. By the way, the word *Fön* (hair dryer) originated from this weather condition. Both spellings, *Föhn* and *Fön,* are acceptable.

C. GRAMMAR AND USAGE

1. The Subjunctive

There are two subjunctive *(der Konjunktiv)* moods in German. Both *Konjunktiv I* and *Konjunktiv II* have four forms derived from certain tenses. Note that the English translations below are approximations.

KONJUNKTIV I / SUBJUNCTIVE I

er gebe	(that) he give (presumably, allegedly)
er werde geben	(that) he will give (presumably, allegedly)
er habe gegeben	(that) he have given (presumably, allegedly)
er werde gegeben haben	(that) he will have given (presumably, allegedly)

KONJUNKTIV II / SUBJUNCTIVE II

er gäbe	(if) he gave
er würde geben	he would give
er hätte gegeben	he would have given
er würde gegeben haben	he would have given

Lesson 20 deals with uses of the *Konjunktiv I,* so we'll set it aside for now. The *Konjunktiv II* is often used in polite requests. The imperfect subjunctive forms *wäre* (would be) and *hätte* (would have), as well as *würde* (would), are most common.

Würden Sie mir bitte ein Rezept geben?
    Would you please give me a prescription?

Was würdest du dazu sagen?
    What would you say about that?

Ich würde mich sehr darüber freuen.
    I'd be very happy about that.

The subjunctive form *würde* (would) can be used with most verbs, but it isn't good style to use *würde* with *haben* (to have) or *sein* (to be). Instead, the subjunctive forms *wäre* (would be) and *hätte* (would have) are used.

Hätten Sie vielleicht einen Einwand?
    Would you perhaps have an objection?

Wären Sie damit einverstanden?
    Would you agree to that?

Wäre es möglich, etwas gegen die Schmerzen zu bekommen?
    Would it be possible to get something for the pain?

Hätten Sie vielleicht eine Medizin dafür?
    Would you possibly have medicine for that?

2. Unreal Conditional

The *Konjunktiv II* is also used to express unreal conditions in "if" sentences. Remember that unreal conditions are the hypothetical kind of conditions, both in English and in German.

Wenn ich mehr Geld hätte, würde ich ein Haus in Hawaii kaufen.
    If I had more money, I would buy a house in Hawaii.

Wenn die Welt perfekt wäre, wären alle Menschen glücklich.
    If the world were perfect, all people would be happy.

The past tense of the *Konjunktiv II* uses *hätte* and *wäre* with a past participle.

Wenn in München kein Föhn gewesen wäre, hätte Klaus keine Kopfschmerzen gehabt.
> If there hadn't been *Föhn* in Munich, Klaus wouldn't have had a headache.

Wenn wir früher gegessen hätten, hätten wir Zeit für einen Film gehabt.
> If we had eaten earlier, we would have had time for a movie.

The verbs *hätte* (would have), *wäre* (would be) and *würde* (would) are most commmonly used. They can express any kind of unreal condition, but every single verb has its own subjunctive forms as well. You can look up *Konjunktiv II* forms of other verbs in the grammar section.

3. *Konjunktiv II* of Modal Verbs

Just like the auxiliaries *haben* and *sein*, most modal verbs are rarely used with *würde* (would). The *Konjunktiv II* forms are: *könnte* (could), *müsste* (would have to), *sollte* (should), *dürfte* (would be allowed to, should [idiom.]), *möchte* (would like), and *wollte* (would want).

Könnten sie mir vielleicht etwas gegen die Kopfschmerzen geben?
> Could you perhaps give me something for the headache?

Wenn Sie die Tabletten nehmen, müssten Sie sich bald besser fühlen.
> If you take the tablets, you ought to feel better soon.

Wenn ich mich nicht irre, sollte Shannon morgen früh nach München kommen.
> If I'm not wrong, Shannon was supposed to come to Munich tomorrow.

Wir möchten ein Zimmer für drei Tage.
   We'd like a room for three nights.

Morgen dürften Sie sich wieder wie ein Fisch im Wasser fühlen.
   Tomorrow you should feel just fine again.

4. Augmentatives

   Unlike German diminutives that make things smaller by adding a suffix, an augmentative makes things larger or extreme by adding a prefix. Some augmentatives can be used with adjectives as well as nouns. The common ones are: *Höchst-* (highest), *Größt-* (largest), *Über-* (over), *Super-* (super), *Erz-* (arch-), *Un-* (un-), *Spitzen-* (peak), *Riesen-* (gigantic), *Best-* (best), *Höllen-* (hell of a), *Affen-* (colloquial—extreme, literally "monkey!"), and *Lieblings-* (favorite).

Das war eine Spitzenleistung.
   That was a peak performance.

Eine Unmenge von Leuten mögen den Föhn.
   A huge amount of people like the *Föhn.*

Die Affenhitze bringt viele Leute auf die Palme.
   This extreme heat drives many people up the walls.

Es gibt eine Riesenanzahl Museen in dieser Stadt.
   There is an abundance of museums in this city.

Es gab einen Höllenlärm auf der Straße.
   There was a hell of a loud noise on the street.

EXERCISES

A. Add the *Konjunktiv II* of the verb in parentheses:

   1. *Es _____ eine Überraschung, wenn das Wetter so bliebe.* (would be)

2. *Wenn er früher nach München kommen* _____ *, hätten wir mehr Zeit.* (would)

3. _____ *Sie vielleicht ein Zimmer frei?* (would have)

4. *Ich* _____ *mich nicht wundern, wenn er sich verspätete.* (would)

5. *Was* _____ *du dazu sagen?* (would)

6. *Wir* _____ *den Fön nicht gesehen, wenn wir später gekommen wären.* (would have)

7. _____ *Sie mir das Buch geben?* (would)

8. *Wenn Klaus sich besser fühlte,* _____ *er in die Stadt gehen.* (would)

9. _____ *er die Handynummer gehabt, hätte er angerufen.* (would have)

10. *Er glaubte, es* _____ *schon Donnerstag.* (would be)

B. Choose the correct translation:

1. Would you like a single room?
   a) *Brauchen sie ein Einzelzimmer?*
   b) *Möchten Sie ein Einzelzimmer?*
   c) *Hätten Sie ein Einzelzimmer?*
   d) *Wären Sie ein Einzelzimmer?*

2. Would you help me, please?
   a) *Wären Sie mir bitte helfen?*
   b) *Hätten Sie mir bitte geholfen?*
   c) *Würden Sie mir bitte helfen?*
   d) *Wären Sie bitte geholfen?*

3. How would you have done that?
   a) *Wie würdest du das machen?*
   b) *Wie solltest du das machen?*

    c) *Wie könntest du das machen?*
    d) *Wie hättest du das gemacht?*

C. Insert the modal verb in its *Konjunktiv II* form:

1. *Das Wetter* _____ *so bleiben. (können)*

2. *Wenn ich mich nicht irre,* _____ *das richtig sein. (müssen)*

3. *Man* _____ *immer einen Plan haben. (sollen)*

4. *Du* _____ *dich morgen besser fühlen! (dürfen)*

5. *Wir* _____ *drei Tage bleiben. (mögen)*

D. Translate these polite requests using the *Konjunktiv II*:

1. Would you have time tomorrow?

2. Could you tell me what time it is?

3. Would you write that down?

4. Would you be so nice?

5. I'd like three of them.

E. Add the correct augmentatives. Several options might be possible: *Über-, Höchst-, Affen-, Un-, Riesen-*

1. *Das ist eine* _____ *hitze!* (That's such hot weather!)

2. *Das war eine* _____ *leistung!* (That was a peak performance!)

3. *Das kostet eine* _____ *summe!* (That is incredibly expensive!)

4. *Eine* _____ *menge von Leuten wartete.* (A huge number of people were waiting.)

5. *Es gab ein* _____ *angebot an Restaurants.* (There was an abundance of restaurants.)

Answer Key

A. 1. *wäre*; 2. *würde*; 3. *Hätten*; 4. *würde*; 5. *würdest*;
6. *hätten*; 7. *Würden*; 8. *würde*; 9. *Hätte*; 10. *wäre*

B. 1. b; 2. c; 3. d.

C. 1. *könnte*; 2. *müsste*; 3. *sollte*; 4. *dürftest*; 5. *möchten*

D. 1. *Hätten Sie morgen Zeit?* 2. *Könnten Sie mir die Uhrzeit sagen? Könnten Sie mir sagen, wie viel Uhr es ist?* 3. *Würden Sie das bitte aufschreiben?* 4. *Wären Sie so nett?* 5. *Ich möchte drei davon!*

E. 1. *Affenhitze*; 2. *Höchstleistung, Riesenleistung*;
3. *Unsumme, Riesensumme*; 4. *Unmenge*;
5. *Überangebot, Riesenangebot*

LESSON 20

POLITISCHE KORREKTHEIT
POLITICAL CORRECTNESS

A. DIALOGUE

1. *Klaus fühlt sich heute wieder ausgezeichnet. Das Fieber und die Kopfschmerzen sind verschwunden. Er trifft sich mit Liza und Shawn im Frühstückszimmer des Hotels.*
   Klaus feels excellent again today. The fever and the headache have disappeared. He meets Liza and Shawn in the breakfast room of the hotel.

2. Liza: **Du siehst heute wirklich viel besser aus. Hast du schon einen Blick aus dem Fenster geworfen? Es ist eine hervorragende Sicht auf die Alpen, und die Luft ist unglaublich klar.**
   You really look much better today. Have you looked outside the window? There is an outstanding view of the Alps, and the air is unbelievably clear.

3. Klaus: **Der Arzt sagte, das sei normal bei Föhnwetter. Angeblich gebe es auch einen bemerkenswerten Sonnenuntergang bei diesem Wetter.**
   The doctor said that this was normal with *Föhn* weather. There is supposed to be a remarkable sunset with this weather as well.

4. Shawn: **Der Rezeptionist sagte, dass der Blick auf die Alpen vom Englischen Garten aus fantastisch sei. Vielleicht sollten wir heute Abend dort in einem Biergarten essen.**
   The receptionist said that the view of the Alps was fantastic from the English Garden. Perhaps we should go eat there tonight in a beer garden.

5. Liza: **Gute Idee! Aber Klaus, sagtest du nicht, dass heute deine amerikanische Bekannte und ihre Freunde aus Hannover nach München kämen?**
Good idea! But Klaus, didn't you say that your American acquaintance and her friends from Hannover were coming to Munich today?

6. Klaus: **Ja, Shannon sagte, sie seien so gegen Mittag hier. Sie sagte, sie wollen versuchen, Zimmer in diesem Hotel zu buchen, aber ich solle sie nach dem Frühstück anrufen.**
Yes, Shannon said that they would be here around noon. She said they want to try to get rooms in this hotel, but I'm supposed to call her after breakfast.

7. Shawn: **Nun, dann möchtest du sicher heute morgen im Hotel bleiben. Liza und ich machen inzwischen einen kleinen Stadtbummel.**
Well, then you probably want to stay in the hotel this morning. Liza and I will have a little stroll through the city in the meantime.

8. Klaus: **Ja, ich muss sowieso wieder zu Kräften kommen. Lass mich mit dem herzhaften Frühstück hier anfangen. Ich habe Hunger wie ein Wolf.**
Yes, I have to get my strength back anyway. Let me start with the hearty breakfast here. I'm as hungry as a wolf.

9. Liza: **Ein gutes Zeichen!**
A good sign!

10. *Shannon, Dorothee und Andreas sind in München angekommen. Glücklicherweise hat Shannon Zimmer im gleichen Hotel bekommen. Jetzt befinden sie sich alle in einem Biergartenrestaurant im Englischen Garten.*

Shannon, Dorothee, and Andreas have arrived in Munich. Luckily, Shannon was able to get rooms at the same hotel. Now, they are all in a beer garden restaurant in the English Garden.

11. Dorothee: **Was für ein glücklicher Zufall jetzt bei Föhn in München zu sein. Die Alpen scheinen so nah, als ob man sie anfassen könnte! Wenn du, Klaus, Shannon nicht überredet hättest, später als geplant nach München zu kommen, hätten wir das alles verpasst!**
What a lucky coincidence to be in Munich during *Föhn*. The Alps seem so close, as if you could touch them! If you, Klaus, hadn't talked Shannon into coming later than planned to Munich, we would have missed all of this.

12. Klaus: **Und glaubt mir, ihr seid nicht einen Tag zu früh gekommen. Gestern ging es mir gar nicht gut!**
And believe me, you didn't come one day too early. Yesterday I didn't feel good at all!

13. Liza: **Ich verstehe nicht, wie die Alpen in einem so hellen purpurnem Licht erstrahlen können. Ich habe noch nie etwas Ähnliches gesehen.**
I don't understand how the Alps can shine in such a bright purple light. I've never seen anything like it.

14. Dorothee: **Ein richtiger Bayer würde sagen, dass es ein himmlischer Segen sei. In Bayern ist alles anders. Auch um politische Korrektheit schert man sich in Bayern selten. Es ist mehr "leben und leben lassen."**
A true Bavarian would say that this was heaven's blessing. In Bavaria everything is different. People don't care much about political correctness, either. It's more like live and let live.

15. Liza: **Sagt man auf Deutsch auch "Politische Korrektheit"?**

Do people also say "political correctness" in German?

16. Dorothee: **Ja, aber es wird mehr und mehr ironisch benutzt. Selbst eine Lehre muss man jetzt Ausbildung nennen.**

Yes, but it's used increasingly in an ironic way. Even an apprenticeship you now have to call vocational training.

17. Shawn: **Ich hab' übrigens die Photos von der Drachenburg ausgedruckt, und ihr werdet es nicht glauben: Der Papagei ist nicht auf dem Photo.**

By the way, I printed out the photos from the Dragon Castle, and you won't believe it: The parrot isn't in the photo.

18. Liza: **Oh, gib es zu, Shawn. Du hast ihn mit dem Computer weggeeditet.**

Oh, admit it Shawn. You edited it out with the computer.

19. Shawn grinst: **Das wird wohl für immer ein Rätsel bleiben!**

Shawn grins: That might remain a mystery forever!

20. *Die Kellnerin bringt sechs Oktoberfestbiere, vier gegrillte Haxen und zwei vegetarische Platten. Niemand hatte bisher bemerkt, dass Shannon and Klaus sich in der Zwischenzeit ausschließlich und intensiv miteinander unterhielten.*

The waitress brings six Oktoberfest beers, four grilled fresh ham shanks and two vegetarian platters. No one had noticed up to now that Shannon and Klaus were occupied with each other exclusively.

21. Shawn: **Nun, wir scheinen hier internationale Barrieren zu durchbrechen. Ich würde eine Hochzeit auf der Drachenburg vorschlagen.**
Well, we seem to be breaking international barriers here. I would suggest a wedding at the Dragon Castle.

22. Dorothee: **Ich würde sagen, sie hätten wirklich eine tolle Geschichte zu erzählen. Wie wär's mit: Ich habe eure Mutter kennengelernt, als sie schwarz gefahren ist.**
I would say they really had a great story to tell. How about: I met your mother when she was dodging the fare.

23. Shawn: **Na dann Prost auf die Zukunft!**
Well, cheers to the future then!

B. NOTES

2. The prefix *un-* is used similarly to the prefix "un-" in English. With many adjectives and adverbs, it indicates the opposite: *unglaublich* (unbelievable), *unklar* (unclear), *unbedeutend* (unmeaningful, unimportant).

6. *das Frühstück* (breakfast) can also be turned into a verb: *frühstücken* (to eat breakfast).

8. *wieder zu Kräften kommen* is idiomatic for getting one's strength back: *Er kommt wieder zu Kräften.* (He's getting his strength back.)

14. *sich nicht scheren um* (not to have a second thought about something): *Ich schere mich nicht um diese Sache.* (I couldn't care less about this thing.)

20. *Oktoberfest* is a renowned Munich celebration, in fact the largest in the city, originally celebrating the

end of the harvest. It usually starts at the end of September with old-fashioned Bavarian music and pret-
zels *(Brezeln)* and beer. The beer is specially brewed
for it and called *Oktoberfestbier.*

   die Zwischenzeit (the meantime) is a noun for
unterdessen (meanwhile) or *inzwischen* (in the
meantime).

22. *toll* is colloquially used for "great." It's very common, as someone would say in English: That's
   absolutely great! *(Das ist wirklich toll!)*

Culture Notes

The term *Politische Korrektheit* (political correctness) has
become a somewhat ironic term since, in some cases, it has
been used to the extreme. It started with the reasonable
replacing of words that might be offensive to members of
certain groups. For instance, *das Fräulein* (Miss) was
replaced by *Frau* for an unmarried woman, and *der Lehrling*
(apprentice) by *der Auszubildende* (vocational trainee). But
then it was applied by some people to more and more areas,
so that even a word like *Fremdenverkehr* (lit.: foreign traffic) was supposed to be replaced by *Tourismus* (tourism). In
education, it was suggested that the modal verb *sollen* (shall,
should) should be eradicated, since it supposedly had a negative impact on students. A dramatic boost up the social lad-
der was given to the *Putzfrau* (cleaning lady), who became
Raumpflegerin (room curator), and the list goes on. While
some term replacements make complete sense, as they were
indeed not *"PK"* or *"PC"* (pron. *peh-tseh*), others are not
taken very seriously and are usually met with smiles.

C. GRAMMAR AND USAGE

1. Indirect Speech

There are three common ways to form indirect or reported speech in German, using the indicative, the *Konjunktiv I*, or the *Konjunktiv II*. The most neutral form is the indicative:

Sie sagte, dass sie heute nach München kommt.
　　She said that she is coming to Munich today.

But the *Konjunktiv I* is more commonly used in indirect speech. Using the *Konjunktiv I* in indirect speech adds distance between the reporting person and what was said by someone else. It is also the form that newspaper reporters use most frequently when reporting someone else's speech, almost with a built-in "allegedly."

Sie sagte, dass sie heute nach München komme.
　　She said that she'd come to Munich today.

Er behauptet, er habe das Auto nicht gesehen.
　　He claims not to have seen the car.

Der Rezeptionist sagt, dass der Blick auf die Alpen sehr gut sei.
　　The receptionist said that the view of the Alps was very good.

Klaus glaubt, dass Shannon gegen Mittag ankommen müsse.
　　Klaus believes that Shannon should arrive around noon.

The *Konjunktiv II* expresses a higher degree of doubt than either the indicative or the *Konjunktiv I*. Compare:

Sie sagte, sie sei um ein Uhr hier.
　　Sie said she would be here at one o'clock.

Sie sagte, sie wäre um ein Uhr hier.
She said she would be here at one o'clock (but I doubt it).

Er fragte, ob das Wetter so bleibe.
He asked if the weather would stay this way.

Er fragte, ob das Wetter so bleiben würde.
He asked if the weather really would stay this way.

2. Special Uses of the Subjunctive

Both subjunctive moods are also used to express wishes, invitations, or instructions. While the *Konjunktiv I* is used more in real wishes or instructions, the *Konjunktiv II* expresses a hypothetical or contrary-to-fact statement.

KONJUNKTIV I:

Man nehme drei Eier und ein halbes Pfund Mehl.
Take three eggs and half a pound of flour.

Das bleibe abzuwarten!
That remains (may remain) to be seen.

KONJUNKTIV II:

Ich wünschte, er nähme seine Medizin.
I wished he'd take his medicine.

Wäre ich doch früher nach München gekommen!
If only I had come to Munich earlier!

Wenn sie doch nur länger bliebe!
If only she were to stay longer!

The *Konjunktiv II* is also used in statements that express a hard-won result or a situation reached with difficulty or effort.

Die Kopfschmerzen wären endlich vorbei!
This headache is finally over!

Damit hätten wir endlich das Ziel erreicht!
    With that we'd finally reached the goal!

The *Konjunktiv II* with *würde* is commonly used to express less certainty when stating an opinion.

Ich würde sagen, es ist spät genug!
    I'd say it's late enough!

Ich würde meinen, das Wetter bleibt so gut!
    I should think the weather will stay so good!

3. Common Subjunctive Constructions

The *Konjunktiv II* is often used with *dass* and *als ob* constructions. Notice that English may use infinitive or gerund constructions.

Das Wetter ist zu schön, als dass wir im Haus bleiben sollten.
    The weather is too beautiful for us to stay in the house.

Die Alpen scheinen so nah, als ob man sie anfassen könnte.
    The Alps seem so close that you could touch them.

Es ist ja nicht, als ob dies das letzte Mal wäre, dass wir zu Besuch kommen!
    It's not as if this were the last time we're coming to visit!

EXERCISES

A. Change the following sentences into indirect speech using the *Konjunktiv I*. There are often two possibilities with regard to word order, depending on whether you use *dass*:

1. *Er sagte: Ich bin um drei Uhr hier.*

2. *Sie glaubt: Das Wetter bleibt so.*

3. *Sie denkt: Sie hat eine interessante Geschichte zu erzählen.*

4. *Er fragte: Wann kommst du wieder?*

5. *Der Hotelangestellte sagte: Der Blick ist ausgezeichnet.*

6. *Sie antwortete: Das ist eine gute Idee.*

7. *Sie sagte: Sie ruft morgen an.*

8. *Der Arzt sagte: Das ist bei diesem Wetter normal.*

9. *Sie fragte: Wo kann man gut essen?*

10. *Er behauptet: Das Photo ist ein Original.*

B. Change the sentences in exercise A into indirect speech with a high degree of doubt by using *Konjunktiv II:*

C. Choose the correct translation.

1. As if that would make a difference!
   a) *Als ob das einen Unterschied machen würde!*
   b) *So dass das einen Unterschied machen würde!*
   c) *Als ob das einen Unterschied möchte!*
   d) *Als dass das einen Unterschied machen!*

2. It looks as if you were right!
   a) *Es sieht so aus, als ob du Recht hättest!*
   b) *Es sieht so aus, als ob du Recht haben!*
   c) *Es sieht so aus, als ob du habest Recht!*
   d) *Es sieht so aus, als ob du rechnest!*

3. The trip was nice, without their getting bored.
   a) *Die Reise war schön, ohne dass sie sich gelangweilt habe.*
   b) *Die Reise war schön, ohne dass sie sich gelangweilt hätten.*
   c) *Die Reise war schön, ohne dass sie sich gelangweilt sei.*

d) *Die Reise war schön, ohne dass sie sich gelang-*
weilt würden.

D. Change the following sentences into an unreal wish
using *Konjunktiv II*. Start with: *Ich wünschte, dass* . . .

1. *Ich kann noch zwei Wochen bleiben.*

2. *Er glaubt es.*

3. *Ich habe mehr Zeit.*

4. *Das Auto ist schneller.*

5. *Es gibt weniger Ausnahmen bei der Grammatik.*

E. Translate the following sentences using *Konjunktiv II*:

1. Finally, we're here!

2. That would be nice of you (familiar).

3. I would have said that as well!

4. With that, we would come to the end of the story.

5. I would think that wouldn't be the end.

Answer Key

A. 1. *Er sagte, er sei um drei Uhr hier. Er sagte, dass er um drei Uhr hier sei.* 2. *Sie glaubt, das Wetter bleibe so. Sie sagt, dass das Wetter so bleibe.* 3. *Sie denkt, sie habe eine interessante Geschichte zu erzählen. Sie denkt, dass sie eine interessante Geschichte zu erzählen habe.* 4. *Er fragte, wann sie wiederkomme.* 5. *Der Hotelangestellte sagte, der Blick sei ausgezeichnet. Der Hotelangestellte sagte, dass der Blick ausgezeichnet sei.* 6. *Sie antwortete, das sei eine gute Idee. Sie antwortete, dass das eine gute Idee sei.* 7. *Sie sagte, sie rufe morgen an. Sie sagte, dass sie morgen anrufe.* 8. *Der Arzt sagte, das sei bei diesem Wetter normal. Der Arzt sagte, dass das bei diesem Wetter normal sei.* 9. *Sie fragte, wo man gut essen könne.* 10. *Er behauptet, das Photo sei ein Original. Er behauptet, dass das Photo ein Original sei.*

B. 1. *Er sagte, er wäre um drei Uhr hier. Er sagte, dass er um drei Uhr hier wäre.* 2. *Sie glaubt, das Wetter bliebe so (würde so bleiben). Sie sagt, dass das Wetter so bliebe (so bleiben würde).* 3. *Sie denkt, sie hätte eine interessante Geschichte zu erzählen. Sie denkt, dass sie eine interessante Geschichte zu erzählen hätte.* 4. *Er fragte, wann sie wiederkäme (wiederkommen würde).* 5. *Der Hotelangestellte sagte, der Blick wäre ausgezeichnet. Der Hotelangestellte sagte, dass der Blick ausgezeichnet wäre.* 6. *Sie antwortete, das wäre eine gute Idee. Sie antwortete, dass das eine gute Idee wäre.* 7. *Sie sagte, sie riefe morgen an (würde morgen anrufen). Sie sagte, dass sie morgen anriefe (anrufen würde).* 8. *Der Arzt sagte, das wäre bei diesem Wetter normal. Der Arzt sagte, dass das bei diesem Wetter normal wäre.* 9. *Sie fragte, wo man gut essen könnte.* 10. *Er behauptet, das Photo wäre ein Original. Er behauptet, dass das Photo ein Original wäre.*

C. 1. a; 2. a; 3. b

D. 1. *Ich wünschte, dass ich noch zwei Wochen bleiben könnte.* 2. *Ich wünschte, dass er es glaubte. Ich wünschte, dass er es glauben würde.* 3. *Ich wünschte, dass ich mehr Zeit hätte.* 4. *Ich wünschte, dass das Auto schneller wäre.* 5. *Ich wünschte, dass es weniger Ausnahmen bei der Grammatik gäbe (geben würde).*

E. 1. *Endlich wären wir hier.* 2. *Das wäre nett von dir.* 3. *Ich hätte das auch gesagt! Das würde ich auch sagen!* 4. *Damit kämen wir zum (ans) Ende der Geschichte.* 5. *Ich würde denken, dass das nicht das Ende wäre.*

SUMMARY OF GERMAN GRAMMAR

1. THE ALPHABET

LETTER	NAME	LETTER	NAME	LETTER	NAME
a	ah	j	yot	s	ess
b	beh	k	kah	t	teh
c	tseh	l	ell	u	oo
d	deh	m	em	v	fauh
e	eh	n	en	w	veh
f	eff	o	oh	x	iks
g	geh	p	peh	y	üpsilon
h	hah	q	ku	z	tsett
i	ee	r	err		

2. THE VOWELS

long **a**	as in "father"	*Vater*
short **a**	as in "but"	*Ratte*
long **ä**	as in "hair"	*spät*
short **ä**	as in "men"	*Männer*
long **e**	as in "dare"	*gehen*
short **e**	as in "bent"	*Adresse*
e	at end of a word as in "pocket"	*heute*
long **i, ie**	as in "meet"	*Liebe*
short **i**	as in "ship"	*Mitte*
long **o**	as in "lone"	*Bohne*
short **o**	as in "off"	*kommen*
long **ö**	similar to *e* in *geben* but with rounded lips	*König*
short **ö**	similar to *ir* in "bird" but with rounded lips	*können*
long **u**	as in "mood"	*Buch*
short **u**	as in "bush"	*dumm*

long **ü**	as long *i* with rounded lips	*früh*
short **ü**	as short *i* but with rounded lips	*Brücke*
y	pronounced as long or short *ü*	*Typ,*
		Mystik

3. THE DIPHTHONGS

ai	as *y* in "by"	*Kai*
ei		*Leine*
au	as *ou* in "house"	*Haus*
äu	as *oy* in "boy"	*häufig*
eu		*Freund*

4. THE CONSONANTS

b	as *b* in "bed," and at the end of a word, as *p* in "trap"
c	as *k* in "keep" and rather rarely like *ts*
d	as *d* in "date," and at the end of a word, like *t* in "but"
f	as *f* in "fly"
g	as *g* in "garden"
h	as *h* in "hundred," sometimes not pronounced at all, as in *Schuh*—"shoe"
j	as *y* in "York"
k	as *c* in "cut"
l	as *l* in "life"
m	as *m* in "man"
n	as *n* in "never"
p	as *p* in "painter"
q	like English *kv*
r	a little more rolled than in English
s	at the beginning of a word, as *z* in "zoo," and at the end of a word or syllable, as *s* in "son"
t	as *t* in "tea"

v	as *f* in "fair"
w	as *v* in "vain"
x	as *x* in "mix"
z	like the English combination *ts*

5. SPECIAL LETTER COMBINATIONS

ch	as *k*, *e.g.*, *Charakter*—character
chs	as *ks*, *e.g.*, *Fuchs*—fox
ch	a sound near the English *h* in "hue," *e.g.*, *Kirche*—church
ch	a guttural sound not existing in English but close to the Scots "loch," *e.g.*, *ach!*—"ah!"
ck	in final position, pronounced as *k*, *e.g.*, *Scheck*—check
ig	as *h* in "hue"
sch	as *sh* in "shoe"
sp or st	when placed at the beginning of the word, also gives the initial sound of *sh* in "shoe," *e.g.*, *Spanien*—Spain
ng	as *ng* in "sing"
tz	is similar to the English *ts*, *e.g.*, *Blitz*—lightning

6. THE GERMAN DECLENSION

  1. Nominative (subject, noun)

Das Buch ist hier.   The book is here.

  2. Genitive (possessive case)

der Name des Lehrers   the name of the teacher

3. Dative (indirect object)

Er gibt dem Kind einen   He gives an apple to the
  Apfel.   child.

4. Accusative (direct object)

Sie hält den Stift.   She is holding the pen.

7. PLURAL OF NOUNS

1. Masculine

a. nominative plus *-e*

der Abend	*die Abende*
der Freund	*die Freunde*

b. nominative plus *-er*

der Geist	*die Geister*
der Leib	*die Leiber*

c. nominative plus *-e* and ¨ (Umlaut) on the last
vowel preceding the word-final *-e*

der Hut	*die Hüte*
der Fall	*die Fälle*

d. nominative plus *-er* and ¨ (Umlaut) on the last
vowel preceding the word-final *-er*

der Mann	*die Männer*
der Rand	*die Ränder*

e. Masculine nouns ending in *-el, -en,* or *-er* do not change.

der Schlüssel	*die Schlüssel*
der Kuchen	*die Kuchen*
der Maler	*die Maler*

2. Feminine

a. Most feminine nouns form their plural by adding *-n* or *-en.*

die Tür	*die Türen*
die Frage	*die Fragen*

b. Some add *-e* or both *-e* and Umlaut on the last vowel preceding the word-final *-e*. Note: An *-s* ending will double in the plural.

die Kenntnis	*die Kenntnisse*
die Frucht	*die Früchte*

c. Feminine words ending in *-in* form their plural with *-innen.*

die Schülerin	*die Schülerinnen*
die Freundin	*die Freundinnen*

3. Neuter
Most neuter nouns form their plural like the masculine, the majority of them with *-e* or *-er.*

das Heft	*die Hefte*
das Licht	*die Lichter*

8. GENDER

German nouns can be masculine, feminine, or neuter. However, there is no rule to determine their gender. Here are a few helpful hints.

1. Masculine nouns include

   a. designations of trade or profession:
   der Maler, der Arzt, der Künstler

   b. titles of nobility:
   der Fürst, der Graf, der König

   c. nouns ending in *-ling*:
   der Sperling, der Jüngling

   d. days of the week and months:
   der Montag, der April

2. Feminine nouns include

   a. feminine designations of trade:
   die Malerin, die Ärztin

   b. feminine titles of nobility:
   die Königin, die Fürstin

   c. names of numbers:
   die Drei, die Null

   d. many names of trees:
   die Tanne, die Eiche

   e. nouns ending in *-ei, -heit, -keit, -schaft, -sucht,* and *-ung: die Freiheit, die Gesellschaft, die Ahnung*

3. Neuter nouns include

   a. diminutives ending in *-chen* or *-lein*:
   das Mädchen, das Büchlein

   b. many nouns ending in *-tum*:
      das Altertum

   c. most names of metals:
      das Gold, das Eisen

   d. most cities:
      das schöne Berlin

   e. most countries:
      das schöne Amerika

   f. colors:
      das Rot

   g. most collective nouns beginning with *ge-*:
      das Gebirge (mountains)

STRESS: German words generally have one strongly accented syllable, and may have two if the word is very long.

1. Short words—The accent is generally on the first syllable:
   Vater, Mutter, Bruder

2. Long words—The accent is generally on the root of the word:
   Empfehlung, Gebirge, Gebäude

3. Separable prefixes are always accented:
   abmachen, zugeben, mitgehen

4. Inseparable prefixes (*be-, emp-, ent-, er-, ge-, ver-, zer-*) are never accented. The accent always falls on the following syllable.
   erhalten, vergessen, zerbrechen

9. THE DEFINITE ARTICLE

1. Unlike English usage, the definite article can be used in front of a first name (*familiar*):
   Der Hans und die Margarete   John and Margaret

2. In front of a title:
   Ist der Herr Doktor da? Is the (Mr.) doctor at home? *Nein, aber die Frau Doktor ist zu Hause.* No, but the (Ms.) doctor is at home.

Remember the declension of the articles:

MASCULINE	FEMININE	NEUTER	PLURAL FOR ALL
N. *der*	N. *die*	N. *das*	N. *die*
G. *des*	G. *der*	G. *des*	G. *der*
D. *dem*	D. *der*	D. *dem*	D. *den*
A. *den*	A. *die*	A. *das*	A. *die*

10. THE INDEFINITE ARTICLE

Notice that in a negation *ein* becomes *kein*.

Er war kein Arzt, sondern ein Zahnarzt.
He was not a physician but a dentist.

MASCULINE	FEMININE	NEUTER
N. *ein*	N. *eine*	N. *ein*
G. *eines*	G. *einer*	G. *eines*
D. *einem*	D. *einer*	D. *einem*
A. *einen*	A. *eine*	A. *ein*

The masculine, feminine, and neuter singular forms of *kein* follow the same declension as *ein*.

PLURAL
N. *keine*
G. *keiner*
D. *keinen*
A. *keine*

11. THE ADJECTIVES

Adjectives are declined in three ways:

1. Without an article or pronoun (Strong Declension)

MASCULINE
N. *roter Wein*
G. *roten Weines*
D. *rotem Wein*
A. *roten Wein*

FEMININE
N. *rote Tinte*
G. *roter Tinte*
D. *roter Tinte*
A. *rote Tinte*

NEUTER
N. *rotes Licht*
G. *roten Lichtes*
D. *rotem Licht*
A. *rotes Licht*

PLURAL (M, F, N)
N. *rote Weine*
G. *roter Weine*
D. *roten Weinen*
A. *rote Weine*

2. With the definite article (Weak Declension)

MASCULINE
N. *der rote Wein*
G. *des roten Weines*
D. *dem roten Wein*
A. *den roten Wein*

FEMININE
N. *die rote Tinte*
G. *der roten Tinte*
D. *der roten Tinte*
A. *die rote Tinte*

NEUTER
N. *das rote Licht*
G. *des roten Lichtes*
D. *dem roten Licht*
A. *das rote Licht*

PLURAL
N. *die roten Weine*
G. *der roten Weine*
D. *den roten Weinen*
A. *die roten Weine*

3. With the indefinite article, possessive adjectives, or *kein* words (Mixed Declension)

MASCULINE

N. *ein roter Wein*
G. *eines roten Weines*
D. *einem roten Wein*
A. *einen roten Wein*

FEMININE

N. *seine rote Tinte*
G. *seiner roten Tinte*
D. *seiner roten Tinte*
A. *seine rote Tinte*

NEUTER

N. *kein rotes Licht*
G. *keines roten Lichtes*
D. *keinem roten Licht*
A. *kein rotes Licht*

PLURAL

N. *meine roten Weine*
G. *meiner roten Weine*
D. *meinen roten Weinen*
A. *meine roten Weine*

12. COMPARATIVE AND SUPERLATIVE

1. The comparative and the superlative are formed as in English by adding *-er* to the adjective for the comparative and *-st* (or *-est*) to the adjective for the superlative.

   Some short adjectives also take an Umlaut on their vowels.

schlecht, schlechter, schlechtest,	bad, worse, worst
alt, älter, ältest	old, older, oldest

2. There are a few adjectives that have an irregular comparative. Here are the most common ones:

POSITIVE	COMPARATIVE	SUPERLATIVE
gut	*besser*	*der (die, das) beste, am besten*
groß	*größer*	*der (die, das) größte, am größten*
hoch	*höher*	*der (die, das) höchste, am höchsten*

nahe	*näher*	*der (die, das) nächste,* *am nächsten*
viel	*mehr*	*der (die, das) meiste,* *am meisten*
gern	*lieber*	*der (die, das) liebste,* *am liebsten*

13. THE PARTITIVE

1. Generally not translated:

   Geben Sie mir Brot!
   Give me some bread.
   Geben Sie mir ein Glas Wein.
   Give me a glass of wine.

2. *Etwas* can also be used to mean a part of something:

   Ich gebe ihm etwas zu trinken.
   I am giving him something to drink.
   Ich gebe ihm etwas davon.
   I give him some of it.

3. The negative *kein* is declined like the indefinite article:

   Ich habe ein Messer, aber keine Gabel.
   I have a knife but no fork.

14. POSSESSIVE ADJECTIVES

1. Possessive adjectives agree in gender and number with the thing possessed:

NOMINATIVE

Before singular nouns:

MASCULINE AND NEUTER	FEMININE	PLURAL	
mein	meine	meine	my
dein	deine	deine	your (*fam.*)
sein	seine	seine	his, its
ihr	ihre	ihre	her
unser	unsere	unsere	our
euer	eure	eure	your (*fam. pl.*)
Ihr	Ihre	Ihre	your (*polite*)
ihr	ihre	ihre	their

2. Examples:

mein Hund	my dog
meine Tante	my aunt
ihr Vater	her father
seine Mutter	his mother
Ihr Buch	your (*polite*) book
ihre Bleistife	their pencils

3. Notice that these adjectives agree in gender not only with the possessor but also with the noun they modify. *Sein* and *seine* may mean "his" or "its":

Hans spricht mit seiner Mutter.
John is talking to his mother.

Das Bier hat seinen Geschmack verloren.
The beer has lost its taste.

Sie liest ihren Roman.
She is reading her (their) novel.

15. POSSESSIVE PRONOUNS

NOMINATIVE

MASCULINE	FEMININE	NEUTER	
meiner	*meine*	*meines*	mine
deiner	*deine*	*deines*	yours (*fam.*)
seiner	*seine*	*seines*	his
ihrer	*ihre*	*ihres*	hers
unser	*unsere*	*unseres*	ours
euer	*eure*	*eures*	yours (*fam. pl.*)
Ihrer	*Ihre*	*Ihres*	yours (*pol.*)
ihrer	*ihre*	*ihres*	theirs

Ist das mein Hut?—Ja, das ist Ihrer. (deiner)
Is that my hat?—Yes, that is yours.

Ist das deine Krawatte?—Ja, das ist meine.
Is that your tie?—Yes, that is mine.

Ist das sein Buch?—Nein, das ist meins. (Note: The *e*
of the neuter *-es* can be dropped.)
Is that his book?—No, that is mine.

Ist das ihr Schirm?—Nein, das ist seiner.
Is that her umbrella?—No, that is his.

16. DEMONSTRATIVE ADJECTIVES

SINGULAR

	MASCULINE	FEMININE	NEUTER	
N.	*dieser*	N. *diese*	N. *dieses*	this *or* that[1]
G.	*dieses*	G. *dieser*	G. *dieses*	
D.	*diesem*	D. *dieser*	D. *diesem*	
A.	*diesen*	A. *diese*	A. *dieses*	

---

[1] *jen (-er, -e, -es)* may also be used, but is less common in conversation.

PLURAL (M, F, N)   these *or* those
N. *diese*
G. *dieser*
D. *diesen*
A. *diese*

Dieses Haus ist schön.
This (that) house is beautiful.

Er sieht diesen Mann.
He sees this man.

Das Haus ist hässlich.
That house is ugly.

Er gibt dieser Frau ein Geschenk.
He gives this woman a present.

17. DEMONSTRATIVE PRONOUNS

Although these forms exist in German, they are not
commonly used.

SINGULAR

MASCULINE	FEMININE	NEUTER
N. *derjenige*	N. *diejenige*	N. *dasjenige*
G. *desjenigen*	G. *derjenigen*	G. *desjenigen*
D. *demjenigen*	D. *derjenigen*	D. *demjenigen*
A. *denjenigen*	A. *diejenige*	A. *dasjenige*

PLURAL
N. *diejenigen*
G. *derjenigen*
D. *denjenigen*
A. *diejenigen*

Mein Buch ist blau. Dasjenige meiner Schwester ist grün.
My book is blue. The one of my sister (My sister's) is green.

18. RELATIVE PRONOUNS

The relative pronoun is like the demonstrative pronoun, but its declension varies in the genitive singular of all genders, and in the genitive and dative plural.

SINGULAR

MASCULINE	FEMININE	NEUTER	
N. *der*	N. *die*	N. *das*	who
G. *dessen*	G. *deren*	G. *dessen*	whose
D. *dem*	D. *der*	D. *dem*	to whom
A. *den*	A. *die*	A. *das*	whom

	PLURAL	
	N. *die*	who
	G. *deren*	whose
	D. *denen*	to whom
	A. *die*	whom

Der Junge, dessen Vater ich kenne, heißt Richard.
The boy whose father I know is named Richard.

Die Frau, deren Tochter die Universität besucht, arbeitet in einen Kaufhaus.
The woman whose daughter attends the university works in a department store.

Welcher can also be used as a relative pronoun and is declined in the same way as the article *der*.

Der Freund, welcher morgen kommt, heißt Max.
The friend who is coming tomorrow is named Max.

NOTES

1. These pronouns must agree in gender and number with the noun to which they refer.

   Das Mädchen, das auf der Straße spielt . . .
   The little girl who is playing on the street . . .

2. A comma should always be used before the relative pronoun.

3. The verb is always placed at the end of the clause that a relative pronoun introduces.

4. Relative pronouns can never be omitted as in English.

   Das Buch, das ich lese . . .
   The book (that) I am reading . . .

19. PERSONAL PRONOUNS

SINGULAR

N. *ich*	*du*	*er*	*sie*	*es*	*Sie* (pol.)
G. *meiner*	*deiner*	*seiner*	*ihrer*	*seines*	*Ihrer* (pol.)
D. *mir*	*dir*	*ihm*	*ihr*	*ihm*	*Ihr* (pol.)
A. *mich*	*dich*	*ihm*	*sie*	*es*	*Sie* (pol.)

PLURAL

N. *wir*	*ihr*	*sie*	*Sie*
G. *unserer*	*eurer*	*ihrer*	*Ihrer*
D. *uns*	*euch*	*ihnen*	*Ihnen*
A. *uns*	*euch*	*sie*	*Sie*

Examples:

Wir geben ihr Blumen.
We are giving her flowers.

Du sprichst mit ihm.
You are speaking with him.

Wir sprechen von Ihnen.
We're talking about you (*polite*).

Diese Geschenke sind für dich.
These presents are for you.

20. INDEFINITE PRONOUNS

man	one
jeder(man)	everybody, everyone
jemand	somebody, someone
niemand	nobody
etwas	something, some

Examples:

Jemand steht vor der Tür.
Someone is standing (before) in front of the door.

Es muss etwas geschehen.
Something has to be done.

Man spricht hier nur Deutsch.
One speaks only German here.

21. POSITION OF PRONOUNS

In a German sentence, the subject pronoun usually comes first and the indirect object generally precedes the direct object.

1. *Er   gibt   dem Bruder   einen Roman.*
   Subj.   Indir. Obj.   Dir. Obj.
   He   gives   the brother   a novel.

2. *Sie schenkt der Mutter eine Ledertasche.*
   She gives her mother a leather handbag.

Dem Bruder and *der Mutter* are indirect objects. If we substituted indirect object pronouns for each indirect object, the sentences would read as follows:

Er gibt <u>ihm</u> einen Roman.
He gives <u>him</u> a novel.
(He gives a novel to <u>him</u>.)

Sie schenkt <u>ihr</u> eine Ledertasche.
She gives <u>her</u> a leather handbag.
(She gives a leather handbag to <u>her</u>.)

3. If we substituted a direct object pronoun for each direct object, the two sentences would read as follows:

Er gibt <u>ihn</u> dem Bruder.
He gives it to the brother.

Sie schenkt <u>sie</u> der Mutter.
She gives it to (her) mother.

4. If we substituted pronouns for both objects in each sentence, we would get:

Er gibt ihn ihm.
He gives it to him.

Sie schenkt sie ihr.
She gives it to her.

22. THE NEGATIVE

A sentence is made negative by using the word *nicht*, generally following the verb. Words may come between the verb and *nicht*.

Ich weiß.	I know.
Ich weiß nicht.	I do not know.
Ich weiß es nicht.	I don't know it.

The negative of *ein* is *kein*.

23. ADVERBS

1. Almost all adjectives can be used as adverbs.

2. The comparative of adverbs is formed the same way as that of adjectives.
   The superlative of adverbs is preceded by *am* instead of by the article, and has the ending *-en*.

Fritz ist ein guter Tänzer.
Fritz is a good dancer.

Fritz tanzt gut.
Fritz dances well.

Karl ist ein besserer Tänzer als Fritz.
Karl is a better dancer than Fritz. Karl dances better than Fritz.

Fred Astaire ist der beste Tänzer.
Fred Astaire is the best dancer.

Fred Astaire tanzt am besten.
Fred Astaire dances the best.

3. A few adverbs have an irregular comparative and superlative. Here are the most common ones:

viel	*mehr*	*am meisten*	much, more, most
gern	*lieber*	*am liebsten*	gladly, preferably, most preferably
bald	*eher*	*am ehesten*	soon, sooner, soonest

4. Adverbs of place:

hier	here
dort	there
fort	away
links	on the left
rechts	on the right
vorne	in front of
irgendwo	somewhere
weg	aside, away
hinten	behind, in the back
unten	down(stairs)
drinnen	inside
draußen	outside
überall	everywhere
nirgendwo, nirgends	nowhere
weit	far
nahe	near
dort oben	up there
dort drüben	over there

5. Adverbs of time:

heute	today
bald	soon
ab und zu	now and then
gerade	just
morgen	tomorrow
gestern	yesterday
vorgestern	the day before yesterday
übermorgen	the day after tomorrow
jetzt	now
dann	then
vorher	before
damals	once, at that time
einmal, ehemals	once, formerly
früh	early
spät	late
oft	often
niemals, nie	never
immer, je, jemals	always, ever
lang, lange	long, for a long time
sofort	at once, right away
manchmal	sometimes
noch	still, yet
nicht mehr	no longer, no more
nachher	afterwards

6. Adverbs of manner:

deshalb	therefore
fast	almost
genau	exactly
sehr	very
sogar	even
überhaupt	at all

sowieso	anyway
gut	well
schlecht	ill, badly
so, somit	thus, so
ähnlich	similarly
andererseits	on the other hand
zusammen	together
viel	much
besonders	above all, especially
absichtlich	on purpose, purposely
ausdrücklich	expressly
gewöhnlich	usually

7. Adverbs of quantity or degree:

viel	much, many
genug	enough
auf einmal	all of a sudden
kaum	not much; hardly
wenig	little
mehr	more
nicht mehr	no more
weniger	less
noch mehr	more, even more
zu viel	too much, too many
so viel	so much, so many

8. Particles and intensifiers:

allerdings	certainly
also	so, well
doch	yes, indeed
eben	exactly, just
ja	certainly, to be sure

mal	just, simply
nämlich	namely
nur	only
schon	already, I (we) suppose
wohl	probably
zwar	to be sure

24. PREPOSITIONS

1. With the Genitive:

während	during
wegen	because of
statt, anstatt	instead of
trotz	in spite of

2. With the Accusative:

durch	through, by
für	for
gegen	against, toward
ohne	without
um	round, about, at (time)

3. With the Dative:

aus	from, out of
bei	at, by, near, with
außer	besides, except
mit	with
nach	after, to (a place)
seit	since
von	of, from, by
zu	to, at

4. With the Dative or Accusative:

an	at, to
auf	on, upon, in
hinter	behind
in	in, into, at
neben	beside, near
über	over, across
unter	under, among
vor	before, ago
zwischen	between

25. Contractions

am	for	*an dem*
ans	for	*an das*
im	for	*in dem*
ins	for	*in das*
beim	for	*bei dem*
vom	for	*von dem*
zum	for	*zu dem*
zur	for	*zu der*
ins	for	*in das*
fürs	for	*für das*
aufs	for	*auf das*

26. Prefixes

Many German verbs have certain prefixes. These often correspond to English prefixed verbs (*over*come, *re*make) or phrasal verbs (come out, do over, go in). They are divided into three groups:

1. *The inseparable prefixes,* which remain attached to the verb and are never accented (just like the

English verbs overthrow, understand, etc.). The past participles of these verbs do not take the prefix *ge-*. These prefixes are: *be-, emp-, ent-, er-, ge-, miss-, ver-, zer-, hinter-,* and *wider-*. Ex.: *empfehlen, gefallen, verstehen.*

2. *The separable prefixes,* which are linked to the verb in the compound tenses; in the other tenses they are separated and generally placed at the end of the sentence. Their past participles place the *ge* between the prefix and the verb form. Ex.: *mitgegangen.* They are always accented. The most common such prefixes are: *ab, an, auf, aus, bei, ein, fort, mit, nach, vor, weg, zu, frei, los, wahr,* and *statt.* There are also compound separable prefixes added to verbs, such as: *hinaus, herauf, hinein, herein, zurück,* and *zusammen.* Ex.: *mitkommen, weggehen, zuschliessen.*

Her indicates a movement toward the person who is speaking:

Kommen Sie herunter!   Come down.

Hin indicates a movement away from the person speaking:

Geh hinaus!   Go out!

The separable prefix is so important in the sentence that the verb is sometimes omitted in short statements:

Herein!   (Come) in!

3. Some prefixes are sometimes separable and sometimes inseparable, depending on the meaning of the verb. They are:

wieder, voll, durch, um, unter, über.

Examples: *Der Schüler wiederholt seine Lektion.*
                  The student repeats his lesson.

Holen Sie das wieder!
Take it back!

Die Polizei hat das ganze Hause durchsucht.
The police searched whole house.

27. THE TENSES OF THE INDICATIVE

SIMPLE TENSES

1. The present tense expresses an uncompleted action in the present. It has several English translations:

ich spreche	I speak, I am speaking, I do speak
ich esse	I eat, I am eating, I do eat

Remember that regular verbs are conjugated with a set of endings, and irregular verbs take the same endings but also have a vowel change.

2. The simple past (narrative past) is mostly used in writing. It sometimes indicates an action that was happening when something else happened. The weak verbs add the following endings to their stems: *te, test, te, tet, ten.*

The strong verbs usually change their stem vowels. The first and third person singular have no ending. The others are as in the present.

Er schlief, als Hans eintrat.	He was sleeping when John entered.
Er sprach oft davon.	He often spoke about that.
Es war dunkel, als er ausging.	It was night (dark) when he went out.

COMPOUND TENSES

1. The future tense is formed by using the auxiliary *werden* plus the infinitive of the verb. It indicates a future action:

Er wird morgen ankommen.	He'll arrive tomorrow.
Ich werde ihm morgen schreiben.	I'll write him (to him) tomorrow.

2. The conversational past tense (also known as the present perfect) is formed by adding the past participle to the present indicative of *haben* or, in some cases, *sein*. It is usually used in spoken German to indicate a past action.

Er hat mir nichts gesagt.	He didn't tell me anything.
Ich habe meine Arbeit beendet.	I finished my work. I have finished my work.
Haben Sie ihn gesehen?	Have you seen him? Did you see him?
Sie sind angekommen.	They arrived.

3. The pluperfect tense is formed by adding the past participle to the imperfect of *haben* or, in some cases, *sein:*

Er hatte es getan.	He had done it.
Als ich zurückkam, war er schon fort gewesen.	When I came back, he had already left.

4. The future perfect tense is formed by adding the past participle to the future of *haben* or, in some cases, *sein.* It translates into the English future perfect:

Er wird bald seine Arbeit beendet haben.	He will soon have finished his work.
In zwei Wochen wird er schon in Spanien gewesen sein.	In two weeks he already will have been in Spain.

Sometimes it indicates probability:

Er wird es ihm zweifellos gesagt haben.	No doubt he will have told him.
Er wird krank gewesen sein.	He probably was sick.
Ich werde mich geirrt haben.	I must have been mistaken.

HABEN AND *SEIN* IN THE COMPOUND PAST TENSES

1. Most compound past tenses are made up of *haben* and the past participle. Some verbs use *sein* instead, namely intransitive verbs of motion and verbs that express a state of being or a change of state.

Er hat gesprochen.   He has spoken.
Sie haben gegessen.   You have eaten.

Ich habe ein Geschenk   I received a present.
  erhalten.
Er hat zuviel getrunken.   He drank too much.

2. The most common intransitive verbs conjugated
   with the verb *sein* are:
   *gehen, ankommen, absteigen, eintreten, ein-
   steigen, sterben, abreisen, bleiben, kommen,
   fallen, zurückkommen, laufen, geboren* and the
   auxiliaries *sein* and *werden*.

Examples:

Ich bin gekommen.   I have come.
Er ist angekommen.   He has come.
Wir sind abgereist.   We have left.
Sie ist geboren.   She was born.

Er ist durch ganz Europa gefahren.
He traveled through Europe.

The verb *fahren* can also be used as a transitive verb,
requiring a direct object. In that case it is conjugated
with *haben*.

Er hat den Mercedes nach Hamburg gefahren.
He drove the Mercedes to Hamburg (the Mercedes is
the direct object of the verb, *fahren*).

28. THE PAST PARTICIPLE

The first syllable of the past participle of the weak
and strong verbs is usually *ge* when the verbs have no

prefix whatsoever. If they do have a separable prefix, then the syllable *ge* stands between the prefix and the past participle. If the verbs have an inseparable prefix, the past participle has no additional *ge*. Most verbs that end in *-ieren* have no *ge* in the past participle.

Infinitive	*Past Participle*
(strong verb without prefix)	
ziehen to pull	*gezogen*
(strong with a separable prefix)	
vorziehen to prefer	*vorgezogen*
(weak without prefix)	
warten to wait	*gewartet*
(weak with a separable prefix)	
abwarten to wait and see	*abgewartet*
(strong verb with an inseparable prefix)	
verlieren to lose	*verloren*
(weak with an inseparable prefix)	
entdecken to discover	*entdeckt*
(*-ieren* verb)	
studieren to study	*studiert*

In the weak verbs, the past participle ends in *t* or *et*.

arbeiten	*gearbeitet*
lernen	*gelernt*

In the strong verbs the past participle ends in *en,* but the vowel of the infinitive stem generally changes. Therefore, when you study the verbs, do not forget to memorize the past participle as well as the other tenses. See table of irregular verbs, page 317.

29. USE OF THE AUXILIARIES *HABEN* AND *SEIN*

Notice that most verbs form the perfect, pluperfect, and future perfect with the auxiliary *haben:*

Ich habe gesehen.	I have seen.
Du hast gesehen.	You have seen.
Ich habe mich gewaschen.	I have washed myself.

However, quite a few verbs, usually intransitive, form these tenses with the auxiliary *sein:*

1. The verbs *sein, werden,* and *bleiben.*

2. Verbs indicating a change of place; chiefly, verbs of motion, such as *gehen, kommen, eilen, fallen, fließen, laufen, reisen, rollen, steigen, sinken, aufstehen, fliegen, begegnen,* etc.

3. Verbs indicating a change in the condition of a thing or a person, such as *aufwachen, einschlafen, wachsen, aufbleiben, verblühen, vergehen, verschwinden, sterben, erhalten, platzen,* and *erkranken.*

30. THE SUBJUNCTIVE

Present subjunctive of *haben, sein,* and *werden*—"to have," "to be," and "to become":

ich habe (hätte)	*ich sei*	*ich werde (würde)*
du habest	*due seiest*	*du werdest*
er, sie, es habe	*er, sie, es sei*	*er, sie, es werde*
wir haben (hätten)	*wir seien*	*wir werden (würden)*

ihr habet	*ihr seiet*	*ihr werdet*
Sie, sie haben	*Sie, sie seien*	*Sie, sie werden*
(hätten)		*(würden)*

The endings of both weak and strong verbs are *e, est, e, en, et, en.* The strong verbs keep the stem vowel in each person.

When the present subjunctive verb forms are identical to the indicative, the imperfect subjunctive verb forms can be used: *Er sagte, dass ich ihn nicht begrüsst hätte* (instead of *begrüsst habe*).

IMPERFECT

ich hätte	*ich wäre*	*ich würde*
du hättest	*du wärest*	*du würdest*
er, sie, es hätte	*er, sie, es wäre*	*er, sie, es würde*
wir hätten	*wir wären*	*wir würden*
ihr hättet	*ihr wäret*	*ihr würdet*
Sie, sie hätten	*Sie, sie wären*	*Sie, sie würden*

Notice that the imperfect tense of the weak verbs is identical in both the indicative and subjunctive. When this occurs, the structure *würde* and a main verb are used. The substitution is therefore with the present conditional tense. Examples:

Indirect Discourse:
Er sagte, dass er es nicht lernen würde.
He said that he would not learn it.

Unreal Conditions:
Wenn er mit mir ins Kino ginge, dann würde ich mich freuen.
If he went with me to the movies, I'd be happy.

Strong verbs have the same endings as the present subjunctive, but take the *Umlaut* if their stem vowel is *a*, *e*, or *u*.

ich tat	I did	*ich täte*	that I did

The past tenses—the past, the pluperfect, and the future—are formed with the past participle of the indicative of the verb plus the auxiliaries *haben, sein,* and *werden* in their respective subjunctive forms. The subjunctive is used to express doubt, wish, eventuality, and unreality. It is also used:

1. in indirect discourse

2. after certain conjunctions and expressions, such as:

als ob	as if
es sei denn, dass	unless

Examples:

Er glaubte, dass er käme.	He believed that he was coming.
Wir helfen ihm, damit er gesund werde.	We help him, so that he may be healthy again.

3. A contrary-to-fact condition in reference to the present or a future time is usually introduced by the conjunction *wenn* (if) and the imperfect subjunctive followed by the result clause in the present conditional:

Example: *Wenn er morgen käme, dann würde ich mit ihm in die Stadt fahren.*

> If he came tomorrow, I would go to the
> city with him.

The "if" clause (*wenn* clause) has transposed word
order (verb in last position), and the main clause has
inverted word order (subject after the verb) whenever
it stands after the subordinate clause. The above sentence may also be expressed as follows:

a. *Ich würde mit ihm in die Stadt fahren, wenn er
   morgen käme.*

b. *Ich führe mit ihm in die Stadt, wenn er käme.*

c. *Ich würde mit ihm in die Stadt fahren, wenn er
   kommen würde.*

Sentence "c" is employed less frequently, since it
employs one conditional verb form in each clause.

4. To express a wish:

Mögen Sie glücklich sein!   May you be happy!
Wärest du doch hier!   Wish you were here!

5. Unreal conditions in reference to past time are
   formed by the past perfect subjunctive in the
   wenn clause, followed by the conditional perfect.
   In modern German, the conditional perfect is
   usually replaced by the pluperfect subjunctive.
   Note that the helping verb may be a form of
   haben or *sein*. Examples:

*Wenn ich Zeit gehabt hätte, wäre ich mit dir zum
Strand gekommen.*
If I had had the time, I would have come to the beach
with you.

Wenn ich die Bahn genommen hätte, (dann) hätte ich ihn rechtzeitig getroffen.
If I had taken the train, (then) I would have met him on time.

31. THE CONDITIONAL

The conditional is most often formed with the auxiliary *werden* in its imperfect subjunctive form.

ich würde	*wir würden*
du würdest	*ihr würdet*
er, sie, es würde	*sie (Sie) würden*

It is generally used in connection with the conjunction *wenn* instead of the subjunctive to express a condition.

Wenn wir Geld hätten, würden wir eine lange Reise machen.
If we had any money, we would go on a long trip.

The past conditional is formed like the past future, but using *würde* instead of *werde*.

32. THE PASSIVE VOICE

The passive voice is formed with the past participle of the verb and the auxiliary *werden* used in the present and in the past.

Die Erde wird von der Sonne beleuchtet.

Earth is lit by the Sun.
"By" is translated by the German *von* (plus dative):

Amerika wurde von Kolumbus entdeckt.
America was discovered by Columbus.

In the past tense (perfect tense) the participle of the auxiliary *werden, geworden,* drops the prefix *ge-* and becomes simply *worden.*
Example:

Das Buch ist von ihm geschrieben worden.
The book has been written by him.

Er war von ihr gesehen worden.
He had been seen by her.

33. THE IMPERATIVE

The imperative of verbs is formed from the present indicative tense.

2nd person singular: Drop the ending *-n* from the infinitive. However, strong verbs that change the vowel *e* to *i* or *ie* in the present indicative form their imperative by dropping the *-st* from this tense.

Lerne! (du lernst)
Nimm! (du nimmst)

1st person plural: Invert the infinitive form with the personal pronoun.

Singen wir! (wir singen)

2nd person plural: Simply insert the second person plural of the present indicative tense and omit the pronoun.

Gebt! (ihr gebt)

Polite 2nd person: Same as the 1st person plural.

Nehmen Sie! Geben Sie!

To express the imperative, the verb *lassen* can also be used; it corresponds to the English "let."

Example:

Lassen Sie das sein!   Let it be!

Imperative of *sein* and *haben:*

sein to be	*haben* to have
sei (fam.)! be!	*habe* (fam.)! have!
seid (fam. pl.)! be!	*habt* (fam. pl.)! have!
seien wir! let us be!	*haben wir!* let us have!
seien Sie! (pol.) be!	*haben Sie!* have! (pol.)

34. THE INFINITIVE

The infinitive is usually preceded by *zu* when used in connection with another verb; however, *zu* is in most instances omitted when the infinitive is used in connection with the following verbs:

werden, können, dürfen, wollen, mögen, müssen, sollen, lassen, machen, hören, sehen, heißen, helfen, lehren, lernen

Examples:

Er bittet ihn, den Brief zu schreiben.	He asks him to write the letter.
Ich werde ihr schreiben.	I shall write to her (future).
Ich helfe ihm den Wagen waschen.	I'm helping him wash the car.
Er lehrt uns schwimmen.	He teaches us to swim.

The infinitive is also used after certain prepositions in connection with *zu:*

um . . . zu (in order to)
ohne . . . zu (without)   the *zu* can be used alone
anstatt . . . zu (instead of)

Examples:

Wir gehen zur Schule, um zu lernen.	We go to school to learn.
Ich kann nicht essen, ohne etwas zu trinken.	I cannot eat without drinking something.
Er faulenzt, anstatt uns zu helfen.	He is lazy instead of helping us.

Words with a separable prefix have the *zu* between the prefix and the infinitive.

Example: *aufmachen*

Er bittet ihn, die Tür aufzumachen.
He asks him to open the door.

35. COMPLEMENTS OF VERBS

Verbs can be followed by:

    a. a preposition: Their complement should be put in the case required by the preposition; for example: *bedecken mit*—"to cover with" (always dative)

Der Tisch ist mit Staub bedeckt.	The table is covered with dust.

b. an object without a preposition: The genitive, accusative, or dative is used, depending on the verb.

Examples:

Er ist des Mordes beschuldigt. (Genitive)	He is accused of murder.
Sie glauben mir nicht. (Dative)	You don't believe me.
Wir lieben ihn. (Accusative)	We love him.

36. CHANGES IN THE NORMAL SEQUENCE OF WORDS WITHIN A SENTENCE

1. *By Transposition:*   putting the verb at the end of a sentence.

In a subordinate clause, that is, a clause beginning with a relative pronoun or a subordinating conjunction, the verb is always placed at the end of the clause.

Die Sprache, die wir lernen, ist Deutsch.
The language that we are learning is German.

Ich kann nicht sehen, weil es dunkel ist.
I cannot see because it is dark.

Ich glaube, dass das Essen in diesem Restaurant gut ist.
I believe that the food in this restaurant is good.

Notice also that a comma is always used before the relative pronoun or conjunction. If the verb is in a compound tense, the *auxiliary* is placed at the end of the sentence.

Ich glaube nicht, dass es morgen regnen wird.
I do not believe that it will rain tomorrow.

In the case of an indirect question or subordinate clause introduced by an interrogative word, such as the pronouns *wer, was,* or *welcher,* or the adverbs *wo, wann,* etc., or the conjunction *ob,* the verb is also placed at the end of the sentence.

Wir wissen nicht, ob er morgen kommt.
We don't know whether he is coming tomorrow.

Können Sie mir sagen, wie weit es von hier bis zum Bahnhof ist?
Can you tell me how far it is from here to the train station?

2. *By Inversion:* putting the verb before the subject. The inversion is necessary:

   a. Usually when a question is asked.

(affirmative)
Er schreibt den Brief.   He writes the letter.
  (interrogative)
Schreibt er den Brief?   Does he write the letter?

   b. In the main clause of any sentence when it is preceded by a subordinate clause.

Wenn wir die Augen schließen, können wir nicht sehen.
If we close our eyes, we cannot see.

   c. Whenever the main clause opens with a word other than the subject.

Morgen werden die Kinder ins Kino gehen.
Tomorrow the children will go to the movies.

Here we have inversion because the sentence does not start with its subject, *die Kinder,* but with an adverb: *morgen.*

Die Kinder werden morgen ins Kino gehen.
The children will go to the movies tomorrow.

The above does not take any inversion because the sentence is started by its subject, *die Kinder.*

37. INDIRECT DISCOURSE

When you want to tell a story or make an indirect quotation in German, you use indirect discourse.

Direct Discourse:
Hans sagt: "Ich gehe zum Bahnhof."
Hans says: "I am going to the station."

Indirect Discourse:
Hans sagt, dass er zum Bahnhof gehe.
Hans says that he is going to the station.

Imperfect:
Hans sagte, dass er zum Bahnhof ginge.
Hans said that he was going to the station.

NOTES

1. The subjunctive should be used (even though you can use the indicative, as many Germans do).

2. The conjunction *dass*—"that"—can be used or omitted.

If it is used, the verb should be placed at the end of the sentence, as in the regular case of transposition.

Er sagt, dass er zum Bahnhof gehe.

3. If it is omitted, the order of the words remains unchanged.

Hans sagt, er gehe zum Bahnhof.
Hans says he is going to the station.

Hans sagte, er ginge zum Bahnhof.
Hans said he was going to the station.

The tense of the verb in indirect discourse does not affect the tense of the inflected verb form in the indirect statement. Examples:

Er berichtet, er nehme (nähme) den Bus. (action in present)
Er berichtet, er habe (hätte) den Bus genommen. (action in past)
Er erzählt uns, er sei (wäre) eine Meile gelaufen. (action in past with an intransitive verb)
Er berichtet, er werde (würde) den Bus nehmen. (action in future)

The subjunctive of indirect discourse is normally used after the following verbs: *behaupten* (to claim), *berichten* (to report), *erklären* (to explain), *glauben* (to believe), *meinen* (to mean), *sagen* (to say), and *schreiben* (to write).

4. Notice that in both instances, a comma is used at the beginning of the second clause.

5. The following sequence of tenses is generally observed in expressing conditional sentences:

For Real Conditions:

The If Clause (*Wenn-Clause*)	Result Clause
Present Indicative	Future or Present Indicative

For Unreal Conditions in Reference to Present or Future Time:

The If Clause (*Wenn-Clause*)	Result Clause
Imperfect Subjunctive	Present Conditional or Imperfect Subjunctive

For Unreal Conditions in Reference to Past Time:

The If Clause (*Wenn-Clause*)	Result Clause
Pluperfect Subjunctive	Pluperfect Subjunctive or Conditional Perfect

38. CONSTRUCTION OF THE SENTENCE (SUMMARY)

1. Main Clauses or Simple Sentences:

   a. Affirmative sentence:

Das Buch ist rot.   The book is red.

   b. Interrogative:

Ist das Buch rot?   Is the book red?

   c. Negative:

Das Buch ist nicht rot.   The book is not red.

d. Past tenses:

Ich habe ein Gedicht gelernt.	I have learned a poem.
Ich lernte ein Gedicht.	I learned a poem.
Ich hatte ein Gedicht gelernt.	I had learned a poem.

e. Infinitive:

Sie brauchen das nicht zu wissen.	You do not need to know that.

2. Subordinate clauses:

a. Transposition:

Ich sehe, dass das Buch rot ist.	I see that the book is red.
Ich kenne den Schüler, der das Gedicht liest.	I know the student who is reading the poem.

b. Inversion:

Wenn das Wetter schön ist, gehe ich gern spazieren.
   (The second clause has inverted word order).
When the weather is fine, I like to take a walk.

c. Indirect discourse:

Sie antwortet ihm, dass sie eine Schülerin $\begin{cases} sei. \\ ist. \end{cases}$

Sie antwortet ihm, sie $\begin{cases} sei \\ ist \end{cases}$ *eine Schülerin.*

She answers (him) that she is a pupil.

39. THE MOST COMMON IRREGULAR VERBS

sein   to be

INFINITIVE

PRESENT	PAST
sein	*gewesen sein*

PARTICIPLES

PRESENT	PAST
seiend	*gewesen*

INDICATIVE

PRESENT	CONVERSATIONAL PAST
ich bin	*bin gewesen*
du bist	*bist gewesen*
er, sie, es ist	*ist gewesen*
wir sind	*sind gewesen*
ihr seid	*seid gewesen*
sie (Sie) sind	*sind gewesen*

SIMPLE PAST	PAST PERFECT
ich war	*war gewesen*
du warst	*warst gewesen*
er, sie, es war	*war gewesen*
wir waren	*waren gewesen*
ihr wart	*wart gewesen*
sie (Sie) waren	*waren gewesen*

FUTURE	PAST FUTURE
ich werde sein	*werde gewesen sein*
du wirst sein	*wirst gewesen sein*
er, sie, es wird sein	*wird gewesen sein*
wir werden sein	*werden gewesen sein*
ihr werdet sein	*werdet gewesen sein*
sie (Sie) werden sein	*werden gewesen sein*

CONDITIONAL

PRESENT	CONDITIONAL PERFECT
ich würde sein	würde gewesen sein
du würdest sein	würdest gewesen sein
er, sie, es würde sein	würde gewesen sein
wir würden sein	würden gewesen sein
ihr würdet sein	würdet gewesen sein
sie (Sie) würden sein	würden gewesen sein

IMPERATIVE

sei!
seien wir!
seid!
seien Sie!

SUBJUNCTIVE

PRESENT	PRESENT PERFECT
ich sei	ich sei gewesen
du seiest	du seiest gewesen
er, sie, es sei	er sei gewesen
wir seien	wir seien gewesen
ihr seiet	ihr seiet gewesen
sie (Sie) seien	sie seien gewesen

IMPERFECT	PAST PERFECT
ich wäre	ich wäre gewesen
du wärest	du wärest gewesen
er, sie, es wäre	er wäre gewesen
wir wären	wir wären gewesen
ihr wäret	ihr wäret gewesen
sie (Sie) wären	sie (Sie) wären gewesen

haben   to have

INFINITIVE

PRESENT
haben

PAST
gehabt haben

PARTICIPLES

PRESENT
habend

PAST
gehabt

INDICATIVE

PRESENT	CONVERSATIONAL PAST
ich habe	*habe gehabt*
du hast	*hast gehabt*
er, sie, es hat	*hat gehabt*
wir haben	*haben gehabt*
ihr habt	*habt gehabt*
sie, Sie haben	*haben gehabt*

SIMPLE PAST	PAST PERFECT
ich hatte	*hatte gehabt*
du hattest	*hattest gehabt*
er hatte	*hatte gehabt*
wir hatten	*hatten gehabt*
ihr hattet	*hattet gehabt*
sie (Sie) hatten	*hatten gehabt*

FUTURE	FUTURE PERFECT
ich werde haben	*werde gehabt haben*
du wirst haben	*wirst gehabt haben*
er, sie, es wird haben	*wird gehabt haben*
wir werden haben	*werden gehabt haben*
ihr werdet haben	*werdet gehabt haben*
sie (Sie) werden haben	*werden gehabt haben*

CONDITIONAL	PAST CONDITIONAL
ich würde haben	würde gehabt haben
du würdest haben	würdest gehabt haben
er, sie, es würde haben	würde gehabt haben
wir würden haben	würden gehabt haben
ihr würdet haben	würdet gehabt haben
sie (Sie) würden haben	würden gehabt haben

IMPERATIVE

Habe!
Haben wir!
Habt!
Haben Sie!

SUBJUNCTIVE

When the subjunctive forms are identical to the indicative forms, you have to use an alternate subjunctive form. These alternates are in parentheses.

PRESENT	PAST
ich habe	ich habe (hätte) gehabt
du habest	du habest gehabt
er, sie, es habe	er, sie, es habe gehabt
wir haben	wir haben (hätten) gehabt
ihr habet	ihr habet gehabt
sie (Sie) haben	sie (Sie) haben (hätten) gehabt

IMPERFECT	PAST PERFECT
ich hätte	ich hätte gehabt
du hättest	du hättest gehabt
er, Sie, es hätte	er, Sie, es hätte gehabt
wir hätten	wir hätten gehabt
ihr hättet	ihr hättet gehabt
sie (Sie) hätten	sie (Sie) hätten gehabt

werden   to become

INFINITIVE

PRESENT	PAST
werden	*geworden sein*

PARTICIPLES

PRESENT	PAST
werdend	*geworden*

INDICATIVE

PRESENT	CONVERSATIONAL PAST
ich werde	*bin geworden*
du wirst	*bist geworden*
er, sie, es wird	*ist geworden*
wir werden	*sind geworden*
ihr werdet	*seid geworden*
sie (Sie) werden	*sind geworden*

SIMPLE PAST	PAST PERFECT
ich wurde	*war geworden*
du wurdest	*warst geworden*
er, sie, es wurde	*war geworden*
wir wurden	*waren geworden*
ihr wurdet	*wart geworden*
sie (Sie) wurden	*waren geworden*

FUTURE	FUTURE PERFECT
ich werde werden	*werde geworden sein*
du wirst werden	*wirst geworden sein*
er, sie, es wird werden	*wird geworden sein*
wir werden werden	*werden geworden sein*
ihr werdet werden	*werdet geworden sein*
sie (Sie) werden werden	*werden geworden sein*

CONDITIONAL	CONDITIONAL PERFECT
ich würde werden	*würde geworden sein*
du würdest werden	*würdest geworden sein*
er, sie, es würde werden	*würde geworden sein*
wir würden werden	*würden geworden sein*
ihr würdet werden	*würdet geworden sein*
sie (Sie) würden werden	*würden geworden sein*

IMPERATIVE

werde!
werden wir!
werdet!
werden Sie!

SUBJUNCTIVE

PRESENT	PRESENT PERFECT
ich werde (würde)	*ich sei geworden*
du werdest	*du seiest gewordeen*
er, sei, es werde	*er, sie, es sei geworden*
wir werden (würden)	*wir seien geworden*
ihr werdet	*ihr seiet geworden*
sie (Sie) werden (würden)	*sie (Sie) seien geworden*

IMPERFECT	PAST PERFECT
ich würde	*ich wäre geworden*
du würdest	*du wärest geworden*
er, sie, es würde	*er, sie, es wäre geworden*
wir würden	*wir wären geworden*
ihr würdet	*ihr wäret geworden*
sie (Sie) würden	*sie (Sie) wären geworden*

können to be able to

INFINITIVE

PRESENT
können

PAST
gekonnt haben

PARTICIPLES

PRESENT
könnend

PAST
gekonnt (können)*

INDICATIVE

PRESENT	CONVERSATIONAL PAST
ich kann	*habe gekonnt**
du kannst	*hast gekonnt*
er, sie, es kann	*hat gekonnt*
wir können	*haben gekonnt*
ihr könnt	*habt gekonnt*
sie (Sie) können	*haben gekonnt*

SIMPLE PAST	PAST PERFECT
ich konnte	*hatte gekonnt*
du konntest	*hattest gekonnt*
er, sie, es konnte	*hatte gekonnt*
wir konnten	*hatten gekonnt*
ihr konntet	*hattet gekonnt*
sie (Sie) konnten	*hatten gekonnt*

* The modal verbs *können, dürfen, müssen, sollen,* and *wollen* appear in the past in their infinitive forms when used with another verb, for example: *er muss es tun* (he has to do it) becomes *er hat es tun müssen* (he had to do it), with a double infinitive, in the past.

FUTURE	FUTURE PERFECT
ich werde können	werde gekonnt haben
du wirst können	wirst gekonnt haben
er, sie, es wird können	wird gekonnt haben
wir werden können	werden gekonnt haben
ihr werdet können	werdet gekonnt haben
sie (Sie) werden können	werden gekonnt haben

CONDITIONAL	CONDITIONAL PERFECT
ich würde können	würde gekonnt haben
du würdest können	würdest gekonnt haben
er, sie, es würde können	würde gekonnt haben
wir würden können	würden gekonnt haben
ihr würdet können	würdet gekonnt haben
sie (Sie) würden können	würden gekonnt haben

SUBJUNCTIVE

PRESENT	PRESENT PERFECT
ich könne	ich (habe) hätte gekonnt
du könnest	du habest gekonnt
er, sie, es könne	er habe gekonnt
wir können (könnten)	wir (haben) hätten gekonnt
ihr könnet	ihr habet gekonnt
sie (Sie) können (könnten)	sie (Sie) (haben) hätten gekonnt

IMPERFECT	PAST PERFECT
ich könnte	ich hätte gekonnt
du könntest	du hättest gekonnt
er, sie, es könnte	er, sie, es hätte gekonnt
wir könnten	wir hätten gekonnt
ihr könntet	ihr hättet gekonnt
sie (Sie) könnten	sie (Sie) hätten gekonnt

dürfen   to be allowed to

INFINITIVE

PRESENT
dürfen

PAST
gedurft haben

PARTICIPLES

PRESENT
dürfend

PAST
gedurft (dürfen)*

INDICATIVE

PRESENT	CONVERSATIONAL PAST
ich darf	*habe gedurft**
du darfst	*hast gedurft*
er, sie, es darf	*hat gedurft*
wir dürfen	*haben gedurft*
ihr dürft	*habt gedurft*
sie, Sie dürfen	*haben gedurft*

SIMPLE PAST	PAST PERFECT
ich durfte	*hatte gedurft*
du durftest	*hattest gedurft*
er, sie, es durfte	*hatte gedurft*
wir durften	*hatten gedurft*
ihr durftet	*hattet gedurft*
sie (Sie) durften	*hatten gedurft*

FUTURE	FUTURE PERFECT
ich werde dürfen	*werde gedurft haben*
du wirst dürfen	*wirst gedurft haben*
er, sie, es wird dürfen	*wird gedurft haben*
wir werden dürfen	*werden gedurft haben*
ihr werdet dürfen	*werdet gedurft haben*
sie (Sie) werden dürfen	*werden gedurft haben*

* See note under *können.*

CONDITIONAL	CONDITIONAL PERFECT
ich würde dürfen	*würde gedurft haben*
du würdest dürfen	*würdest gedurft haben*
er, sie, es würde dürfen	*würde gedurft haben*
wir würden dürfen	*würden gedurft haben*
ihr würdet dürfen	*würdet gedurft haben*
sie (Sie) würden dürfen	*würden gedurft haben*

SUBJUNCTIVE

PRESENT	PRESENT PERFECT
ich dürfe	*ich habe (hätte) gedurft*
du dürfest	*du habest gedurft*
er, sie, es dürfe	*er habe gedurft*
wir dürfen (dürften)	*wir haben (hätten) gedurft*
ihr dürfet	*ihr habet gedurft*
sie (Sie) dürfen (dürften)	*sie (Sie) haben (hätten) gedurft.*

IMPERFECT	PAST PERFECT
ich dürfte	*ich hätte gedurft*
du dürftest	*du hättest gedurft*
er, sie, es dürfte	*er hätte gedurft*
wir dürften	*wir hätten gedurft*
ihr dürftet	*ihr hättet gedurft*
sie (Sie) dürften	*sie hätten gedurft*

müssen   to be obliged to, to have to

INFINITIVE

PRESENT	PAST
müssen	*gemusst haben*

PARTICIPLES

PRESENT	PAST
müssend	*gemusst (müssen)**

INDICATIVE

PRESENT	CONVERSATIONAL PAST
ich muss	*habe gemusst**
du musst	*hast gemusst*
er, sie, es muss	*hat gemusst*
wir müssen	*haben gemusst*
ihr müsst	*habt gemusst*
sie, (Sie) müssen	*haben gemusst*

SIMPLE PAST	PAST PERFECT
ich musste	*hatte gemusst*
du musstest	*hattest gemusst*
er, sie, es musste	*hatte gemusst*
wir mussten	*hatten gemusst*
ihr musstet	*hattet gemusst*
sie (Sie) mussten	*hatten gemusst*

FUTURE	FUTURE PERFECT
ich werde müssen	*werde gemusst haben*
du wirst müssen	*wirst gemusst haben*
er, sie, es wird müssen	*wird gemusst haben*
wir werden müssen	*werden gemusst haben*
ihr werdet müssen	*werdet gemusst haben*
sie (Sie) werden müssen	*werden gemusst haben*

CONDITIONAL	CONDITIONAL PERFECT
ich würde müssen	*würde gemusst haben*
du würdest müssen	*würdest gemusst haben*

* See note under *können*.

er, sie, es würde müssen	*würde gemusst haben*
wir würden müssen	*würden gemusst haben*
ihr würdet müssen	*würdet gemusst haben*
sie (Sie) würden müssen	*würden gemusst haben*

SUBJUNCTIVE

PRESENT	PRESENT PERFECT
ich müsse	*ich habe (hätte) gemusst*
du müssest	*du habest gemusst*
er, sie, es müsse	*er, sie, es habe gemusst*
wir müssen (müssten)	*wir haben (hätten) gemusst*
ihr müsset	*ihr habet gemusst*
sie, Sie müssen (müssten)	*sie, Sie haben (hätten) gemusst*

IMPERFECT	PAST PERFECT
ich müsste	*ich hätte gemusst*
du müsstest	*du hättest gemusst*
er, sie, es müsse	*er, sie, es hätte gemusst*
wir müssten	*wir hätten gemusst*
ihr müsstet	*ihr hättet gemusst*
sie, Sie müssten	*sie (Sie) hätten gemusst*

wissen   to know

INFINITIVE

PRESENT	PAST
wissen	*gewusst haben*

PARTICIPLES

PRESENT	PAST
wissend	*gewusst*

INDICATIVE

PRESENT	CONVERSATIONAL PAST
ich weiß	*habe gewusst*
du weißt	*hast gewusst*
er, sie, es weiß	*hat gewusst*
wir wissen	*haben gewusst*
ihr wisst	*habt gewusst*
sie, Sie wissen	*haben gewusst*

SIMPLE PAST	PAST PERFECT
ich wusste	*hatte gewusst*
du wusstest	*hattest gewusst*
er, sie, es wusste	*hatte gewusst*
wir wussten	*hatten gewusst*
ihr wusstet	*hattet gewusst*
sie (Sie) wussten	*hatten gewusst*

FUTURE	FUTURE PERFECT
ich werde wissen	*werde gewusst haben*
du wirst wissen	*wirst gewusst haben*
er, sie, es wird wissen	*wird gewusst haben*
wir werden wissen	*werden gewusst haben*
ihr werdet wissen	*werdet gewusst haben*
sie (Sie) werden wissen	*werden gewusst haben*

CONDITIONAL	CONDITIONAL PERFECT
ich würde wissen	*würde gewusst haben*
du würdest wissen	*würdest gewusst haben*
er, sie, es würde wissen	*würde gewusst haben*
wir würden wissen	*würden gewusst haben*
ihr würdet wissen	*würdet gewusst haben*
sie (Sie) würden wissen	*würden gewusst haben*

IMPERATIVE

wisse!
wissen wir!

wisst!
wissen Sie!

SUBJUNCTIVE

PRESENT	PRESENT PERFECT
ich wisse	*ich habe hätte gewusst*
du wissest	*du habest gewusst*
er, sie, es wisse	*er habe gewusst*
wir wissen (wüssten)	*wir haben (hätten) gewusst*
ihr wisset	*ihr habet gewusst*
sie (Sie) wissen (wüssten)	*sie (Sie) haben (hätten) gewusst*

IMPERFECT	PAST PERFECT
ich wüsste	*ich hätte gewusst*
du wüsstest	*du hättest gewusst*
er, sie, es wüsste	*er, sie, es hätte gewusst*
wir wüssten	*wir hätten gewusst*
ihr wüsstet	*ihr hättet gewusst*
sie (Sie) wüssten	*sie (Sie) hätten gewusst*

gehen   to go

INFINITIVE

PRESENT	PAST
gehen	*gegangen sein*

PARTICIPLES

PRESENT	PAST
gehend	*gegangen*

INDICATIVE

PRESENT	CONVERSATIONAL PAST
ich gehe	*bin gegangen*
du gehst	*bist gegangen*

er, sie, es geht	*ist gegangen*
wir gehen	*sind gegangen*
ihr geht	*seid gegangen*
sie (Sie) gehen	*sind gegangen*

SIMPLE PAST	PAST PERFECT
ich ging	*war gegangen*
du gingst	*warst gegangen*
er, sie, es ging	*war gegangen*
wir gingen	*waren gegangen*
ihr gingt	*wart gegangen*
sie (Sie) gingen	*waren gegangen*

FUTURE	FUTURE PERFECT
ich werde gehen	*werde gegangen sein*
du wirst gehen	*wirst gegangen sein*
er, sie, es wird gehen	*wird gegangen sein*
wir werden gehen	*werden gegangen sein*
ihr werdet gehen	*werdet gegangen sein*
sie (Sie) werden gehen	*werden gegangen sein*

CONDITIONAL	CONDITIONAL PERFECT
ich würde gehen	*würde gegangen sein*
du würdest gehen	*würdest gegangen sein*
er, sie, es würde gehen	*würde gegangen sein*
wir würden gehen	*würden gegangen sein*
ihr würdet gehen	*würdet gegangen sein*
sie (Sie) würden gehen	*würden gegangen sein*

IMPERATIVE

gehe!
gehen wir!
geht!
gehen Sie!

SUBJUNCTIVE

PRESENT	PRESENT PERFECT
ich (gehe) ginge	*ich sei gegangen*
du gehest	*du seiest gegangen*
er, sie, es gehe	*er sei gegangen*
wir (gehen) gingen	*wir seien gegangen*
ihr gehet	*ihr seid gegangen*
sie (Sie) (gehen) gingen	*sie (Sie) seien gegangen*

IMPERFECT	PAST PERFECT
ich ginge	*ich wäre gegangen*
du gingest	*du wärest gegangen*
er, sie, es ginge	*er wäre gegangen*
wir gingen	*wir wären gegangen*
ihr ginget	*ihr wäret gegangen*
sie (Sie) gingen	*sie wären gegangen*

kommen   to come

INFINITIVE

PRESENT	PAST
kommen	*gekommen sein*

PARTICIPLES

PRESENT	PAST
kommend	*gekommen*

INDICATIVE

PRESENT	CONVERSATIONAL PAST
ich komme	*bin gekommen*
du kommst	*bist gekommen*
er, sie, es kommt	*ist gekommen*
wir kommen	*sind gekommen*

ihr kommt	*seid gekommen*
sie, Sie kommen	*sind gekommen*

SIMPLE PAST	PAST PERFECT
ich kam	*war gekommen*
du kamst	*warst gekommen*
er, sie, es kam	*war gekommen*
wir kamen	*waren gekommen*
ihr kamt	*wart gekommen*
sie (Sie) kamen	*waren gekommen*

FUTURE	FUTURE PERFECT
ich werde kommen	*werde gekommen sein*
du wirst kommen	*wirst gekommen sein*
er, sie, es wird kommen	*wird gekommen sein*
wir werden kommen	*werden gekommen sein*
ihr werdet kommen	*werdet gekommen sein*
sie (Sie) werden kommen	*werden gekommen sein*

CONDITIONAL	CONDITIONAL PERFECT
ich würde kommen	*würde gekommen sein*
du würdest kommen	*würdest gekommen sein*
er, sie, es würde kommen	*würde gekommen sein*
wir würden kommen	*würden gekommen sein*
ihr würdet kommen	*würdet gekommen sein*
sie (Sie) würden kommen	*würden gekommen sein*

IMPERATIVE

komm!
kommen wir!
kommt!
kommen Sie!

SUBJUNCTIVE

PRESENT	PRESENT PERFECT
ich (komme) käme	*ich sei gekommen*
dass du kommest	*du seiest gekommen*

er, sie, es komme

wir (kommen) kämen

ihr kommet

sie (Sie) (kommen)
   kämen

er, sie, es sei gekommen

wir seien gekommen

ihr seid gekommen

sie seien gekommen

IMPERFECT	PAST PERFECT
ich käme	*ich wäre gekommen*
du kämest	*du wärest gekommen*
er, sie, es käme	*er, sie, es wäre gekommen*
wir kämen	*wir wären gekommen*
ihr kämet	*ihr wäret gekommen*
sie (Sie) kämen	*sie wären gekommen*

40. OTHER IRREGULAR VERBS

When the present subjunctive form is in parentheses, it indicates that it is identical to the present indicative. Whenever this occurs, the imperfect or the past perfect subjunctive form is used. .

Infinitive: *beginnen,* to begin

Pres. Part.: *beginnend*

Present Indicative: *ich beginne, du beginnst, er beginnt, wir beginnen, ihr beginnt, Sie beginnen, sie beginnen*

Present Subjunctive: *(ich beginne), du beginnest, er beginne, wir beginnen, ihr beginnet, (Sie beginnen), sie (beginnen)*

Simple Past: *ich begann*

Imperfect Subjunctive: *Ich begänne (begönne)*

Past Part.: *begonnen*

Conversational Past: *ich habe begonnen*

Past Perfect Indicative: *ich hatte begonnen*

Past Perfect Subjunctive: *ich hätte begonnen*

Future: *ich werde beginnen*

Future Perfect: *ich werde begonnen haben*

Conditional: *ich würde beginnen*
Conditional Perfect: *ich würde begonnen haben*
Imperative: *beginn! beginnen wir! beginnt! beginnen Sie!*

Infinitive: *bleiben*, to remain
Pres. Part.: *bleibend*
Present Indicative: *ich bleibe, du bleibst, er bleibt, wir bleiben, ihr bleibt, Sie bleiben, sie bleiben*
Present Subjunctive: *ich bleibe, du bleibest, er bleibe, wir bleiben, ihr bleibet, Sie bleiben, sie bleiben*
Simple Past: *ich blieb*
Imperfect Subjunctive: *ich bliebe*
Past Part.: *geblieben*
Conversational Past: *ich bin geblieben*
Past Perfect Indicative: *ich war geblieben*
Present Perfect Subjunctive: *ich sei geblieben*
Past Perfect Subjunctive: *ich wäre geblieben*
Future: *ich werde bleiben*
Future Perfect: *ich werde geblieben sein*
Conditional: *ich würde bleiben*
Conditional Perfect: *ich würde geblieben sein*
Imperative: *bleib! bleiben wir! bleibt! bleiben Sie!*

Infinitive: *bringen*, to bring
Pres. Part.: *bringend*
Present Indicative: *ich bringe, du bringst, er bringt, wir bringen, ihr bringt, Sie bringen, sie bringen*
Present Subjunctive: *(ich bringe), du bringest, er bringe, (wir bringen), ihr bringet, (Sie bringen, sie bringen)*
Simple Past: *ich brachte*
Imperfect Subjunctive: *ich brächte*
Past Part.: *gebracht*
Conversational Past: *ich habe gebracht*
Past Perfect Indicative; *ich hatte gebracht*
Present Perfect Subjunctive: *ich habe (hatte) gebracht*
Past Perfect Subjunctive: *ich hätte gebracht*

Future: *ich werde bringen*
Future Perfect: *ich werde gebracht haben*
Conditional: *ich würde bringen*
Conditional Perfect: *ich würde gebracht haben*
Imperative: *bring! bringen wir! bringt! bringen Sie!*

Infinitive: *denken,* to think
Pres. Part.: *denkend*
Present Indicative: *ich denke, du denkst, er denkt, wir denken, ihr denkt, Sie denken, sie denken*
Present Subjunctive: *(ich denke), du denkest, er denke, (wir denken), ihr denket, (Sie denken, sie denken)*
Simple Past: *ich dachte*
Imperfect Subjunctive: *ich dächte*
Past Part.: *gedacht*
Conversational Past: *ich habe gedacht*
Past Perfect Indicative: *ich hatte gedacht*
Present Perfect Subjunctive: *(ich habe gedacht)*
Past Perfect Subjunctive: *ich hätte gedacht*
Future: *ich werde denken*
Future Perfect: *ich werde gedacht haben*
Conditional: *ich würde denken*
Conditional Perfect: *ich würde gedacht haben*
Imperative: *denke! (denk!) denken wir! denkt! denken Sie!*

Infinitive: *essen,* to eat
Pres. Part.: *essend*
Present Indicative: *ich esse, du isst, er isst, wir essen, ihr esst, Sie essen, sie essen*
Present Subjunctive: *(ich esse), du essest, er esse, (wir essen), ihr esset, (Sie essen, sie essen)*
Simple Past: *ich aß*
Imperfect Subjunctive: *ich äße*
Past Part.: *gegessen*
Conversational Past: *ich habe gegessen*
Past Perfect Indicative: *ich hatte gegessen*

Present Perfect Subjunctive: *ich (hatte) habe gegessen*
Past Perfect Subjunctive: *ich hätte gegessen*
Future: *ich werde essen*
Future Perfect: *ich werde gegessen haben*
Conditional: *ich würde essen*
Conditional Perfect: *ich würde gegessen haben*
Imperative: *iss! essen wir! esst! essen Sie!*

Infinitive: *fahren*, to drive
Pres. Part.: *fahrend*
Present Indicative: *ich fahre, du fährst, er fährt, wir fahren, ihr fahrt, Sie fahren, sie fahren*
Present Subjunctive: *ich (fahre) führe, du fahrest, er fahre, (wir fahren), ihr fahret, (Sie fahren, sie fahren)*
Simple Past: *ich fuhr*
Imperfect Subjunctive: *ich führe*
Past Part.: *gefahren*
Conversational Past: *ich bin gefahren*
Past Perfect Indicative: *ich war gefahren*
Present Perfect Subjunctive: *ich sei gefahren*
Past Perfect Subjunctive: *ich wäre gefahren*
Future: *ich werde fahren*
Future Perfect: *ich werde gefahren sein*
Conditional: *ich würde fahren*
Conditional Perfect: *ich würde gefahren sein*
Imperative: *fahr! fahren wir! fahrt! fahren Sie!*

Infinitive: *fallen*, to fall
Pres. Part.: *fallend*
Present Indicative: *ich falle, du fällst, er fällt, wir fallen, ihr fallt, Sie fallen, sie fallen*
Present Subjunctive: *ich (falle) fiele, du fallest, er falle, (wir fallen), ihr fallet, (Sie fallen, sie fallen)*
Simple Past: *ich fiel*
Imperfect Subjunctive: *ich fiele*
Past Part.: *gefallen*
Conversational Past: *ich bin gefallen*

Past Perfect Indicative: *ich war gefallen*
Present Perfect Subjunctive: *ich sei gefallen*
Past Perfect Subjunctive: *ich wäre gefallen*
Future: *ich werde fallen*
Future Perfect: *ich werde gefallen sein*
Conditional: *ich würde fallen*
Conditional Perfect: *ich würde gefallen sein*
Imperative: *falle! fall! fallen wir! fallt! fallen Sie!*

Infinitive: *finden*, to find
Pres. Part.: *findend*
Present Indicative: *ich finde, du findest, er findet, wir finden, ihr findet, Sie finden, sie finden*
Present Subjunctive: *ich (finde) fände, du findest, er finde, (wir finden), ihr findet, (Sie finden, sie finden)*
Simple Past: *ich fand*
Imperfect Subjunctive: *ich fände*
Past Part.: *gefunden*
Conversational Past: *ich habe gefunden*
Past Perfect Indicative: *ich hatte gefunden*
Present Perfect Subjunctive: *ich habe gefunden*
Past Perfect Subjunctive: *ich hätte gefunden*
Future: *ich werde finden*
Future Perfect: *ich werde gefunden haben*
Conditional: *ich würde finden*
Conditional Perfect: *ich würde gefunden haben*
Imperative: *finde! finden wir! findet! finden Sie!*

Infinitive: *fliegen*, to fly
Pres. Part.: *fliegend*
Present Indicative: *ich fliege, du fliegst, er fliegt, wir fliegen, ihr fliegt, Sie fliegen, sie fliegen*
Present Subjunctive: *ich (fliege) flöge, du fliegest, er fliege, (wir fliegen), ihr flieget, Sie fliegen, (sie fliegen)*
Simple Past: *ich flog*
Imperfect Subjunctive: *ich flöge*
Past Part.: *geflogen*

Conversational Past: *ich bin geflogen*
Past Perfect Indicative: *ich war geflogen*
Present Perfect Subjunctive: *ich sei geflogen*
Past Perfect Subjunctive: *ich wäre geflogen*
Future: *ich werde fliegen*
Future Perfect: *ich werde geflogen sein*
Conditional: *ich würde fliegen*
Conditional Perfect: *ich würde geflogen sein*
Imperative: *fliege! fliegen wir! fliegt! fliegen Sie!*

Infinitive: *heißen,* to be called
Pres. Part.: *heißend*
Present Indicative: *ich heiße, du heißt, er heißt, wir heißen, ihr heißt, Sie heißen, sie heißen*
Present Subjunctive: *ich (heiße) heiße, du heißest, er heiße, (wir heißen), ihr heißet, (Sie heißen, sie heißen)*
Simple Past: *ich hieß*
Imperfect Subjunctive: *ich hieße*
Past Part.: *geheißen*
Conversational Past: *ich habe geheißen*
Past Perfect Indicative: *ich hatte geheißen*
Present Perfect Subjunctive: *ich (habe) hätte geheißen*
Past Perfect Subjunctive: *ich hätte geheißen*
Future: *ich werde heißen*
Future Perfect: *ich werde geheißen haben*
Conditional: *ich würde heißen*
Conditional Perfect: *ich würde geheißen haben*
Imperative: *heiße! heißen wir! heißt! heißen Sie!*

Infinitive: *helfen,* to help
Pres. Part.: *helfend*
Present Indicative: *ich helfe, du hilfst, er hilft, wir helfen, ihr helft, Sie helfen, sie helfen*
Present Subjunctive: *(ich helfe), du helfest, er helfe, (wir helfen), ihr helfet, (Sie helfen, sie helfen)*
Simple Past: *ich half*
Imperfect Subjunctive: *ich hälfe (also: ich hülfe)*

Past Part.: *geholfen*
Conversational Past: *ich habe geholfen*
Past Perfect Indicative: *ich hatte geholfen*
Present Perfect Subjunctive: *ich (habe) hätte geholfen*
Past Perfect Subjunctive: *ich hätte geholfen*
Future: *ich werde helfen*
Future Perfect: *ich werde geholfen haben*
Conditional: *ich würde helfen*
Conditional Perfect: *ich würde geholfen haben*
Imperative: *hilf! helfen wir! helft! helfen Sie!*

Infinitive: *kennen,* to know
Pres. Part.: *kennend*
Present Indicative: *ich kenne, du kennst, er kennt, wir kennen, ihr kennt, Sie kennen, sie kennen*
Present Subjunctive: *ich (kenne) kennte, du kennest, er kenne, (wir kennen), ihr kennet, (Sie kennen, sie kennen)*
Simple Past: *ich kannte*
Imperfect Subjunctive: *ich kannte*
Past Part.: *gekannt*
Conversational Past: *ich habe gekannt*
Past Perfect Indicative: *ich hatte gekannt*
Present Perfect Subjunctive: *ich (habe) hätte gekannt*
Past Perfect Subjunctive: *ich hätte gekannt*
Future: *ich werde kennen*
Future Perfect: *ich werde gekannt haben*
Conditional: *ich würde kennen*
Conditional Perfect: *ich würde gekannt haben*
Imperative: *kenne! kennen wir! kennt! kennen Sie!*

Infinitive: *laden,* to load
Pres. Part.: *ladend*
Present Indicative: *ich lade, du lädst, er lädt, wir laden, ihr ladet, Sie laden, sie laden*
Present Subjunctive: *ich (lade) lüde, du ladest, er lad, (wir laden), ihr ladet, (Sie laden, sie laden)*
Simple Past: *ich lud*

Imperfect Subjunctive: *ich lüde*
Past Part.: *geladen*
Conversational Past: *ich habe geladen*
Past Perfect Indicative: *ich hatte geladen*
Present Perfect Subjunctive: *ich (habe) hätte geladen*
Past Perfect Subjunctive: *ich hätte geladen*
Future: *ich werde laden*
Future Perfect: *ich werde geladen haben*
Conditional: *ich würde laden*
Conditional Perfect: *ich würde geladen haben*
Imperative: *lade! laden wir! ladet! laden Sie!*

Infinitive: *lassen,* to let
Pres. Part.: *lassend*
Present Indicative: *ich lasse, du lässt, er lässt, wir lassen, ihr lasst, Sie lassen, sie lassen*
Present Subjunctive: *ich (lasse) ließe, du lassest, er lasse, (wir lassen), ihr lasset, Sie lassen, (sie lassen)*
Simple Past: *ich ließ*
Imperfect Subjunctive: *ich ließe*
Past Part.: *gelassen*
Conversational Past: *ich habe gelassen*
Past Perfect Indicative: *ich hatte gelassen*
Present Perfect Subjunctive: *ich (habe) hätte gelassen*
Past Perfect Subjunctive: *ich hätte gelassen*
Future: *ich werde lassen*
Future Perfect: *ich werde gelassen haben*
Conditional: *ich würde lassen*
Conditional Perfect: *ich würde gelassen haben*
Imperative: *lass! lassen wir! lasst! lassen Sie!*

Infinitive: *laufen,* to run
Pres. Part.: *laufend*
Present Indicative: *ich laufe, du läufst, er läuft, wir laufen, ihr lauft, Sie laufen, sie laufen*
Present Subjunctive: *ich (laufe) liefe, du laufest, er laufe, (wir laufen), ihr laufet, Sie laufen, (sie laufen)*

Simple Past: *ich lief*
Imperfect Subjunctive: *ich liefe*
Past Part.: *gelaufen*
Conversational Past: *ich bin gelaufen*
Past Perfect Indicative: *ich war gelaufen*
Present Perfect Subjunctive: *ich sei gelaufen*
Past Perfect Subjunctive: *ich wäre gelaufen*
Future: *ich werde laufen*
Future Perfect: *ich werde gelaufen sein*
Conditional: *ich würde laufen*
Conditional Perfect: *ich würde gelaufen sein*
Imperative: *lauf! laufen wir! lauft! laufen Sie!*

Infinitive: *leiden*, to suffer, endure
Pres. Part.: *leidend*
Present Indicative: *ich leide, du leidest, er leidet, wir leiden, ihr leidet, Sie leiden, sie leiden*
Present Subjunctive: *ich (leide) litte, du leidest, er leide, (wir leiden), ihr leidet, Sie leiden, (sie leiden)*
Simple Past: *ich litt*
Imperfect Subjunctive: *ich litte*
Past Part.: *gelitten*
Conversational Past: *ich habe gelitten*
Past Perfect Indicative: *ich hatte gelitten*
Present Perfect Subjunctive: *ich (habe) hätte gelitten*
Past Perfect Subjunctive: *ich hätte gelitten*
Future: *ich werde leiden*
Future Perfect: *ich werde gelitten haben*
Conditional: *ich würde leiden*
Conditional Perfect: *ich würde gelitten haben*
Imperative: *leide! leiden wir! leidet! leiden Sie!*

Infinitive: *lesen*, to read
Pres. Part.: *lesend*
Present Indicative: *ich lese, du liest, er liest, wir lesen, ihr lest, Sie lesen, sie lesen*

Present Subjunctive: *ich (lese) läse, du lesest, er lese, (wir lesen), ihr leset, (Sie lesen, sie lesen)*
Simple Past: *ich las*
Imperfect Subjunctive: *ich läse*
Past Part.: *gelesen*
Conversational Past: *ich habe gelesen*
Past Perfect Indicative: *ich hatte gelesen*
Present Perfect Subjunctive: *ich (habe) hätte gelesen*
Past Perfect Subjunctive: *ich hätte gelesen*
Future: *ich werde lesen*
Future Perfect: *ich werde gelesen haben*
Conditional: *ich würde lesen*
Conditional Perfect: *ich würde gelesen haben*
Imperative: *lies! lesen wir! lest! lesen Sie!*

Infinitive: *liegen*, to lie (recline)
Pres. Part.: *liegend*
Present Indicative: *ich liege, du liegst, er liegt, wir liegen, ihr liegt, Sie liegen, sie liegen*
Present Subjunctive: *ich (liege) läge, du liegest, er liege, (wir liegen), ihr lieget, (Sie liegen, sie liegen)*
Simple Past: *ich lag*
Imperfect Subjunctive: *ich läge*
Past Part.: *gelegen*
Conversational Past: *ich habe gelegen*
Past Perfect Indicative: *ich hatte gelegen*
Present Perfect Subjunctive: *ich (habe) hätte gelegen*
Past Perfect Subjunctive: *ich hätte gelegen*
Future: *ich werde liegen*
Future Perfect: *ich werde gelegen haben*
Conditional: *ich würde liegen*
Conditional Perfect: *ich würde gelegen haben*
Imperative: *liege! liegen wir! liegt! liegen Sie!*

Infinitive: *lügen*, to lie (say something untrue)
Pres. Part.: *lügend*

Present Indicative: *ich lüge, du lügst, er lügt, wir lügen, ihr lügt, Sie lügen, sie lügen*
Present Subjunctive: *ich lüge, du lügest, er lüge, wir lügen, ihr lüget, Sie lügen, sie lügen*
Simple Past: *ich log*
Imperfect Subjunctive: *ich löge*
Past Part.: *gelogen*
Conversational Past: *ich habe gelogen*
Past Perfect Indicative: *ich hatte gelogen*
Present Perfect Subjunctive: *ich (habe) hätte gelogen*
Past Perfect Subjunctive: *ich hätte gelogen*
Future: *ich werde lügen*
Future Perfect: *ich werde gelogen haben*
Conditional: *ich würde lügen*
Conditional Perfect: *ich würde gelogen haben*
Imperative: *lüge! lügen wir! lügt! lügen Sie!*

Infinitive: *nehmen,* to take
Pres. Part.: *nehmend*
Present Indicative: *ich nehme, du nimmst, er nimmt, wir nehmen, ihr nehmt, Sie nehmen, sie nehmen*
Present Subjunctive: *ich (nehme) nähme, du nehmest, er nehme, (wir nehmen), ihr nehmet, (Sie nehmen, sie nehmen.)*
Simple Past: *ich nahm*
Imperfect Subjunctive: *ich nähme*
Past Part.: *genommen*
Conversational Past: *ich habe genommen*
Past Perfect Indicative: *ich hatte genommen*
Present Perfect Subjunctive: *ich (habe) hätte genommen*
Past Perfect Subjunctive: *ich hätte genommen*
Future: *ich werde nehmen*
Future Perfect: *ich werde genommen haben*
Conditional: *ich würde nehmen*
Conditional Perfect: *ich würde genommen haben*
Imperative: *nimm! nehmen wir! nehmt! nehmen Sie!*

Infinitive: *nennen,* to name
Pres. Part.: *nennend*
Present Indicative: *ich nenne, du nennst, er nennt, wir nennen, ihr nennt, Sie nennen, sie nennen*
Present Subjunctive: *ich (nenne) nennte, du nennest, er nenne, (wir nennen), ihr nennet, (Sie nennen, sie nennen)*
Simple Past: *ich nannte*
Imperfect Subjunctive: *ich nennte*
Past Part.: *genannt*
Conversational Past: *ich habe genannt*
Past Perfect Indicative: *ich hatte genannt*
Present Perfect Subjunctive: *ich (habe) hätte genannt*
Past Perfect Subjunctive: *ich hätte genannt*
Future: *ich werde nennen*
Future Perfect: *ich werde genannt haben*
Conditional: *ich würde nennen*
Conditional Perfect: *ich würde genannt haben*
Imperative: *nenne! nennen wir! nennt! nennen Sie!*

Infinitive: *rufen,* to call
Pres. Part.: *rufend*
Present Indicative: *ich rufe, du rufst, er ruft, wir rufen, ihr ruft, Sie rufen, sie rufen*
Present Subjunctive: *ich (rufe) riefe, du rufest, er rufe, (wir rufen), rufet, (Sie rufen, sie rufen)*
Simple Past: *ich rief*
Imperfect Subjunctive: *ich riefe*
Past Part.: *gerufen*
Conversational Past: *ich habe gerufen*
Past Perfect Indicative: *ich hatte gerufen*
Present Perfect Subjunctive: *ich (habe) hätte gerufen*
Past Perfect Subjunctive: *ich hätte gerufen*
Future: *ich werde rufen*
Future Perfect: *ich werde gerufen haben*
Conditional: *ich würde rufen*

Conditional Perfect: *ich würde gerufen haben*
Imperative: *ruf! rufen wir! ruft! rufen Sie!*

Infinitive: *schaffen*, to create
Pres. Part.: *schaffend*
Present Indicative: *ich schaffe, du schaffst, er schafft, wir schaffen, ihr schafft, Sie schaffen, sie schaffen*
Present Subjunctive: *ich (schaffe) schüfe, du schaffest, er schaffe, (wir schaffen), ihr schaffet, (Sie schaffen, sie schaffen)*
Simple Plan: *ich schuf*
Imperfect Subjunctive: *ich schüfe*
Past Part.: *geschaffen*
Conversational Past: *ich habe geschaffen*
Past Perfect Indicative: *ich hatte geschaffen*
Present Perfect Subjunctive: *ich (habe) hätte geschaffen*
Past Perfect Subjunctive: *ich hätte geschaffen*
Future: *ich werde schaffen*
Future Perfect: *ich werde geschaffen haben*
Conditional: *ich würde schaffen*
Conditional Perfect: *ich würde geschaffen haben*
Imperative: *schaffe! schaffen wir! schafft! schaffen Sie!*

Infinitive: *schlafen*, to sleep
Pres. Part.: *schlafend*
Present Indicative: *ich schlafe, du schläfst, er schläft, wir schlafen, ihr schlaft, Sie schlafen, sie schlafen*
Present Subjunctive: *ich (schlafe) schliefe, du schlafest, er schlafe, (wir schlafen), ihr schlafet, (Sie schlafen, sie schlafen)*
Simple Past: *ich schlief*
Imperfect Subjunctive: *ich schliefe*
Past Part.: *geschlafen*
Conversational Past: *ich habe geschlafen*
Past Perfect Indicative: *ich hatte geschlafen*
Present Perfect Subjunctive: *ich (habe) hätte geschlafen*

Past Perfect Subjunctive: *ich hätte geschlafen*
Future: *ich werde schlafen*
Future Perfect: *ich werde geschlafen haben*
Conditional: *ich würde schlafen*
Conditional Perfect: *ich würde geschlafen haben*
Imperative: *schlafe! schlafen wir! schlaft! schlafen Sie!*

Infinitive: *schlagen,* to beat, to strike
Pres. Part.: *schlagend*
Present Indicative: *ich schlage, du schlägst, er schlägt, wir schlagen, ihr schlagt, Sie schlagen, sie schlagen*
Present Subjunctive: *ich (schlage) schlüge, du schlagest, er schlage, (wir schlagen), ihr schlaget, (Sie schlagen, sie schlagen)*
Simple Past: *ich schlug*
Imperfect Subjunctive: *ich schlüge*
Past Part.: *geschlagen*
Conversational Past: *ich habe geschlagen*
Past Perfect Indicative: *ich hatte geschlagen*
Present Perfect Subjunctive: *ich (habe) hätte geschlagen*
Past Perfect Subjunctive: *ich hätte geschlagen*
Future: *ich werde schlagen*
Future Perfect: *ich werde geschlagen haben*
Conditional: *ich würde schlagen*
Conditional Perfect: *ich würde geschlagen haben*
Imperative: *schlage! (schlag!) schlagen wir! schlagt! schlagen Sie!*

Infinitive: *schreiben,* to write
Pres. Part.: *schreibend*
Present Indicative: *ich schreibe, du schreibst, er schreibt, wir schreiben, ihr schreibt, Sie schreiben, sie schreiben*
Present Subjunctive: *ich (schreibe) schriebe, du schreibest, er schreibe, (wir schreiben), ihr schreibet, (Sie schreiben, sie schreiben)*

Simple Past: *ich schrieb*
Imperfect Subjunctive: *ich schriebe*
Past Part.: *geschrieben*
Conversational Past: *ich habe geschrieben*
Past Perfect Indicative: *ich hatte geschrieben*
Present Perfect Subjunctive: *ich (habe) hätte geschrieben*
Past Perfect Subjunctive: *ich hätte geschrieben*
Future: *ich werde schreiben*
Future Perfect: *ich werde geschrieben haben*
Conditional: *ich würde schreiben*
Conditional Perfect: *ich würde geschrieben haben*
Imperative: *schreib! schreiben wir! schreibt! schreiben Sie!*

Infinitive: *schwimmen,* to swim
Pres. Part.: *schwimmend*
Present Indicative: *ich schwimme, du schwimmst, er schwimmt, wir schwimmen, ihr schwimmt, Sie schwimmen, sie schwimmen*
Present Subjunctive: *ich (schwimme) schwömme, du schwimmest, er schwimme, (wir schwimmen), ihr schwimmet, (Sie schwimmen, sie schwimmen)*
Simple Past: *ich schwamm*
Imperfect Subjunctive: *ich schwömme (schwämme)*
Past Part.: *geschwommen*
Conversational Past: *ich bin geschwommen*
Past Perfect Indicative: *ich war geschwommen*
Present Perfect Subjunctive: *ich sei geschwommen*
Past Perfect Subjunctive: *ich wäre geschwommen*
Future: *ich werde schwimmen*
Future Perfect: *ich werde geschwommen sein*
Conditional: *ich würde schwimmen*
Conditional Perfect: *ich würde geschwommen sein*
Imperative: *schwimm! schwimmen wir! schwimmt! schwimmen Sie!*

Infinitive: *senden,* to send, to broadcast
Pres. Part.: *sendend*
Present Indicative: *ich sende, du sendest, er sendet, wir senden, ihr sendet, Sie senden, sie senden*
Present Subjunctive: *ich (sende) sendete, du sendest, er sendet, (wir senden), ihr sendet, (Sie senden, sie senden)*
Simple Past: *ich sandte* (or *sendete*)
Imperfect Subjunctive: *ich sendete*
Past Part.: *gesandt (gesendet)**
Conversational Past: *ich habe gesandt (gesendet)*
Past Perfect Indicative: *ich hatte gesandt (gesendet)*
Present Perfect Subjunctive: *ich (habe) hätte gesandt (gesendet)*
Past Perfect Subjunctive: *ich hätte gesandt (gesendet)*
Future: *ich werde senden*
Future Perfect: *ich werde gesandt (gesendet) haben*
Conditional: *ich würde senden*
Conditional Perfect: *ich würde gesandt (gesendet) haben*
Imperative: *sende! senden wir! sendet! senden Sie!*

Infinitive: *singen,* to sing
Pres. Part.: *singend*
Present Indicative: *ich singe, du singst, er singt, wir singen, ihr singt, Sie singen, sie singen*
Present Subjunctive: *ich (singe) sänge, du singest, er singe, (wir singen), ihr singet, (Sie singen, sie singen)*
Simple Past: *ich sang*
Imperfect Subjunctive: *ich sänge*
Past Part.: *gesungen*
Conversational Past: *ich habe gesungen*
Past Perfect Indicative: *ich hatte gesungen*

***Senden** has two simple past and two past participle forms, depending on the meaning: *sandte, gesandt* (sent) and *sendete, gesendet* (broadcast).

Present Perfect Subjunctive: *ich (habe) hatte gesungen*
Past Perfect Subjunctive: *ich hätte gesungen*
Future: *ich werde singen*
Future Perfect: *ich werde gesungen haben*
Conditional: *ich würde singen*
Conditional Perfect: *ich würde gesungen haben*
Imperative: *sing! singen wir! singt! singen Sie!*

Infinitive: *sitzen*, to sit
Pres. Part.: *sitzend*
Present Indicative: *ich sitze, du sitzt, er sitzt, wir sitzen, ihr sitzt, Sie sitzen, sie sitzen*
Present Subjunctive: *ich (sitze) sässe, du sitzest, er sitze, (wir sitzen), ihr sitzet, (Sie sitzen, sie sitzen)*
Simple Past: *ich sass*
Imperfect Subjunctive: *ich sässe*
Past Part.: *gesessen*
Conversational Past: *ich habe gesessen*
Past Perfect Indicative: *ich hatte gesessen*
Present Perfect Subjunctive: *ich (habe) hätte gesessen*
Past Perfect Subjunctive: *ich hätte gesessen*
Future: *ich werde sitzen*
Future Perfect: *ich werde gesessen haben*
Conditional: *ich würde sitzen*
Conditional Perfect: *ich würde gesessen haben*
Imperative: *sitz! sitzen wir! sitzt! sitzen Sie!*

Infinitive: *stehen*, to stand
Pres. Part.: *stehend*
Present Indicative: *ich stehe, du stehst, er steht, wir stehen, ihr steht, Sie stehen, sie stehen*
Present Subjunctive: *ich (stehe) stünde/stände du stehest, er stehe, (wir stehen), ihr stehet, (Sie stehen, sie stehen)*
Simple Past: *ich stand*
Imperfect Subjunctive: *ich stünde* or *stände*
Past Part.: *gestanden*

Conversational Past: *ich habe gestanden*
Past Perfect Indicative: *ich hatte gestanden*
Present Perfect Subjunctive: *ich (habe) hätte gestanden*
Past Perfect Subjunctive: *ich hätte gestanden*
Future: *ich werde stehen*
Future Perfect: *ich werde gestanden haben*
Conditional: *ich würde stehen*
Conditional Perfect: *ich würde gestanden haben*
Imperative: *steh! stehen wir! steht! stehen Sie!*

Infinitive: *stehlen,* to steal
Pres. Part.: *stehlend*
Present Indicative: *ich stehle, du stiehlst, er stiehlt, wir stehlen, ihr stehlt, Sie stehlen, sie stehlen*
Present Subjunctive: *ich (stehle) stöhle/stähle, du stehlest, er stehle, (wir stehlen), ihr stehlet, (Sie stehlen, sie stehlen)*
Simple Past: *ich stahl*
Imperfect Subjunctive: *ich stöhle/stähle*
Past Part.: *gestohlen*
Conversational Past: *ich habe gestohlen*
Past Perfect Indicative: *ich hatte gestohlen*
Present Perfect Subjunctive: *ich (habe) hätte gestohlen*
Past Perfect Subjunctive: *ich hätte gestohlen*
Future: *ich werde stehlen*
Future Perfect: *ich werde gestohlen haben*
Conditional: *ich würde stehlen*
Conditional Perfect: *ich würde gestohlen haben*
Imperative: *stiehl! stehlen wir! stehlt! stehlen Sie!*

Infinitive: *springen,* to jump
Pres. Part.: *springend*
Present Indicative: *ich springe, du springst, er springt, wir springen, ihr springt, Sie springen, sie springen*
Present Subjunctive: *ich (springe) spränge, du springest, er springe, (wir springen), ihr springet, (Sie springen, sie springen)*

Simple Past: *ich sprang*
Imperfect Subjunctive: *ich spränge*
Past Part.: *gesprungen*
Conversational Past: *ich bin gesprungen*
Past Perfect Indicative: *ich war gesprungen*
Present Perfect Subjunctive: *ich sei gesprungen*
Past Perfect Subjunctive: *ich wäre gesprungen*
Future: *ich werde springen*
Future Perfect: *ich werde gesprungen sein*
Conditional: *ich würde springen*
Conditional Perfect: *ich würde gesprungen sein*
Imperative: *spring! springen wir! springt! springen Sie!*

Infinitive: *tragen*, to carry
Pres. Part.: *tragend*
Present Indicative: *ich trage, du trägst, er trägt, wir tragen, ihr tragt, Sie tragen, sie tragen*
Present Subjunctive: *ich (trage) trüge, du tragest, er trage, (wir tragen), ihr traget, (Sie tragen, sie tragen)*
Simple Past: *ich trug*
Imperfect Subjunctive: *ich trüge*
Past Part.: *getragen*
Conversational Past: *ich (habe) hätte getragen*
Past Perfect Indicative: *ich hatte getragen*
Present Perfect Subjunctive: *ich habe getragen*
Past Perfect Subjunctive: *ich hätte getragen*
Future: *ich werde tragen*
Future Perfect: *ich werde getragen haben*
Conditional: *ich würde tragen*
Conditional Perfect: *ich würde getragen haben*
Imperative: *trag! tragen wir! tragt! tragen Sie!*

Infinitive: *treffen*, to meet
Pres. Part.: *treffend*
Present Indicative: *ich treffe, du triffst, er trifft, wir treffen, ihr trefft, Sie treffen, sie treffen*

Present Subjunctive: *ich (treffe) träfe, du treffest, er treffe, (wir treffen), ihr treffet, (Sie treffen, sie treffen)*
Simple Past: *ich traf*
Imperfect Subjunctive: *ich träfe*
Past Part.: *getroffen*
Conversational Past: *ich habe getroffen*
Past Perfect Indicative: *ich hätte getroffen*
Present Perfect Subjunctive: *ich (habe) hätte getroffen*
Past Perfect Subjunctive: *ich hätte getroffen*
Future: *ich werde treffen*
Future Perfect: *ich werde getroffen haben*
Conditional: *ich würde treffen*
Conditional Perfect: *ich würde getroffen haben*
Imperative: *triff! treffen wir! trefft! treffen Sie!*

Infinitive: *trinken,* to drink
Pres. Part.: *trinkend*
Present Indicative: *ich trinke, du trinkst, er trinkt, wir trinken, ihr trinkt, Sie trinken, sie trinken*
Present Subjunctive: *ich (trinke) tränke, du trinkest, er trinke, (wir trinken), ihr trinket, (Sie trinken, sie trinken)*
Simple Past: *ich trank*
Imperfect Subjunctive: *ich tränke*
Past Part.: *getrunken*
Conversational Past: *ich habe getrunken*
Past Perfect Indicative: *ich hatte getrunken*
Present Perfect Subjunctive: *ich (habe) hätte getrunken*
Past Perfect Subjunctive: *ich hätte getrunken*
Future: *ich werde trinken*
Future Perfect: *ich werde getrunken haben*
Conditional: *ich würde trinken*
Conditional Perfect: *ich würde getrunken haben*
Imperative: *trink! trinken wir! trinkt! trinken Sie!*

Infinitive: *tun,* to do
Pres. Part.: *tuend*

Present Indicative: *ich tue, du tust, er tut, wir tun, ihr tut, Sie tun, sie tun*
Present Subjunctive: *ich (tue) täte, du tuest, er tue, (wir tun), ihr tuet, (Sie tun, sie tun)*
Simple Past: *ich tat*
Imperfect Subjunctive: *ich täte*
Past Part.: *getan*
Conversational Past: *ich habe getan*
Past Perfect Indicative: *ich hatte getan*
Present Perfect Subjunctive: *ich (habe) hätte getan*
Past Perfect Subjunctive: *ich hätte getan*
Future: *ich werde tun*
Future Perfect: *ich werde getan haben*
Conditional: *ich würde tun*
Conditional Perfect: *ich würde getan haben*
Imperative: *tue! tun wir! tut! tun Sie!*

Infinitive: *vergessen*, to forget
Pres. Part.: *vergessend*
Present Indicative: *ich vergesse, du vergisst, er vergisst, wir vergessen, ihr vergesst, Sie vergessen, sie vergessen*
Present Subjunctive: *ich (vergesse) vergäße, du vergessest, er vergesse, (wir vergessen), ihr vergesset, (Sie vergessen, sie vergessen)*
Simple Past: *ich vergaß*
Imperfect Subjunctive: *ich vergäße*
Past Part.: *vergessen*
Conversational Past: *ich habe vergessen*
Past Perfect Indicative: *ich hatte vergessen*
Present Perfect Subjunctive: *ich (habe) hätte vergessen*
Past Perfect Subjunctive: *ich hätte vergessen*
Future: *ich werde vergessen*
Future Perfect: *ich werde vergessen haben*
Conditional: *ich würde vergessen*
Conditional Perfect: *ich würde vergessen haben*

Imperative: *vergiss! vergessen wir! vergesst! vergessen Sie!*

Infinitive: *verlieren,* to lose
Pres. Part.: *verlierend*
Present Indicative: *ich verliere, du verlierst, er verliert, wir verlieren, ihr verliert, Sie verlieren, sie verlieren*
Present Subjunctive: *ich (verliere) verlöre, du verlierest, er verliere, (wir verlieren), ihr verlieret, (Sie verlieren, sie verlieren)*
Simple Past: *ich verlor*
Imperfect Subjunctive: *ich verlöre*
Past Part.: *verloren*
Conversational Past: *ich habe verloren*
Past Perfect Indicative: *ich hatte verloren*
Present Perfect Subjunctive: *ich (habe) hätte verloren*
Past Perfect Subjunctive: *ich hätte verloren*
Future: *ich werde verlieren*
Future Perfect: *ich werde verloren haben*
Conditional: *ich würde verlieren*
Conditional Perfect: *ich würde verloren haben*
Imperative: *verlier(e)! verlieren wir! verliert! verlieren Sie!*

LETTER WRITING

A. Thank-You Notes

Berlin, den 6. Januar 2005

Sehr geehrte Frau Zimmermann,

   Ich möchte Ihnen herzlich für Ihr wunderbares Geschenk danken. Das Bild entspricht ganz meinem Geschmack und passt so gut zu den neuen Möbeln in meinem Wohnzimmer.
   Meinen allerherzlichsten Dank.

      Mit verbindlichen Grüßen
      Lotte Schäfer

Berlin, January 6, 2005

Dear Mrs. Zimmermann,

   I should (would) like to thank you for your delightful present. The picture is entirely to my taste and matches the new furniture in my living room perfectly.
   Thank you ever so much.

      Sincerely yours,
      Lotte Schäfer

B. BUSINESS LETTERS

> *H. Molz*
> *Kantstraße 16*
> *D-10623 Berlin*
>
> *Berlin, den 2. Mai 2005*

Verlag Peter Basten
Kurfürstendamm 10
D-10719 Berlin

Anbei übersende ich Ihnen einen Scheck über €100, für ein Jahresabonnement Ihrer Zeitschrift "Merkur."

> *Hochachtungsvoll!*
> *Heinrich Molz*

ANLAGE

> H. Mulz
> 16 Kant Street
> D-10623 Berlin
>
> May 2, 2005

Peter Basten Press
Kurfürstendamm 10
D-10719 Berlin

Gentlemen:

Enclosed please find a check for 100 euros for a year's subscription to your magazine *Merkur.*

> Very truly yours,
> Heinrich Molz

(Encl.)

Schwarzkopf & Co.
Breite Straße 6
D-13597 Berlin

Berlin, den 30. Sept. 2005

Firma
Paul Gerber & Co.
Goethestraße 20
D-12207 Berlin

Ihre Anfrage 8.8.05

Sehr geehrte Herren,

   In Beantwortung Ihrer Anfrage vom 8. d.M. bestäti-
gen wir Ihnen gerne nochmals die Aufgabe der Sendung
per Postpaket am 13. August.

Hochachtungsvoll
Ernst Schwarzkopf

Schwarzkopf & Co.
6 Breite Straße
D-13597 Berlin

Sept. 30, 2005

Paul Gerber & Co.
Goethestraße 20
D-12207 Berlin

Re: Inquiry of 8/8/05

Gentlemen:

In reply to your letter ("inquiry") of the eighth of this
month, we wish to confirm once more that the merchandise was mailed to you parcel post on August 13.

Very truly yours,
Ernst Schwarzkopf

C. INFORMAL LETTERS

7. März 2005

Lieber Helmut,
   ich habe mich sehr über deinen letzten Brief gefreut.
Zunächst habe ich eine gute Nachricht für dich.
Anfang April beabsichtige ich, zwei Wochen in Berlin
zu verbringen. Ich freue mich schon sehr darauf, mit
dir und deiner Familie zusammenzukommen und hoffe,
dass es euch allen gut geht.
   Irene begleitet mich auf dieser Reise. Sie freut sich
sehr, nun endlich deine Frau kennenzulernen. Auf
diese Weise wird es uns gelingen, die berühmten
Sehenswürdigkeiten des alten und des neuen Berlins

zu besichtigen. Wir beide können uns lange unterhalten, wie wir es in der Schule immer getan haben.

Meine Praxis läuft ganz gut zur Zeit. Ich werde versuchen, nicht zu viele neue Patienten im April anzunehmen, obwohl ich glaube, dass es sehr schwierig sein wird. Neulich habe ich mich mit Müller getroffen. Er hat nach dir gefragt und lässt dich herzlich grüßen. Man kann es kaum glauben, dass der „kleine Fritz" zwei Kaufhäuser und mehrere Restaurants besitzt.

Fast hätte ich die Hauptsache vergessen. Ich wäre dir sehr dankbar, wenn du mir ein Zimmer im Hilton Hotel für den fünften April reservieren könntest. Du tätest mir einen großen Gefallen.

Ich hoffe bald von dir zu hören. Grüße an Deine Frau.

> *Dein*
> *Klaus*

March 7, 2005

Dear Helmut,

I was very happy to receive your last letter. First of all, I have some good news for you. I intend to spend two weeks in Berlin at the beginning of April. I'm already looking forward to getting together with you and your family and hope you are all well.

Irene is going to accompany me on this trip. She is looking forward to meeting your wife. That way we will be able to visit the sights of the old and new Berlin. The two of us will be able to chat as we always used to in school.

Presently, my practice is going quite well. I'll try not to take on too many new patients during the month of April, although I believe that it will be very difficult.

Recently I met with Müller. He asked about you. He sends you his best. One can hardly believe that "little Fritz" owns two department stores and several restaurants.

I almost forgot the most important thing. I would be very grateful if you (were able to) could reserve a room for me at the Hilton Hotel for the fifth of April. You would be doing me a big favor.

I hope to hear from you soon. Regards to your wife.

Yours,
Klaus

D.   FORMS OF SALUTATIONS AND COMPLIMENTARY CLOSINGS

SALUTATIONS:

FORMAL

Sehr geehrter Herr Professor,	Dear Professor (Smith),
Sehr geehrter Herr Bürgermeister,	Dear Mayor (Smith),
Sehr geehrter Herr Rechtsanwalt, *Sehr geehrter Herr Doktor*	Dear Lawyer (Smith), (Lawyers are often addressed as *Doktor* in Germany.)
Sehr geehrte Frau Schmitt,	Dear Mrs. Schmitt,
Sehr geehrte Herren,	Gentlemen:
Sehr geehrter Herr Pulver,	Dear Mr. Pulver,

INFORMAL

Mein lieber Karl,	Dear Karl,
Meine liebe Franziska,	Dear Frances,
Mein Liebling,	My darling (*m.* and *f.*),

Mein Liebster,	My darling (*m.*),
Meine Liebste,	My darling (*f.*),
Lieber Franz,	Dear Frank,
Liebe Paula,	Dear Paula,
Meine Lieben,	My dear ones,

COMPLIMENTARY CLOSINGS:

FORMAL

1. *Hochachtungsvoll!*[1] Very truly yours,
   ("Most respectfully")
2. *Mit vorzüglicher Hochach-* Very truly yours,
   tung!
   ("With the most excellent
   and highest regard")
3. *Mit besten Grüßen,* Yours truly,
   ("With best greetings")
4. *Wir empfehlen uns* Yours truly,
   mit besten Grüßen,
   ("We commend ourselves
   with best regards")

INFORMAL

1. *Mit herzlichem* Very sincerely, love
   Gruß
   ("With hearty
   greeting")
2. *Bitte grüße deine* Please give my regards
   Mutter von mir to your mother
3. *Meine besten Grüße* Give my regards to your
   an die Deinen family
4. *Grüße und Küsse* My love to everybody
   an euch alle
   ("Greetings and
   kisses to you all")

E. FORM OF THE ENVELOPE

Letters to an individual are addressed:

Herrn	*Herrn Peter Müller*	(Mr.)
Frau	*Frau Else Schneider*	(Ms.)

E-MAIL AND INTERNET RESOURCES

A. SAMPLE E-MAIL

Sehr geehrte Frau Schüler,
Auf Grund Ihrer Anfrage nach Textilmustern für die
Neudekoration Ihres Konferenzraumes übersende ich
Ihnen hiermit die Muster als angehängte Datei.

Ich habe auch Ihre vorherige und eine Kopie dieser
Mail an Ihren Innenarchitekten weitergeleitet.

Wären sie so nett, mir sobald wie möglich Ihre
Entscheidung zurückzumailen?

Mit freundlichen Grüßen
Karl Schulze
Textilimport Hamburg

Dear Ms. Schüler,
On the basis of your inquiry for textile samples for
the remodeling of your conference room, I hereby
send you the samples as an attachment.

I also forwarded your previous e-mail and a copy of
this one to your interior designer.

Would you be so kind as to e-mail your decision back to me as soon as possible?

With best regards,
Karl Schulze
Textile Import Hamburg

B. INTERNET RESOURCES

The following is a list of useful Web sites for those students who would like to enhance their language abilities.

For a comprehensive German online dictionary: *www.leo.org*

The German National Tourist Board: *www.germany-tourism.de*
Austria: *www.austria-tourism.at*
Switzerland: *www.switzerlandtourism.ch*
Liechtenstein: *www.liechtenstein.li*

If you would like to listen to live news broadcasts over the Internet: *www.deutschewelle.de*

The German online magazine *Der Spiegel* with articles about politics and current events: *www.spiegel.de*

The German magazine *Der Stern* with a large variety of articles on entertainment and current affairs: *www.stern.de*

If you want to order German delicacies online: *www.german-grocery.com*

Thousands of traditional German recipes can be found at: *www.daskochrezept.de*

For more modern German dishes go to: *www.theotherhalf.tv*

If you are looking for a hotel log onto *www.hotel.de*

For inexpensive lodging youth hostels: *www.jugendherberge.de*

To find an apartment in German speaking countries visit: *www.wohnung.de*

For travel by train: *www.bahn.de*

THE GERMAN
SPELLING REFORM OF 1998

The educational ministries of all German states have agreed upon a spelling reform, which is supposed to make German spelling a little easier on students and natives alike. The spelling reform became mandatory in the year 1998. The following are the most important new rules.

- After short vowels *ß* becomes *ss*. *ß* remains *ß* after long vowels, if the stem of the word shows no more consonants: *Fass* (keg) but *Straße* (street).

- Double consonants after a stressed short vowel: *nummerieren* (to number), *Ass* (ace), *Tipp* (tip).

- Always write as two separate words: verb combinations with *sein* such as *pleite sein* (to be destitute), combinations of two verbs such as *kennen lernen* (to get to know), combinations of verb and participle such as *gesagt haben* (to have said), combinations of verb plus noun such as *Rad fahren* (to ride a bicycle), combinations of verb and adverb such as *beiseite legen* (to set aside), combinations of verb plus adjective such as *gut lesen* (to read well), and verb + *-ig, -isch, -lich,* such as *lästig fallen* (to be a burden).

- Capitalize all nouns and derivatives of nouns: *Trimm-dich-Pfad* (fitness trail), *Leid tun* (to be sorry), *das Dutzend* (the dozen), *im Deutschen* (in German), *Schweizer Käse* (Swiss cheese).

- Write out all letters that meet: *Schiff + Fahrt = Schifffahrt* (boat ride).

- In letters, *du* (you), *dir* (to you), *dein* (your), *eure* (your [pl.]), etc., are written in lowercase.

- Many foreign words receive a "Germanized" spelling: *Fotograf* (photographer).

- Words separate after spoken syllables: *Fens-ter* (window), *Bä-der* (bathroom), *A-bend* (evening).

- Commas are no longer necessary before *und* or *oder*.

INDEX